The
Bamboo
Bracelet

Merilyn Brason

Matador
9 Priory Business Park,
Wistow Road, Kibworth Beauchamp,
Leicestershire. LE8 0RX
Tel: 0116 279 2299
Email: books@troubador.co.uk
Web: www.troubador.co.uk/matador
Twitter: @matadorbooks

ISBN 978 1838593 322

British Library Cataloguing in Publication Data.
A catalogue record for this book is available from the British Library.

Printed and bound by CPI Group (UK) Ltd, Croydon, CR0 4YY
Typeset in 12pt Adobe Jenson Pro by Troubador Publishing Ltd, Leicester, UK

Matador is an imprint of Troubador Publishing Ltd

For Ben, Adam and Luke

Ronny's *Philippines Entry Document 1941*

PREFACE

It all started one cathartic February afternoon when my spirits were as low as the direction of the rain hammering on the windows. I was in my sister's flat in the Channel Islands, going through her possessions, on the day following her funeral. My task of trying to separate the detritus of her life seemed endless and deeply depressing. Catherine was a hoarder. She lived alone and had crammed her flat with our familial history, refusing to examine or jettison any of my parents' possessions as they had passed into her care. I was turning from one box to another, totally overwhelmed, when I came to a halt suddenly.

There beneath my fingers was a treasure trove of my mother's familiar handwritten notes and a bamboo bracelet. In the notes, she (Ronny) recalled her years of incarceration in a Japanese prisoner-of-war camp throughout World War II. Courageous and determined, she had given birth and brought up my sister in the camp, and, by confronting the Japanese authority, engineered a reunion with my father.

My father, Pat, was one of a generation who protected himself by not revisiting his experience of internment, no matter how hard he was coaxed. His fellow internee, my godfather Reg, was also tight-lipped, but Ronny intended to write her story herself. I recall many evenings when I was growing up when she sat at her Chinese writing desk, positioned so that she could keep one eye on the television as she scribbled away. She was always able to multitask, and her energy levels were impressive. We often listened to her internment stories. She spoke of the humour and inventiveness displayed in camp, and the way the prisoners, in their adversity, adapted and created a self-governing society to lessen their individual pain and distress. Ronny was part of this mini-world that developed its own structure with only one aim: to survive when it became evident that rescue was a distant fantasy. She soft-pedalled the despair, and I was only to learn the degree of the horror from the books and accounts of other survivors.

I abandoned my executor duties and spent the next few days immersed in reading Ronny's copious notes as the certainty grew that I needed to complete her discarded task. My mother's recollections are the basis of this book, researched and clarified with the considerable help I received from the network of ex-internees, some of whom personally recall my mother and father. The world has not changed so much. There are men and women who will relate to my mother's story as they are experiencing something akin to it today. There are different protagonists and different horrors, but it is the same story for the innocents whose only fault is being caught in the wrong place at the wrong time.

Ronny and Pat's story, with all its horror and unfair challenges, is theirs alone.

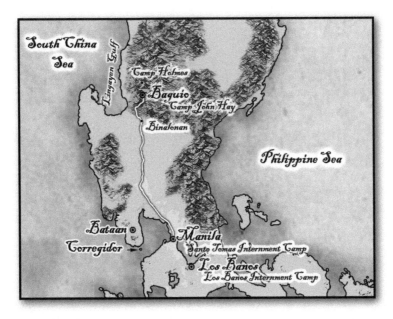

Map of Philippines *(created courtesy of Robelyn Balbuena Brason)*

ONE

8th December 1941

Ronny felt the invasion first, as a vibration in her chest, before it assailed her ears. She was leaning out over the balcony, inhaling the early blossom of the creamy-white gardenias, relishing the early morning warmth and anticipating a beautiful Philippines day to come. Her mind struggled to make sense of it, and then the sound crashed into her a second later. It was as if a monstrous cymbal had been smashed over her head. Its very suddenness stunned her. Her panicked eyes swept the manicured, green lawns and the sweeping hotel drive, and then her gaze rose through the gaps in the bordering pines towards the paddy fields, which climbed in steps to the distant blue mountains. Instinctively, she looked up at the silver glint of a plane against the cloudless sky. It was threateningly low and very loud. The explosion of noise reverberated round the mountains, as she realised that this was not one plane, but a dense shoal of them. Squinting up, against the glare, she saw the red circle of the Rising Sun on each of their wings. These were Japanese planes, and their menace was unmistakable.

1

Ronny's world blinked.

The huge explosions, seconds later, came from the direction of Baguio city. Trembling violently, she hung onto the balcony rail and stared in the direction of the incomprehensible sound. The tall palm trees behind the hotel obstructed her view. The planes had vanished, and the serenity of the sky belied the attack that had just occurred, except for the slow plumes of smoke that rose in billows into the blue.

There followed silence: no birdsong. Was she going mad? Had this really happened? As the world woke up, she uncurled her grip on the balustrade and leaned over, seeking reassurance.

Below her was a flurry of activity. Gardeners, who had been watering plants indolently, were running, shouting and gesticulating wildly. Doors banged in the corridor. She heard the hammer of feet down the stairs, accompanied by reverberating booms of voices. The stampede of activity dictated that she ought to be doing something or going somewhere, but she felt suspended in a surreal dream, still unable to grasp any sense of reality.

Paralysed, she remained on the balcony.

It was only when the second assault arrived, with the suddenness of the first, that Ronny's limbs responded. This time, she needed no urging to flee. She flung herself back into her cool, shaded bedroom, and – with one arm cradling her belly – she scrambled under the protection of the high, wrought-iron bed. She was six months' pregnant, and her movements were hampered as she pulled herself along the wooden floor. Curled up in a foetal position with her hands pressed against her ears, she felt the vibration of the second wave of bombs through the hard floorboards. Her trembling started again, and she could not stop it. Fear for herself and fear for her baby flooded her. The attack felt personal. They were out to get her.

Once again there was a deathly silence. Was she in the best place to survive? Unable to move, she could only lie there and pray that this was not her time, that the onslaught of bombs on Baguio would be precise and that there would be no stray missiles landing on her hotel. Like she was in a monstrous game of hide and seek, she held her breath for fear of being found. She dared not hope the attack was over, and she was right not to hope.

Two more waves of planes roared over as menacingly as the previous ones, until, finally, the strange silence following the raids gave way to indications of life. The sounds of birds started, and Ronny heard vehicles start up and fly off along the gravel. There were noises in the corridor again, shouts and the stamp of feet, as the hotel woke up. And still she lay there. She found that she had been crying for herself, for her baby and for the shattering of her world.

At last, Ronny felt able to move and face her situation. Slowly, she levered herself up, wiped away her tears and rinsed her face with cold water. She needed to leave the room to seek the company of others.

––×––×––

As Ronny descended the gracious stairs slowly, heading towards the hubbub in the hotel lobby, she caught sight of herself in a long, gilt mirror. She was thirty-four years old and a good-looking woman with long, wavy, auburn hair and grey-green eyes. With a slim outline and great legs, she made more of her presence than would be assumed from her five feet and three inches. At that time, the figure in the mirror on the stairwell was dominated by the roundness of her stomach – the outward sign of her six-month fecundity, which then defined her in the glance of strangers.

Ronny looked down on the sea of people gathered in the entrance hall. The floors of white marble gleamed and were adorned with richly fronded plants set in mosaic containers. The overhead fans whirred, forbidding the entrance of the heat from outside. The setting shouted elegance, but excited noise rose to a crescendo as frantic people gathered. Ronny stood alone, overlooking the bustle. Her pregnancy had made her vulnerable, and it was with trepidation that she viewed the crowd beneath her.

"Mrs Rynd, Mrs Rynd! Please let me help you." The speaker was the Filipina receptionist who had signed her in the previous day. The girl ushered her down the remaining steps and into a small private room. "I remember you arrived yesterday. This is not a good place for you to be," the receptionist declared.

Sinking into the comfort of a chair, Ronny smiled her gratitude. "Thank you so much. Can you tell me what's happened?"

"The Japanese have bombed Camp John Hay. There has been a lot of damage, and I think people have been killed. I am so sorry that you are here, Mrs Rynd. This is a terrible time. May I ask you where your husband is? You should not be here on your own."

"The Japanese? I don't understand! Why? Why have they done this?"

"The camp is the American military base where they train my people. It is a big recreation centre. It is a very important place for the Americans here, but, luckily, it's not so close to this hotel. They must have been seeking out the other American bases as well as attacking Pearl Harbor."

"Pearl Harbor? What?" Ronny struggled to take in the girl's words. The name meant nothing to her.

"Yes, this morning; only a few hours ago. We heard it on the radio. Japan is at war with the US. They have sunk the US ships at Pearl Harbor in Hawaii." The pretty girl squatted beside Ronny. "I think that you are not American, Mrs Rynd. Please, where is your husband? Why are you here?"

Ronny answered automatically, but her head was spinning. "Yes, I'm English, and my husband's in Manila. He works for the Hong Kong and Shanghai Bank. He couldn't get away, so I'm here for a holiday on my own before my baby's due." She had wanted to catch up on sleep after the sultry nights she endured in Manila. She had sought the cool mountain air and the flower-scented breezes here, where the vegetation was green and lush.

"How sad that you are here alone."

Ronny, sensing judgement, leapt to Pat's defence. "We thought that if he put in the extra time now, he'd be able to have time off closer to the birth. We haven't been in the Philippines long, and there's so much to prepare. I took this time before the build up to Christmas."

"I am sure you have nothing to worry about. The Americans will not let the Japanese get away with it. They were taken by surprise in Hawaii. Now the Americans know they are under attack, they will soon put the Japanese in their place."

"I can't believe that we left the war with Germany behind only to end up in a new one here."

"I am sure we have nothing to fear. We are not at war with the Japanese. We don't want trouble."

Suddenly, the receptionist's formal English revealed a tremor, and Ronny became aware of the extreme youth of this girl. This was not Ronny's homeland. The reassurance should be coming from her and going to the Filipina girl. It was the Philippines that was being bombed and violated this beautiful morning. Ronny felt ashamed.

"Where are your family? Are they safe? Have you heard from them?" Ronny asked.

"You are kind, Mrs Rynd. I am sure my family is safe, thank you. They are village people: Igorot people. I will go back to see them when I am not needed here," the girl confirmed.

Ronny felt the need for a stiff drink and, thanking the receptionist, negotiated the noisy lobby again to seek the hotel bar. Stunned disbelief was evident amongst the groups of people there, and their exchanges were quiet and subdued. She spotted Eric, an American who had been pleasant to her the evening before. He was alone, so Ronny settled next to him. With his bulging eyes, high colour and a receding chin, he reminded her of a wise tortoise.

Ronny concentrated on him. "I know I'm being naïve, but I really don't understand why this has happened."

"You're not naïve, my dear. You've got the excuse of being new to the East. You would have been concentrating on the war in Europe, so why should you be aware of the clouds gathering here?" he questioned.

"But Pearl Harbor? And now this? Why the attack on American interests? It doesn't make sense."

"Oh, I can't imagine it was as much of a surprise to the White House as it was to the rest of us!"

"How can you say that? Surely it's madness for the Japs to attack the US?"

There was a sudden burst of noise from the lobby as a group of people flocked in, talking excitedly. Ronny had to lean forwards to hear Eric's answer.

"Japan's interest in taking over China is at the root of it and that goes back to 1937. There's always been hostility between the two Far Eastern powers. It's easy for the West to lump the two together, but their cultures are very different. They've always been in some state of war or aggression with each other," he explained.

Only then did she remember that Eric could be long-winded.

"I'm ashamed that I know so little about it. I think I've been blinkered about the political situation," stated Ronny.

"Well, I've always been interested in Asian history, which is why I jumped at the chance to come here when the opportunity arose."

Ronny reflected on how badly timed this move to the Far East had been. Why hadn't she been more aware of the undertow? She had been so wrapped up in the little miracle that was growing within her, that she apparently had blundered into a war zone.

"Go on, please," she requested.

"The Japanese have always wanted to take over China and reduce it to a colony of Japan. By 1939 they were really getting a foothold. They had taken over the whole of the China coast and had gone up the Yangtze Valley to Hangchow. Chaing Kai-shek and the Chinese government had fled to Chungking. The Japanese wanted to press for a settlement that would completely wipe out the power of the Chinese once and for all." Eric broke off suddenly as his wife, Eleanor, joined them, and, searching her face he enquired. "Are you feeling better, my dear?"

Eleanor nodded and joined them without a word.

The American woman had the face of a faded beauty: a rose turning to dust. Her flared nostrils and high cheekbones would once have been magnificent, but the fine lines of tension round her mouth and eyes spoke of a habit of anxiety. The two women exchanged a hug, and Ronny felt a tremor running through the woman, like an over stimulated racehorse. The older woman settled down close to her on the brocade lounger and waved to Eric to continue, obviously used to him holding forth.

He duly obliged, saying, "By August last year they'd managed to occupy the whole of northern Indio-China, and that is where Europe and the rest of the world came in. Germany and Italy signed a tripartite pact with Japan in September, which was a smart move. Then they signed a non-aggression pact with Russia. All eyes were on the battle in Europe, and I guess they were trying to complete the takeover of China whilst nobody noticed."

Ronny was struggling to concentrate. It was hard to relate this flow of logic to the bombardment she had experienced upstairs. She leaned closer in and said, "In London, we were only thinking of Hitler. The Philippines posting seemed such a wonderful adventure for us. How would it help the Japs to attack American bases?"

"Well, in July, the Japanese government signed a joint-protectorate agreement with the French Vichy government for the whole of Indo-China. And that's when we, the US, woke up!" Eric signalled to the barman for pink gins for Ronny and his wife.

He resumed. "Our interests in Southeast Asia were being threatened by Japanese imperialism and especially our interests in the Philippines! We imposed sanctions, severing all trade with them. The Dutch, with their interests in Indonesia, and the British followed suit."

Ronny felt awkward in the overly quiet company of Eleanor, but she felt they had a complicit understanding that they would talk later. She asked, "Why would that be enough to make any difference?"

"Oil, my dear. Always look at the role of oil in any conflict or war. The problem for the Japanese is that without oil from the Dutch East Indies they can't continue their takeover, and they are powerless to complete their move! They're so close to their dreams of total dominance of China that there are only two options for them. They either capitulate to America, or—"

Ronny knew this one. "Lose face?"

"Yes, either lose face or they make a bid for the East Indies oil fields. That meant striking when nobody was watching. It was inevitable. Pearl Harbor was inexorable given their choices. And we, my dear, just happen to be here at the wrong moment."

"So you, too, are shocked?"

His face darkened. "The theory is one thing, but reality is quite different. Although I'd been watching, I, too, am shocked at the suddenness of it all. I suppose I thought there would be more sabre-rattling before a confrontation. This morning, the Japanese have achieved their first objective. Pearl Harbor is a huge blow. I fear we are trapped in the middle of a battle. We've got enough troops in the Philippines to push the Japanese back. It is just a question of time." And, as if on cue, Eric excused himself and left the room with a sense of purpose.

Eleanor sighed and, immediately the atmosphere became more personal. They exchanged accounts of the morning and when that was exhausted, moved on to what was to come next. "Have you heard anything from your husband? What are you going to do?"

This was an obvious question to which she had no answer. "I don't know Eleanor."

"Please call me Ellie. I think sharing this catastrophe makes us friends."

Ronny smiled. "In which case, Ronny is what I like to be called. My full name is Charis Veronica, but with my hair colouring, I got fed up with being called 'Carrots' at school, so that name is strictly off limits!"

Eleanor laughed. "But that's so unusual. I've never heard that name before."

"My father was passionate about the composer Elgar. Apparently, Elgar called his daughter Carise, and my father thought he'd copy it. Something got lost in translation, so my name was a mistake right from the beginning! Ellie, I shall try to get to the phone once the scrum has died down. I can't push my way through that lot."

"I'm sure your husband will come and collect you," Eleanor said blandly, as if that would be the answer to all problems.

Ronny was not so sure! There was only one telephone booth in the hotel lobby, so she foresaw endless queuing to use it.

Over the next two weeks, Ronny managed to talk to Pat on three of the countless occasions they tried to make contact. It was a relief to hear his familiar voice, but the conversations always ran along the same lines and ended badly.

"But, Pat, we should be facing this together. I don't want to stay here, when you're there!" she cried. She knew Pat's mantra by heart, which was 'When in doubt, do nothing', but it was not her mantra!

Pat's voice was firm. "You must stay in Baguio. It's really important that you're in the best possible place for the baby. I can't get you off the islands, and Manila's no place for you at the moment."

"But the baby isn't due till March, and this will be resolved by then. The Yanks won't let the Japs get away with it. There are far too many of them in the Philippines, so they're bound to make it a priority. Lots of people are returning to Manila, so I'm sure that I could find a lift."

"No, poppet, I absolutely forbid you to come back down. Believe me, you're in the best place. This humidity is ghastly, and the city is in chaos. It's just not safe here!"

"Well then, you must come here. I need you here. There are lots of people who have come up, so of course you must."

"I can't leave the bank. We're needed to stay in our place so that people can access their funds."

Pat was immovable. She knew that he would never desert his work post. She also knew he genuinely believed that encouraging her to stay in Baguio was his way of looking after her.

She could feel her frustration building and could not back off. "No, your place is here with me, especially in my condition. I'm sure you could get compassionate leave to come in these circumstances."

"I'm not going to do that, Ronny. This is my job, our livelihood, and I have to stay," he reiterated.

"You're putting your job in front of your wife and your baby! You could come if you wanted to; I know you could. I need you here. If you loved me, you would want to be here to protect me." She could feel the tension of her rising anger reflected in her voice.

"It is not a matter of choice. You know that. I've no choice."

He was an honourable man of the static variety, but, right then, she wanted a dishonourable man who would fight, lie and steal for her. However, she knew that the more pressure she put on him, the more immovable he would be.

"You and your bloody loyalty to the bank! You should be protecting me!" she exclaimed.

Her anger rose like a constricting buzz, and the calls all ended with her losing her control and slamming down the phone. She was helpless to overcome this pattern and could not get back to him to apologise.

Five months of pregnancy had opened up a vulnerability in Ronny. Once she would have worked her charm and hitched a lift down, no matter what reception awaited her, but just then she hesitated. What should she do? She faced an uncertain future, alone amidst a crowd of strangers in an unfamiliar land, and she was frightened.

TWO

17th December 1941

Ronny sat in the foyer of the hotel, with her packed suitcase beside her. She was tense with anticipation over her coming ride, and checked and rechecked her handbag.

The last ten days had been spent in a daze of unreality; her holiday had turned into a nightmare, and she felt useless. Not a day had passed without Japanese aeroplanes flying low on bombing raids, but they no longer generated the same frantic panic. A bomb shelter had been constructed hastily in front of the hotel, and teams of Americans tried to prepare for the anticipated Japanese invasion. Blackout practices had started, and everyone followed directions with concentration.

Ronny had felt in limbo. Pat had been adamant about her remaining in Baguio, so she had sought some role to concentrate on and fill the endless hours. However, all her offers had been met with rejection because, as a pregnant woman, she was considered to be nothing but a liability by the American men on the committees.

The hotel bar had become the main source of information. Rumours had been rife over the last few days. A fleet of ninety ships had been reported to be steaming up the Lingayn Gulf and heading in their direction. The American forces had cleared out of Baguio, reportedly to join the forces in Bataan and Corregidor to regroup and come back stronger. Plane and train links across the island had been commandeered by the military and Filipino hierarchy. The American chief of police had left Baguio supposedly, and the message was that officials thought Manila should be better defended. Ronny had heard that the Red Cross representative had gone down there with all the funds, and she considered that that was a clear message that Baguio had been abandoned.

She had found it easier to deny her fear by taking long, solitary walks away from the hotel, which by then overflowed with American civilians fleeing the south. At 3,000 feet above sea level, the temperature was pleasant, and she was always greeted on her walks by smiling Filipinos, making her feel safe. As she walked, her inner conversations had tormented her. She hated Pat's rigid stance and the indecision this generated within her. She was used to making decisions and being master of her own destiny, but being pregnant had complicated things. Would she be safer here in the face of the Japanese advance, as Pat insisted? Or would Manila, with Pat and the bank to support her, be the better option? She missed her husband and wanted to be with him, so as to face the invasion with him at her side.

Then, two days ago, her indecision had vanished as an incident triggered Ronny's resolve to act.

On one of her walks, she had come upon some impromptu markets that shrewd locals had set up. Guarded by smiling teenagers, household belongings were piled on the pavements in front of their dwellings. It was here she had spotted a delightful little sewing basket amidst a pile of goods for sale. She had stopped to examine it and found it well equipped. Pat had ensured that she had money available at the local bank. Ronny loved sewing and was sure she would make good use of it. She deserved it and, after the compulsory haggling, she had purchased it.

It was then as she had turned away that her peace had been shattered when the bark of shots had rung out. She had spun towards the sound, shocked, and she had seen that a group of jostling men were advancing in that quiet backstreet, shooting their weapons indiscriminately into the air in the vain attempt to attack an enemy plane. The local Filipinos had acquired arms apparently, but this burst of gunfire had been far too close for comfort. Ronny felt exposed. These menacing enthusiasts appeared far more dangerous than the distant plane, and Ronny had been frozen on the spot watching them. The calm morning had felt suddenly oppressive and hostile. What had she thought she was doing, strolling alone as if everything was normal? She had to get out of Baguio. She had decided then that she had to return to the safety of their little flat in the city, to be with Pat, no matter what his views on the matter. She was vulnerable and desperately lonely. Her mind was made up. She had to return to Manila immediately before it was too late.

She had hurried back to the main thoroughfare, where she had flagged down one of the taxis, which – with sprigs of vegetation as camouflage fixed to their radiator caps – drove around erratically, looking for rides.

—*+--*+—

Ronny fidgeted on the sofa and checked her watch again.

Over the last two days, Ronny had approached brazenly everyone she had come across for the prospect of a lift down to the lowlands. She had been met with disbelief and even open hostility. No one would take responsibility for a six-months-pregnant woman on what could be a hazardous journey at the best of times. Her determination had increased with every rejection until, finally, her luck had changed last night.

———×—×———

As she had entered the bar, she had noticed new faces. A scruffy, young couple – with their heads together – had been discussing earnestly a planned dash down south. She had introduced herself and made her request.

She had been met by an ironic stare. The girl had excused herself hastily, and Ronny had steeled herself for the expected refusal. Thus, the negotiations began.

"I'm not sure we can accommodate you. Don't get me wrong, I've nothing against taking you to Manila, but you do realise that we're talking about a 150 mile journey over rough roads?" asked the man.

"Forgive me, but I overheard that you'll be making the trip anyway. I've only got one small suitcase, and I could make it worth your while," cajoled Ronny. Had she detected a flicker of interest? "How about if I paid for my share of the petrol?"

No, he had not been interested.

"All right, I'll pay for all the petrol to get us there," she declared.

He had seemed to be hooked. "We're leaving tomorrow morning. If I agree to take you, I'll need the full amount to pay for the juice. Petrol prices have rocketed. I'll have to buy it on the black market."

"I'm happy to pay if you take me. How much are we talking about?"

He then mentioned a sum that staggered her, and she had looked at him in shock.

"Would you be prepared to accept half now and my husband will give you the other half when we arrive?" She was counting on Pat having the funds and paying up, despite being angry that she had ignored his advice.

"No, lady, that's not how it works. Cash up front or there'll be no trip."

She knew he could name his price, so what option had she got? "That's impossible. I'm going to need money to pay the hotel bill."

Actually, she had drawn out the amount he had demanded that morning. Pregnant she might be, but stupid she was not! Payment at the far end of her journey would be good insurance that she would get there. They had weighed each other up.

"No offence, but how do I know I'll get paid when we deliver you?" had asked the man.

"My husband works for the Hong Kong Shanghai Bank. He knows I'm coming and has already said he will have the money waiting," she explained.

She had watched the young man whilst he considered the proposition.

"All right, but I'm going to need the half-payment immediately so I can get the car filled up, before the prices go up even further," he capitulated.

Ronny had suspected his need was as desperate as hers, but turned her back decisively on her instinctive distrust. She had needed to believe he would honour his side of the bargain and deliver her safely. She had had no choice. The man had then become accommodating, and had waited whilst she went and collected money from her room. A pick-up time had been arranged for the next morning.

And there she was waiting.

Ronny looked at her watch again and felt a nudge of uneasiness. She persuaded herself that she had been too punctual in her anxiety and was pleased to be diverted when Eric plopped himself down next to her.

"Are you off then, my dear?" he queried.

"Yes, as soon as my lift arrives. I'm pleased to see you and have something to ask you," Ronny elaborated.

"Ask away!"

"I keep hearing mention of Nanking, but nobody explains. Will you tell me what's significant about it?"

"I don't want to scare you unnecessarily, but as you've asked." He hesitated. "In the summer of 1937, 50,000 of the Japanese Imperial Army [the Imperial Army] set out to conquer all of China. The emperor had declared it had to be taken in three months. They'd been met with stubborn resistance by Chinese troops in Shanghai, so by the time they reached the capital Nanking in December they were in no mood for leniency. Around 90,000 Chinese soldiers rapidly surrendered to them."

Ronny was surprised. "Why? The Chinese had superior numbers obviously."

"Yes, but they were ill-equipped and intimidated by the reputation of the Japs. The surrendered soldiers were rounded up and trucked out to remote areas and were killed systematically in the most barbaric manner possible. They were used for bayonet practice, beheaded, mown down by machine guns, or doused with petrol and burned alive. We know all this because the Japs filmed it all for posterity."

"That's horrible. How could they justify that after the Chinese had surrendered?"

"The concept of surrender is considered cowardly and unacceptable to the Japanese. They deemed their captives both military and civilian unworthy of life."

"They turned on the civilians?"

Eric paused. "Ronny, dear, well over 20,000 women were gang raped by the soldiers, and then shot or bayoneted to death. No one was spared. Children and the elderly were included in the frenzy. Pregnant women were attacked and, after being raped, had their bellies slashed open. Their babies were torn from them."

Ronny tasted bile in the back of her throat. Her arms closed over her stomach instinctively, and she wished she had never asked. Tears sprang to her eyes, and she thought she was going to be sick. Eric apologised, but Ronny was determined to hear it all.

After a searching look, Eric continued quietly, "Families were deliberately barricaded into houses and burned alive. Indiscriminate acts of murder were commonplace. Soldiers fired rifles into fleeing crowds. Storekeepers were butchered, and their shops were looted. The city burned, and there were corpses on every street corner. It took over six weeks before the blood lust was sated."

Ronny concentrated on Eric's eyes and heard his voice as a distant monotone. "Six weeks of bloodshed? How could it have been allowed? Why didn't the world intervene?" she whispered.

"The rest of the world didn't believe it! The Japanese newspapers took pride in their vivid accounts of the massacre, but the civilised world didn't believe it. A small group of Americans and Europeans verified what had happened finally. They'd been trapped in the centre of the carnage. They showed enormous courage in declaring an international safety zone in the middle of the city. Amazingly, they managed to defend it using Red Cross flags to mark the area as off limits to the Japanese."

Ronny was silent as Eric's voice pounded on.

"Of the population of 60,000 Chinese citizens of Nanking, 30,000 were butchered. Only those who managed to stay inside the zone survived," he confirmed.

This was the reputation that the Japanese Army brought with them, and Ronny had every reason to fear the coming days. She had to get down to Manila and face the Japanese with Pat. She looked at her watch again and felt her baby move.

Eric left her after a warm farewell.

Her lift was by then over an hour late. Her growing conviction that she had been left behind built to a powerful certainty, but she would still not give way to her bitter disappointment.

Ronny sat alone in the busy foyer for another hour before she admitted that she had been taken for a fool and was defeated.

—⚔️—⚔️—

The news that the Japanese had landed in the centre of the island, effectively blocking off the north from the south, came just three weeks after the initial bombing. By then communications were totally severed. Ronny could no longer get in touch with Pat. There was nothing she could do but walk, read and write letters that she suspected would never be read. Food stores were closing down due to lack of stock, so she joined others in the scramble to get what she could, whilst she could. She contented herself in buying a supply of soap, cigarettes for barter, underwear, tins of food and powdered milk. Convincing herself that normality would soon be restored, she did not buy any baby things. She continued to stay at the hotel, and watched and waited.

In the bar, Ronny sought the company of the informative Eric.

He explained, "The committee has decided to declare Baguio as an open city for the Japanese. It's the only way to protect ourselves. It'll let the Imperial Army know that there will be no opposition. All arms will be given up. Brent Boarding School [Brent] has been chosen as the place where we'll gather together to meet them. The committee is doing everything it can to avoid another Nanking. The school will be our safety zone! We will all move there on Boxing Day, so that we'll greet them under one roof to lessen the danger. The school will be the best place for us to appease the invaders."

With Nanking in mind, Ronny wondered if surrendering *en masse* was actually the wisest move, but she had no other option.

———✳——✳———

On Christmas Day, the murmur of voices in the hotel dining room was patchy, with long silences followed by attempts at forced high spirits. Ronny had made an effort for the celebration meal. She had piled her hair into a coil on her head, and put on her soft, green dress and jade earrings. Every table had been taken. The hotel had produced some semblance of Christmas past, complete with turkey and roast potatoes for the guests. A growing black market had sprung up in the city, and the local staff struggled to make the day memorable. Paper crackers and decorations graced the gleaming, white tablecloths, and balloons hung from the ceiling. The staff, comprised mostly of women, displayed their familiar smiles, although they must have been as frightened by the tales of Japanese atrocities as the guests were.

Ronny was sharing the table with Eleanor and Eric. As she had come to know them better, she was aware of the complicated balance of their relationship. Eleanor had a fragility about her and a nervous, childlike dependence on her solid husband. She had a brain, but it seemed to disengage rapidly when disturbed. Eric obviously adored her, but he controlled every aspect of her life.

Ronny made an attempt at light conversation. "My sisters were very envious when we were assigned to come to the Philippines! They were stuck in London at the mercy of the Luftwaffe, doing their bit for the war effort. Joy is a physiotherapist at the Brompton Hospital, specialising in lung disorders, and my younger sister Felicity drives an ambulance."

Eleanor asked, "What did you do before you got married?"

"I'm a physical education [PE] teacher. One of my jobs was as a games hostess on the Australia route with Orient Line cruises. I was rather proud that I was the first woman to get that job."

"Was that fun?"

"Yes, it was! It meant organising the leisure activities of the guests, which ranged from deck quoits to fitness classes, quizzes and dances. I'm good at organising, which is why I find it so frustrating that I'm not being allowed to do anything useful here. Let's hope that, this time next year, we'll be joking about all this."

Eric responded. "We have to be realistic. Hitler shows no sign of retreating, and the Allies don't seem to be getting anywhere. Why should this situation with the Japs be any different?"

Eleanor had her answer: "Because it's our country that's been attacked! Our boys will teach them a lesson before they know it! You'll see!"

"Are you ready for the move to the school tomorrow?" Eric asked Ronny.

"Yes, I'm as ready as possible. I've collected a few useful things for the next couple of days. I've just the one small suitcase and a bedroll," Ronny confirmed.

"How's your money situation? I'm so sorry that bounder took you for a ride over the lift. We may need money for bribes in the coming days, and I want you to know I can help you out if you run short," offered Eric generously.

Eleanor interjected, "Last night, I sewed bank notes into the hems of my dresses, just in case."

Ronny had done the same thing, only into the base of her toilet bag. "It's too late to get any more supplies, and it will only be for a few nights at most. I'm taking a notebook and pencils with me to record what's happening. I just wish I had returned to

Manila when it was possible. And then I got tricked, which was stupid of me. Have you heard any news of what's going on down south? I wish…" She tailed off.

"Ronny, what are you planning to wear tomorrow? I don't want to upset you, but I've only seen you wearing dresses. Do you have a pair of slacks with you?" Eric enquired.

"Eric, don't!" said Eleanor, appalled.

"No, my dear, I'm only trying to look after her as I do you," he explained.

"It's fine," Ronny responded, "You're not suggesting anything I haven't been thinking about. Yes, Eric, I'll certainly be wearing slacks." She tried to lighten her dread. "And no lipstick!"

Eleanor cut in, "I don't want to talk about rape as a possibility. Nanking was more to do with the hostility between the Nips and the Chinese. It was a historical thing. We're not in the same category. We're innocent bystanders, and they've no reason to hurt us."

"Ellie, my dear, you've no experience of men in a war situation. Sadly, finer considerations get blunted and brutalised. These Japs have left their women at home, and if their commanders see rape as important in the degradation of their captives, then it is going to happen," stated Eric.

"Eric, that's enough." Tears started in Eleanor's eyes.

"No, Ellie, it's not enough." He looked from face to face. "Ronny, Ellie, you must be so very careful. There must be no sign of anything that makes you stand out and no show of individuality. Conceal your attractiveness. Do nothing to draw attention to yourselves. That's the only way to survive. These first few days are going to be the most dangerous ones. They've a point to make, and we've no idea what threat we may present to them. We're dealing with people whose culture requires them never to be taken prisoner, so we'll be the lowest of the low already, just by surrendering."

Eleanor was adamant. "They can't be as bad as they're made out to be. I've heard they love children."

Ronny could not follow this logic. "They love their children. Who's to say they'll love ours?"

Eric stuck to his point. "You need to be totally submissive, no matter what happens."

"Please, Eric. Enough! Can't we just try, for today, to enjoy what we have? This Christmas is certainly not of our choosing, but let's make the most of it. We've ample food and this wonderful wine. Please let's enjoy the meal and deal with the rest when we've left the table," Eleanor pleaded.

The fear and uncertainty were camouflaged for a little while. They ate automatically and talked about their families back home. Finally, the crackers were pulled and the coffee served, and they wandered out onto the terrace. Christmas Day felt like the last day of the world as they knew it.

—⚔—⚔—

Later, in her room, Ronny felt a wave of homesickness. She thought about her parents. Her father was in Palestine with his job in the oil business, and her mother was in South Africa raising funds for the war effort. Ronny had learned at an early age that she had to take care of herself, as her parents were vibrant and dynamic but not the most attentive to their children. She wondered if her family even knew of her situation or had received any of her letters.

That night Ronny felt utterly alone and terribly frightened as she soaked in the beauty of the scene from her balcony. The sunset sky was flooded with glorious shades of peach and vibrant gold, against which the mountains loomed deep purple and menacing. This was not a nightmare from which she would wake up when things got too serious. This horror was real, and tomorrow she would need all her strength and courage to survive.

THREE

—‡—‡—

27th December 1941

Ronny dragged her suitcase through the dormitories, looking for the bunk beds she had assumed they were going to sleep on, but there were none to be seen. Brent Boarding School was smaller than she had expected, and it was obvious that, despite forward planning, the committee had grossly underestimated the numbers who would show up. She had arrived too late. Most of the floor space had been taken up by families and their piles of mosquito nets, mattress rolls and household possessions, resembling the chaos prior to a jumble sale. Hot and tired, she pushed her way into room after room, looking for a niche. She saw familiar faces from the hotel, Eric and Eleanor amongst them, but they showed no inclination to leave their firmly established patch. Ronny had imagined the school would be like a basic hostel, but the reality was that there would be no segregation, and she was lumped in with men, women, children and babies. There would be no special consideration for a woman in her condition. Someone had put up signs to segregate the toilet areas, but it was evident that the facilities were going to be totally inadequate.

Finally, she found a little vacant patch and – dumping her newly purchased bedroll, mosquito net and suitcase – she slid down with her back to the wall to rest her aching legs. Looking around at her neighbours, she realised the move had been easier for her than for those who came straight from their homes. Mattresses bore witness to peoples' decisions on what to bring. She noticed one that was piled high with children's toys, obviously at the cost of more adult needs. She stared at the patchwork of humanity that surrounded her. The temperature of the overcrowded room became rapidly uncomfortable, with the overhead fan failing to combat the heat.

The noise was considerable.

A large woman near her sobbed, "I can't bear it. He knew we were deserting him."

Her husband seemed helpless. "My dear, we had no option! You know dogs aren't allowed to come. Ruby will look after him."

"He won't understand! Did you see his face? We never leave him!"

"We have to trust the maid! She'll look after him. It won't be for long!"

"The servants don't love him the way we do! Ruby won't give him his treats. We should never have agreed to this." The woman was as distraught as if she had left a child behind, and no words of comfort from her husband could console her.

The overwhelming majority of those gathered were American. Ronny found only a smattering of Europeans and no Filipinos. Although they were giving up the city to the Japanese, everyone believed the situation would be short-lived and that the American forces would strike back immediately. What would happen in the next few days was the fear, and this was the reason they were all huddled together in the hope that there would be safety in numbers. Of course Ronny was frightened and she was wearing slacks, as were most of the women, but her greatest concern was for her baby. Would her pregnancy make her more vulnerable or less?

The hours passed slowly, and she tried to lose herself in a book, but gave up after reading pages without assimilating them. To stretch her legs, she explored, and she found that all the dormitories were already totally occupied. People were camping in classrooms, despite the fixed-to-the-floor desks that were a menace to the latecomers trying to set up camp between them. And yet more people continued to arrive.

The mosquitoes came as evening turned into a humid night. The floor was hard, her back hurt, and there was little peace. Ronny found it almost impossible to sleep propped against the wall under her net. Throughout the night, families continued to arrive. Some had come voluntarily, but many had been rousted by Japanese soldiers and had been driven to the school in their own cars, which were then requisitioned.

Ronny heard a whispered conversation between two women, one of whom had newly joined the other on a mat near her.

"Thank God, you're all right. It must have been terrifying," said the woman who was there first.

"It was. I didn't know what to expect. The first thing I knew was the banging on the door. I was asleep. They shouted a lot. It was humiliating," replied the new arrival.

"Humiliating?"

"They made me get dressed in front of them. They just stood there and watched."

"They didn't touch you?"

"No. They just acted angry and impatient. I didn't have time to grab anything, and they used my car to bring me in!"

Ronny was relieved to hear that no violation had taken place.

Mayor Halsema announced on the local radio that Baguio was under the control of the Imperial Army, and word spread through the dormitory. It was official. There were by then over 300 people crammed into the school, where even the front hall looked like a flop house.

It was around dawn when Ronny opened her eyes to her first sight of Japanese soldiers. They were there suddenly, clad in khaki and with bayonets fixed to their guns. They were small, swarthy men who smelled foreign. She sat very still and watched them warily. By that point, it had really begun. In a show of open aggression, the soldiers stomped their way through the crowded room. Children wailed, frightened, as bayonets were thrust into bedding and piles of possessions were overturned. Incomprehensible orders were barked, and men and women were shoved around in a blatant display of dominance. Exhaustion and confusion reigned. Guards placed themselves at the doors, and movement was restricted immediately to the room that they were in. Even going to the by then filthy toilet was only by permission and with the supervision of a guard.

As the morning wore on, Ronny sat alone amidst the crush of people, and witnessed how tempers flared and distress increased. The noise became unbearable, with fractious children whining at being thirsty, hungry and contained. Parents did their best, but the increasing heat throughout the day did little to alleviate their problems. She knew she had limited energy and tried to distance herself from it all by reading. The long night had taken its toll, and she had finished her bottled water. Generosity vanished as everyone looked after their own.

A child's screams became intolerable, and she met the eyes of an elderly woman neighbour and commiserated, "Surely they'll let the women and children go? Isn't that the rule of war for civilians?"

"You would certainly hope so, but I'm concerned that they won't follow the Geneva Convention. They've an axe to grind," the woman replied.

"What do you mean?"

"I'm thinking about the Japanese expatriates whom the Americans rounded up and took to Camp John Hay after the first bombings. They thought the Americans had used them as a human shield. They were just left there without food and water when the military took off. It was five days before the civilian authorities learned about them, and they wouldn't have survived if it hadn't been for Mayor Halsema and Elmer Herold bringing them food and water. If we're treated well it's those two we need to thank."

A sharp faced woman butted in. "It's unbelievable that our troops left us unprotected like this, and now you tell me they left us open to revenge treatment too!"

"We shouldn't be held responsible for the military," retorted the older woman, and Ronny heard the tension in her voice.

Another voice cut in. "Surely if Japs were being held at Camp John Hay, their air force wouldn't have continued to bomb it? I heard that they suffered some direct hits."

There was no shortage of opinions on offer as everyone waited for something to happen.

By lunch time, increased thirst and hunger overrode all other issues. No provisions had been supplied by the Imperial Army. There was no way of knowing where her next drink or meal was coming from, so – unhygienic as it was – Ronny kept herself going by drinking from the toilet washbasin. She was thankful she only had herself to look after, as there were several unaccompanied mothers with small children to entertain. She considered them the brave ones. They had to keep them amused whilst dealing with their own fear. Ronny sighed, abandoned her book, produced a pack of playing cards and passed the time teaching one little nine-year-old how to play a simple card game.

The khaki-clad guards, with their big boots, appeared to be waiting for higher authorities, and so afternoon turned to evening. That night, chaos erupted again as everyone who had been sleeping in the classrooms and corridors were forced to move into the overcrowded dormitories. There were no arguments in the face of the bayonets, and angry scenes ensued as people piled in. On the floor of Ronny's room, there simply was no space. She was jammed in, shoulder to shoulder, and the jostling and noise of the family next to her made her finally snap.

"It's no good. Can't you see it's impossible for me to move over any further? You're spilling right onto me," she declared.

"Well, I can't help it. My kids need to lie down. You can't expect them to sleep sitting up," a voice replied.

"They don't look as if they're going to sleep anyhow and nor are we, with the racket they're making," chimed in someone else.

"You wait till you have kids, then you'll understand!" stated the father.

There was no answer to this, and Ronny closed her eyes and tried to ignore the pain in her back. Utterly weary, she was desperate to lie down and blot out her surroundings.

After midnight, just as she was dozing off, she was startled awake by shouted orders to file out into the hall of the administration block. It was a relief to be out of the dormitory, even though it meant joining an endless queue to be interrogated. However, the joy of being free to move around soon wore off, as children wailed and the line dragged itself forwards at a snail's pace. A corridor of armed guards funnelled them along, avoiding all eye contact, and it was whispered that some expatriate Baguio Japanese had been spotted amongst them.

Finally, Ronny stepped forwards to meet the clinical stare of the beautifully turned out Japanese officer positioned behind a large desk. His shirt was pristinely white, and his gestures were precise. He spoke English and, in a bored manner, asked for her name, age and occupation. He questioned where her husband was, grunted and dismissed her when she answered, "Manila."

Ronny returned to the dormitory to face the rest of the fetid night. She re-draped her mosquito net over her body and elbowed her way back into her secured wall space, which she was not going to relinquish. Intermittently, she dozed, squeezed between the encroaching shoulders. The night seemed endless. Men and women could leave the room in order to go to relieve themselves, under escort, and queues formed. Driven by thirst and a constricted bladder, Ronny was forced to join the shuffling line. The wait became distressing and when she could bear it no longer, she left her place in line, approached a guard and, using mime, she tried to make her desperation understood. The young and uncertain guard looked alarmed, but, to her relief, after rapid conversation with a colleague, escorted her to the toilet. She was able to smile later at his obvious conviction that she had been about to give birth there and then.

By the morning, the emotional state in the room had become a dark presence all of its own. Tempers were uncontrollable and neighbourliness had long departed. The noise from children and crying babies was intolerable, and the unending squabbling of the family near her became more than she could bear.

Ronny pleaded, "Look, just get them to shut up. Whatever it takes!"

"Don't shout at me! I didn't cause this mess. You can't expect the kids to understand. They're just overtired and scared!" declared the father.

"Aren't we all!" Ronny muttered. She withdrew into an icy anger that was directed against her guards, her neighbours, her distant family, her husband and the world in general.

It was impossible to maintain order in the room, as the guards walked through systematically in their brutal boots, upending mats with their bayonets. They confiscated money, cameras, watches and jewellery, and Ronny watched as one guard even took tins of food that he came across in his search. Rings were taken off fingers and she was grateful that her own gold wedding ring was covered with a platinum layer, so that, to the casual observer, it appeared to have no real value. They took her watch, her last connection to her absent mother, which really upset her. It meant more to her than the little jewellery of value she possessed, which had been left behind in Manila. Ronny noticed one neighbour checking that her ring was secured, sewn under a large button on her jacket, and made a note to do the same herself as soon as she had the opportunity.

In the early afternoon, they were ordered out to the tennis courts. The nets had been removed and they trailed onto the hot tarmac, which was surrounded by armed guards. Four machine guns were already in place, directed towards the courts. The number of internees had swelled to about 500, and panic grew as everyone was segregated. Children were separated from their parents, causing further fear. The old and infirm were directed to one side, women and infants to another and, finally, just the men were left. Ronny felt her heart constrict. Divided like this, they appeared so vulnerable. Could this be the time when the women and children would be released? She was desperate for this nightmare to end. Surely they would let her go? She looked at the pain on the faces surrounding her, the separated families, and found herself conflicted. She had yet to witness violence first-hand in her life, and this nightmare still had the substance of a dream. Part of her prayed for her own release and part prayed that everyone would be kept together.

The Japanese officer who had interrogated them the night before mounted a block in the centre of the group and, with the ease of natural authority, introduced himself as Major Mukaibo. After the curt efficiency of the previous night, it was a surprise when he launched into an angry rant, laying down the rules and regulations for his prisoners. He threatened death for a number of crimes. Death for the failure to hand in a weapon or to report anyone who was holding one. Death for any attempt to escape or for withholding information about an attempted escape. Five men and five women would be shot as the penalty for any infraction. The word 'shot' hammered into Ronny's heart. All hope of release vanished as she believed utterly that her captors would follow through with their threats. Lost in a downward spiral of fear, she barely heard the last pronouncement that they were to prepare for immediate departure and form a line in front of the school.

Chaos followed the announcement. Ronny was caught up in the dash to ready themselves, taking only what they could carry. Back in the dormitory she saw men and women putting on several layers of clothing so that they could carry more in their bundles or suitcases. She managed to squeeze everything into the suitcase that she had packed in a different world, two days ago. Her slim bedroll did not weigh much, but she was anxious to know how far she was supposed to carry everything. Already weak from the lack of food and water over the last two days, Ronny knew that pregnancy had lessened her stamina, and she dreaded the prospect of the trek ahead of her.

—⊬—⊬—

Major Mukaibo stood by the gate whilst the soldiers organised the exodus, with the men first, women second, children third and, finally, the elderly. Ronny shuffled into line. The sun bore down hotly on her head.

They set off, flanked by soldiers, but it soon became evident that not everyone was going to manage the walk. Almost immediately, the elderly and sick were holding everyone up. The sun was merciless, and the heat bounced off the dusty road. The walking pace had slowed to a crawl as Japanese soldiers, with shouts and shoves, tried to regulate the march. Filipinos had been organised to line the route to witness the humiliation of the Americans, but, in reality, the witnesses were subdued and sympathetic. Many people had attempted to carry too much, so the Filipinos benefitted as desperate walkers gave up the unequal struggle and offloaded their possessions en route. Ronny found the walk gruelling. Her throat was parched and her head swam. Her misery was heightened by the lack of knowledge as to how far away their destination was.

The next enforced stop brought the soldiers along the line, and they started separating out those who were clearly unfit to continue. Instinctively, Ronny stepped forwards, thrusting out her belly to exaggerate her pregnancy. The guard nodded. She stepped into the secondary line and then, for one awful moment, wondered whether she was headed to her death. Would the weak be disposed of once the fit had marched on? It was too late to change her mind, and indeed she was almost past caring. She could not take another step.

Ronny edged into the shade thrown out by the roadside trees and sunk down on the stubbly grass. Her throat ached and sweat dripped, stinging her eyes. The heat haze danced on the road surface as the wait by the road seemed interminable. No one in the group broke the silence as they watched the departing prisoners. Ronny was desperately relieved when a lorry arrived finally and it came to be her turn to be bundled aboard.

FOUR

———⊣⊢——⊣⊢———

29th December 1941

2 days in captivity

It was bruising travelling in the open well of the lorry as Ronny was driven the four miles to Camp John Hay. This former American retreat, with its fabulous golf course and velvet lawns, was the very place where Japanese civilians had been imprisoned after the first bombing attack. As she was driven through the gates, Ronny saw bomb craters pitting those legendary fairways, the lawns were churned up, and the roof of the clubhouse had bomb damage at one end of it. The location and far reaching views were still special, but the former Igorot scout barracks were surrounded by glistening, new barbed wire.

The barely functional buildings, which had housed eighty soldiers, were filthy and totally unsuitable for the wave of 500 exhausted incomers. The leaders of the representative committee organised the dormitory, placing men near the front entrances, and women and children closer to the toilets. Adults were allocated a two-by-seven-foot floor area on which to place their bedroll, mattress and possessions. Ronny slumped down where she was told, too tired to compete for a better slot.

Angry strident voices were raised near her. "No. Absolutely not. I'm not going next to that mob of towheads. I had enough of them at Brent."

It was answered immediately with, "Well, you can think again if you think I want you snivelling next to me."

Ronny allowed the voices to wash over her, only registering when they reached a certain peak. The jostling for position continued without dignity. Some were reduced to tears and some slumped silently on the floor. Ronny was used to her gnawing hunger and accompanying light-headedness, but her raging thirst was frightening. The guards were inundated with requests and, finally, commandeered Filipinos came round with drinking water, for which Ronny was desperately grateful.

—⊁—⊁—

At the roll call, Nakamura Takeshi introduced himself as the commandant in charge of the camp. Being slightly taller than most Japanese, he had large hands and a solid appearance. He and his family had lived in Baguio for many years. He belonged to civic clubs, played golf at Camp John Hay and was well connected. He was a 'perfect plant', some muttered. As a result of being employed by the Heald Lumber Company as a carpenter, he spoke fluent American English, his language peppered with profanities picked up from his co-workers and he appeared ignorant of the offence he caused.

The camp would be run by a committee of eminent men: Dr Richard Walker; Jim Halsema, who was the former mayor of Baguio; the tall and charming Reverend Carl Eschbach; and Elmer Herold, who had been the general manager of the Heald

Lumber Company. Nakamura awarded his former boss and that man's wife a semi-private cubicle which made them unpopular with other internees.

—⊁⋅⊁—

Ronny lay on her bedroll and closed her eyes. There was so much that she needed to get used to in order to survive. She thought about an incident she had witnessed. A woman standing smoking on the grass flicked away the butt of a cigarette casually and was slapped hard across the face by a nearby guard. The woman was more frightened than hurt, and the guard – satisfied he had delivered his message – continued on his rounds. This instant physical reprimand was used not just on them but also on the guards themselves by their superiors. Ronny was determined to learn how to stay out of trouble.

—⊁⋅⊁—

The committee organised their first meal that day, a soup containing rice, and food was the primary subject in the conversations around her.

Next to her, a reed-thin woman was holding forth: "The Nips have made it clear that the army have no money to feed us."

Ronny was curious. "How do you know that?"

"One of the guys from the organising committee told me the Imperial Army will only provide us with rice. They've given us permission to use the remnants of the canned goods and staples left in the camp by the US Army."

"I did hear that a truck has been sent back to collect rice, sugar, oatmeal and tinned food from the Brent kitchen." She closed her eyes to rest them.

"The committee is asking us to pool what resources we have."

A woman hissed, "They can ask as much as they like, I'm not sharing mine! I'm not supporting anyone who hadn't the foresight to stock up!"

Ronny wondered what the face would look like if she opened her eyes and thought better of it. She mumbled, "You won't be allowed to keep it!"

The thin woman continued, "It's tough, but if everyone gives as much as they can, it ensures we have a shared staple diet. Do you know Mr Trimble, who owns the refrigeration store in Baguio? He's going to ship into camp all the contents he has in storage, mostly imported meat."

Ronny made an effort. "If we all chip in, we'll survive until our boys come back. You'll see! It won't be for long."

The reality was that none of them had any idea as to how long this unfunded imprisonment would last. It was obvious that strict rations should be imposed from the outset.

—⊁——⊁—

Ronny was disturbed as the committee reorganised the floor space. Shame and gain tactics were used on families too confused or depressed to think for themselves. Mothers with children were awarded extra space. Mattresses were re-laid several times, leaving narrow corridors between the sleeping areas, which had to be negotiated with care. The dormitory was claustrophobic, and the accommodation squares resembled a patchwork of dumped debris with mosquito nets draped over bedding areas or nailed to ceiling structures. The noise level, especially from distressed infants, was unremitting. Ronny retreated back out into the fresh air of the grounds, which was infinitely preferable, even though it was under the scrutiny of the guards. The buildings lacked electricity due to the bombing, which made the coming of darkness that first evening even more fraught.

That night was Ronny's first experience of how bodies lying so close together had to accommodate themselves for the greater good. Turning over had a domino effect forcing strangers to shift their positions. The constant trickle of people trying to negotiate their way to the toilet between sleeping bodies led to yelps at misplaced feet, and general mutters about encroachment. Ronny was dog tired and grateful to be able to lie down, but she feared what trials the next day would bring.

—⊬—⊬—

There was jubilation when the electricity and intermittent water were restored. After three days, the stench from the overloaded toilets became overpowering. The one bathroom had been designed for military men and was totally inadequate, so long queues formed. Everything from teeth brushing to nappy washing had to be done in a single metal sink, and Ronny was convinced it would affect their hygiene as well as their morale. In order to relieve the congestion, the men organised themselves into a work group and dug a urinal ditch protected by the roof of an adjacent hut. In theory it was intended for men only, but the women started to use it so a system of half-hourly segregation was set up. Toilet paper was rationed to two pieces per visit.

Some semblance of a routine established itself, but it was a sordid sort of life. Ronny found the lack of privacy, both physical and emotional, was hardest to bear. Dressing and undressing in a room with no respect for gender was just one aspect, and, initially, due to her distended belly, she had found herself an object of interest from the children. Luckily, that passed as all sorts of private idiosyncrasies were revealed. There were ladies whose immaculate hair turned out to be wigs and many whose teeth were removed at night. Children giggled at one poor man who removed his leg before going to bed. Averting eyes became second nature, but eavesdropping was harder to avoid.

Ronny felt desperately alone and wondered continually what had happened to Pat. She paced the grounds under the eyes of the guards and, in her turn, watched her captors doing their daily exercise routines. The Japanese officers in charge were formally dressed, with long swords trailing to the ground. The khaki-clad soldiers were not impressive in stature, but they were wiry and energetic, and their gestures would have been funny at times, were it not for the menace they exuded. Armed with guns and the terrifying sharp bayonets, they were a chilling reminder of the slaughter in Nanking. Their practice sessions ended with the stiff bow from the waist, which the prisoners were required to perform whenever they were passing their Japanese captors in the camp.

The lack of food was the major problem. Ten days had passed since Boxing Day, and the Japanese still had provided no food. The pooled supply of tins, brought into the camp, was nearly finished. The thin soup that was their staple diet became little more than flavoured water when stretched to feed so many. The committee was worried about the health of infants, breastfeeding mothers and the pregnant ladies, so an extra snack was allocated to Ronny every day.

With nothing to do, depression was rife. Even normally active people lay around in the dormitory or on the grass, unable to summon the energy to do anything other than the bare minimum needed to exist. Ronny was frightened of succumbing to this numbness of mind and body. The elderly were especially vulnerable, and she watched as those with the least reserves of mental and physical stamina showed signs of giving up. Everyone felt powerless and were waiting desperately for the liberating Americans to arrive.

Finally, Nakamura gave permission for the men, under guard, to haul in extra water that was brought to the camp by trucks. A new toilet trench was dug, and this one was more sophisticated, with a segregating piece of galvanised iron in place for gender privacy. It had boards for the placement of feet and could even be sluiced down at intervals.

—⊁—⊁—

Ronny and Eleanor were lying on the grass, looking bleakly at their empty coconut bowls that acted as plates.

A heavily made-up woman slumped down beside them and whined, "They're going to starve us to death. It's as simple as that."

Her clothing announced she was well heeled, and Ronny thought her attitude to lesser mortals around her was reflected by her heavy nasal breathing.

Ronny replied, "I don't think they even thought about how they were going to feed us. It obviously wasn't in the emperor's mind in the great scheme of things."

"Eric says the Jap soldiers were expected to live off the land as they went along. Holding us in one place presents a very different problem," offered Eleanor, as she stared at the useless grass.

The woman continued, "The committee is petitioning Nakamura every day, but getting nowhere. He's an idiot if he doesn't allow our Filipino servants to bring in food for us."

Ronny fumed, "You're lucky to have Filipino servants who are prepared to do that. Some of us don't have that option!"

"Of course we'll pay them. We know our staff are lining up at the gate every day, but the guards won't allow the food to come in," the woman responded.

"I've seen them being turned away." Eleanor agreed.

"That's what I mean. It's deliberate. They're starving us to death. I'm so hungry that I can't think straight. I wish we'd taken to the hills whilst we could. We should never have been persuaded to give ourselves up. We'd have been better off with the guerrillas," the woman complained.

Ronny was irritated. "You've got no idea what it would have been like. I imagine it's no picnic for the guerrillas either."

Ronny wished the woman would go away, but instead she wailed on, "At least they have choices. We don't. This life is so degrading. I can't bear it. I'd sooner be dead."

Ronny and Eleanor exchanged glances.

Day followed day, and life deteriorated without structure, as they all waited for the Americans to arrive and rescue them. The first cases of dysentery were reported. Internees went down with sickness, and Ronny was torn between fear of what the tap water might contain and her constant drive to relieve her thirst. She became withdrawn and fixated on her concern for her unborn baby. She was naturally a doer, and the powerlessness of her situation, coupled with her pregnancy, conspired against her.

The camp population was divided between missionaries, miners, lumber-workers and other commercial tradespeople, and, inevitably, there was a chasm between groups and their reasons for being in the Pacific region. There were over 200 missionaries in camp from several different denominations, and most of them were young, American families who had been working in China. The Roman Catholic Philippines had been a safe haven after fleeing mainland China. In Ronny's cramped dormitory, an extended family group of missionaries gathered every evening to share prayers and songs.

One evening, a missionary called Helen Angeny was showing Ronny how to put her hair up into two plaits, in the Swiss style. Helen was dark-haired with a ready smile and calm strength.

And, most importantly to Ronny, she was almost nine-months pregnant with her first child. Her husband, Ed was in camp too.

Helen chatted whilst plaiting. "You really do have beautiful hair. Have you heard Dr Dana Nance is getting involved in what's going on in camp?"

"The doctor from the Notre Dame Hospital? How come he's involved when he's not interned?" Ronny queried.

"He heard about the water situation here and read the riot act to Nakamura. How do you like your hair?"

Ronny had no mirror, but had already decided it took more effort than she was prepared to put in. "It feels lovely and much cooler. Thank you. Why would he think he could make a difference?"

"Dr Nance is special; he's the son of Chinese missionaries and a skilled surgeon. He's renowned for helping the Japanese community before the war. I don't think Nakamura can afford to ignore him."

"Why isn't he interned?"

"As I said, he has special standing, and, actually, we're better off with him on the outside. He knows about the dysentery and he's going to provide medicines from the hospital."

"Will Major Mukaibo allow it?"

"Yes. Mukaibo's a strange one. Did you know that he's a Methodist minister? One of the women recognised him from a seminary in Philadelphia! Apparently, he was educated in a college in the US, hence the perfect English."

Ronny laughed. "And the American accent! I never quite understand what his role is."

The pair stopped talking as a Japanese soldier strolled by. Boredom afflicted the guards as well as the guarded, and this perambulation was a means of passing time, rather than a diligent inspection. Ronny looked at the man's pockmarked, young face and wondered what was going on behind his uncommunicative eyes. She found oriental faces impossible to read.

He passed, and Helen resumed. "Without a doubt, Mukaibo's involved with Japanese intelligence, which is why Nakamura is so cautious around him. Mukaibo's a powerful man. It's a strange notion to think that he's a saviour of souls. What a complicated world we live in."

Dr Nance lived up to his reputation and delivered the medicines. The wave of dysentery lessened, and the interned doctors inoculated the elderly and the children in the camp. Dr Nance's next proposal was to make use of the empty Camp John Hay military hospital, which was full of medical supplies. The move to separate the sick from the healthy made such sense that Nakamura could not refuse. The fear of an epidemic within the barracks decreased, and there was a general lifting of spirits. Dr Nance may have made one demand too many, for shortly after this he was forced to join their ranks as an internee.

Nance was not popular with everyone and was rumoured to have a drinking problem. Ronny felt more secure with the warm-mannered Dr Beulah Allen, who was already a mother and in the early stages of her own second pregnancy. Dr Allen's husband, Sam, was away fighting alongside the American forces, so Ronny felt a connection with her. It was an open secret that Dr Allen and Dr Nance had diametrically opposed views, and they were actively hostile to each other.

"I've just heard the Japs have agreed to pay a per capita allowance to the camp. It may be minimal, but it's better than nothing." Eleanor was excited, but Ronny ignored her as she considered her breakfast.

A stout woman joined the conversation. "And Nakamura is allowing us our food packages. I can't wait for some home cooking. Yesterday, our boys had to wait two hours to deliver food through the guardhouse, but I am sure it'll get easier."

Ronny growled, "Some of us don't have that luxury!" She stirred the spoonful of syrup into her breakfast rice. Lunch was always a form of soup. Dinner was rice or a potato-like vegetable, a touch of meat and whatever else could be bought.

Eleanor placated her by saying, "Think of it this way, Ronny. There will be fewer of us eating the communal fare, so you'll get bigger helpings."

"Oh, and that's supposed to make me feel better?" questioned Ronny.

"I personally think chef Alex is doing a fantastic job! It's no mean feat what he produces!" cried Eleanor.

The stout woman contributed, "I expect being Russian helps!"

Ronny rounded on her. "What's that got to do with it? It's more to do with his contacts as the manager of the Pines Hotel."

"Ray Hale is a help. It was a smart move to appoint him as daily driver to shop in Baguio. Ray's useful. His wife is a Filipina, and he speaks the lingo and can barter," the woman explained.

Ronny smiled. "I did ask chef Alex how he managed to make such a small amount go round, and he tapped the side of his nose and said in his funny accent 'Better not to ask!'"

The stout woman had the last negative word. "We'd be in trouble if Nakamura didn't allow the men to forage for wood to feed the old cooker. What's going to happen when the wood runs out?"

—⊬⸱⸱⊬—

The sound of cheers intruded on Ronny's siesta one afternoon. She found she was continually tired and valued her escape into afternoon naps. Stumbling out of the dormitory, her mind still in another world, she was greeted by celebrating crowds.

"We've done it. The committee's done it. Nakamura's letting the men move into the other barracks," someone explained.

Eleanor was excited. "It made so much sense and it's ridiculous that we had to petition for so long."

But some were not happy; one person grumbled, "There's a lot of bomb damage, and the men must work to make it habitable."

"There's nothing structural that our men can't do, and we can help with scrubbing and painting," Eleanor elaborated.

Ronny was delighted. "It's wonderful news. I can't wait to have the dormitory to ourselves."

"You must be mad," muttered a long face. "With the men gone, we've got no protection from the soldiers. They could do anything to us if the men aren't there."

"I don't think you have to worry about that," replied Eleanor.

"Of course I'm worried," the woman responded, "They come in at least twice a night to check up on us and poke about. I won't sleep a wink now. We'll have no protection, and they'll be able to do anything they please."

"I think some of our room sisters are bigger and tougher than most of the men!" Ronny chuckled. "I'll name no names, but I'd put money on them as protectors rather than any man."

Eleanor mused, "I'll miss Eric, but it's only the sleeping arrangements that are changed. It'll give us all much more room. Eric's too nice to say it, but I'm sure he'll be happy not to have to share with young children any more!"

The men set to work with enthusiasm and the barracks was patched up and made serviceable. The floors were scrubbed, and everyone benefitted from this positive aim of bettering their lot. Ronny helped the other women clean the old dormitory and re-lay the mattresses to take advantage of the extra room. The barracks bathroom, which had been such a cause of embarrassment with its long row of toilets without stalls, acquired some curtain material suddenly, which was tacked up between the toilets for privacy. There was still no mirror, but that was a low priority under the circumstances. Ronny was sure some women missed sleeping next to their men, but overall there was a feeling of relief all round.

It had been a busy morning, and Ronny lay on her mattress at siesta time, idly stroking her taut belly. Her baby moved and kicked her regularly, and she valued this interlude as her legs and back ached from the extra load.

Helen lowered herself carefully down on a neighbouring mattress, wiped a damp lock of hair from her eyes and said, "You seem to be in your element on the floor."

"It really suits my back," Ronny confirmed.

"Have you always had problems with your back?"

"It comes from a childhood folly! I was so stupid and did this damage to myself! I was nine years old, and my parents were entertaining friends in the garden." She recalled the warm, English day and could almost smell the newly cut grass. "I was supposed to be confined to my room for something I'd done wrong. I can't remember what. I thought it would be fun to climb out of my bedroom window and up onto the roof so that I could to listen to their conversation."

"Ronny! You didn't!"

"Yes, I did. But my route was easier in my imagination than in reality. Warm slippery tiles were my downfall."

"You must have been mad. You fell?"

"I'll never forget the feeling. That awful scrabbling at the tiles. The helplessness of frantic slipping with nothing to hold on to, then falling through space till I landed flat on my back on the grass. The pain was awful. I really thought I'd never get breath into my lungs again." The recollection was still vivid.

"You could have died! Your parents must have been worried sick."

"They never knew. They don't to this day. I never got over the top of the roof, so I fell on the far side from them. I lay there for any awfully long time, but, finally, I got back into the house and back to my bedroom."

"You never told them?"

"Of course not! I was always in trouble, so I wasn't going to add to it. I only saw the damage when I had an x-ray in college many years later."

"I knew you were mad the first time I saw you."

The two women laughed. Pat was the only other person who knew the story, and Ronny wondered what he was doing at that moment.

Her mood changed, and Helen picked it up, asking, "What do you miss most about not having your husband here?"

Ronny frowned and studied her hands. "I guess it's the shared history. The connection to the life we've lived together." Ronny smiled at her friend and diverted the question. "And you?"

"Ed and I laugh a lot. We laugh at things that would be meaningless to others. We know and love the same people."

"Yes, I can relate to that. Pat knows me inside out. I don't have to explain things to him as we grew up in the same household." At Helen's look of enquiry, she continued, "We knew each other from childhood. I don't have to pretend with him; I don't have to justify my behaviour. He knows me warts and all."

"Ed's only in the next barracks, but I still miss him."

They were quiet, each deep in their own worlds. They could hear the sounds of life outside the dormitory, a murmured conversation on the grass and the echo of the distant banging of men at work.

Ronny broke the silence. "Pat's the kind and solid one. I'm the one with all the ideas and energy, and he supports me. I can be impatient sometimes, and he always stays calm. He drives me to distraction!"

"It sounds like a good mixture!"

"He's two years older than me, but I'm the practical one."

Helen considered this. "I have great faith that Ed and I will be all right. I'm lucky to have my missionary group. I don't understand God's purpose in all this, but I have the utmost belief that we'll be stronger for it."

At least Ronny by then knew where Pat was! The Japanese had put up a list of names of all civilians in Manila who had been interned at the Santo Tomas University. Pat was amongst the 3,000 civilian prisoners in the camp there.

FIVE

12th January 1942

16 days in captivity

Ronny was carefully adding another safety pin to the chain that expanded her slacks, when she heard a commotion outside. Word had spread that Japanese officials had arrived, directed by Major Mukaibo, and the guards became threatening immediately. Women were confined to the barracks and men to the tennis court.

To avoid being jostled in the crowd of women looking out of the window, Ronny contented herself with their commentary. In small groups, the men were forced to retrieve any cash and valuables in their possession and hand them over. Ronny could hear raised voices as the Japanese were trashing the men's quarters.

Ignored children wailed as frantic women blocked the light.

"What's happening now?" asked Ronny.

"They seem to be taking an interest in Wally Moore. They've singled him out and are taking him away," said the woman with the clearest view out of the window.

"What's he done? He's not the type to cause trouble. He's the president of our bank," declared Eleanor.

"That's it then. They'll force him to open the vaults and our safety deposit boxes!" a tall woman exclaimed.

"They'll be after any jewellery they've not already taken!" stated the woman near the window.

Feverish activity ensued as the women attempted to hide their precious things.

Ronny had already sewn her wedding ring under her cardigan button. She checked her toilet bag and the peso bills sewn into the base were well hidden.

"I can't move it! It's stuck!" Ronny heard the panic in the voice of the woman standing next to her. The distraught woman was ashen, sweat glistening on her forehead.

"They'll be here in a minute. What's the matter?" asked Ronny.

The woman's baby-blue eyes were wide with fear. "They're going to want my gold ring and I can't get it off. They're going to cut my finger off!" The sobbing woman frantically tugged at the ring that had become embedded over the years.

"Wait. Hold still. Let me help you," offered Ronny. She found her soap sliver, lubricated the swollen finger and helped the trembling woman ease the gold band off. "Now swallow it!" Ronny commanded.

"What?"

"If you want to save it, swallow it. Now!"

Ronny spun at the sound of the door crashing open. The woman forgotten, she followed the exodus as, in their turn, they were ordered outside onto the tennis court. When she saw her neighbour again the woman was shaking visibly, and, as their eyes met, the woman gave a covert nod of her head. Ronny stared at her. She hadn't, had she? Ronny had not imagined the woman would follow her command! She was pretty sure that she wouldn't have!

In small groups, it was their turn to be escorted to their dormitories to hand over their valuables. Ronny was one of the last to be summoned. Their orderly dormitory had been trashed. Possessions were strewn everywhere, some smashed, and mattresses gaped open from bayonet slashes. She watched, humiliated, as the soldiers, grunting from their exertions, went through her precious suitcase handling her personal things. A soldier with a scar across his chin demanded that she stand and patted down her chest, arms and legs as she stared at him daring him to touch her stomach. He found neither the ring nor the hidden cash that could be useful for barter later.

The soldiers left, and the atmosphere in the dormitory was ugly. Nakamura had assured the women that any confiscated goods would be returned in due course, but no one believed him. The thefts were the only topic of conversation, and misplaced anger boiled over suddenly, souring relationships between fellow victims. She noticed that her neighbour with the ring remained unusually quiet, and Ronny watched her, riddled with guilt.

Two days later, the woman greeted her with a Cheshire-cat smile.

Ronny could sit as she worked with Eleanor and Pam on the tedious task of removing weevils and debris from uncooked rice. The fine stones would easily have broken teeth, and the weevils, although edible, were in competition for their food supply. These dull-reddish-brown insects were tiny and able to fly, but easy to spot and squash promptly. Pam, a dizzy, young American housewife, whose dark roots betrayed her blonde hair, always found it hard to concentrate. The rice was spread out over the long table in the kitchen, and the three women were intent on the sifting process.

Eleanor commented, "Have you heard the latest rule that Nakamura's made up?"

"Clearly, it's all going too smoothly, so of course he's got to spoil it. What is it?" Ronny responded.

"He's said that the only time that men and women will be allowed to get together is for one hour on Sunday evenings between six and seven o'clock in the evening," explained Eleanor.

The flighty Pam chuckled. "Do you mean that we'll be allowed special time in the barracks at that time? Bob'll love that. It's pretty limiting, but with some ingenuity I guess it's better than nothing."

"No, you don't understand. That one hour is to be on the tennis court under the eyes of the guards. He called it 'commingling'. That's the only time women will be allowed to spend any time with their husbands. And strictly no touching!" Eleanor elaborated.

Pam was aghast. "That can't be all we're allowed? Surely we'll be together for meals at least?"

"No. The food queues are going to be segregated too. They're painting a seven-foot corridor on the tennis court to establish a no-contact zone."

Ronny mashed a weevil between her fingers. "Why do they keep punishing us? No one's tried to escape or done anything against the rules. That lecture from Mukaibo at Brent about shooting us was enough to keep me in line. What do they gain by making us so miserable and angry?"

"Maybe Nakamura has personal reasons, and this is pay back. He was imprisoned here in Camp John Hay by the US after the first bombings," posited Eleanor.

Pam interjected, "Did you hear that Mukaibo has asked for some of our younger girls to attend to visiting Jap officers at the Pines Hotel?"

The work halted.

"No. Absolutely not! No parents are going to let their girls do that," stated Eleanor, aghast.

"I think it's aimed at the girls from Brent whose parents are interned in Manila. They said it was to work as waitresses for extra food at the hotel and possibly to stay the night. Waitresses? Who's he trying to kid?" Pam was all-wise.

"The answer is absolutely no. I suggest that we give a clear message to the committee that it's not going to happen." Ronny glared at the rice.

"How are we going to get messages to the committee, if we are to be separated?" queried Pam.

"Those poor boarding-school kids have suffered enough by being away from their families. They're vulnerable. Perhaps we should each adopt a particular girl, to make sure that nothing untoward can happen to her?" Ronny had been a boarder as a child and felt a strong empathy for these abandoned children. "Don't let's kid ourselves that any of us are safe with the Japs. They're soldiers far from home. Never think they aren't capable of 'anything' if the opportunity arises." Ronny could feel herself going into crusading mode, and had to draw back and consider her own vulnerability. She was not actually in any position to go campaigning.

Ronny had her own worries. Her due date was getting ever closer, and the unknown frightened her. Her dormitory mates veered between telling her that her labour would be fine and seemingly being intent on frightening her to death with their childbirth tales:

"The first time is always the worst. You get torn."

"My friend had a forty-two hour labour and they had to get the forceps at the end. Poor dear, her baby was never the same!"

"I'm sure that won't happen to you, dear!"

These were comments she could do without!

She felt unprepared for her new responsibility and turned to Helen more and more. Her pretty friend went into labour towards the end of January. She was whisked out to the Notre Dame Hospital, accompanied by Dr Nance, and news filtered through that after a twenty-seven-hour labour, she had given birth to a little girl. Due to an administration hitch, Helen stayed in the hospital for three weeks, and Ronny missed her. When Helen returned, she was immediately housed in the barracks' jailhouse with other mothers and newborn babies.

Ronny visited her friend there whenever she could. Helen was coping well with the tiny, dependant infant.

"Ronny, just relax. You seem really anxious about it all. I wish you'd just trust yourself and rely on your instinct," said Helen.

The baby, Carol, lay like a slithery seal on her mother's supporting hand, whilst Helen soaped her gently in the warm water. Her bath was a commandeered fire bucket, and mother and child seemed in perfect harmony.

Ronny pulled a face. "What instinct, Helen? I'm scared. I'm thirty-four years old and I simply don't know how I'm going to manage. I've avoided babies ever since I was a kid."

"You told me that you were the middle one of three girls. Surely you had experience of smaller children?" asked Helen.

"Not really. I was ten when my little sister was born. Felicity was an afterthought, and I hated her. She took all my parents attention and even took my name!" Ronny watched as Helen lifted the little slippery body and patted her daughter dry.

"She took your name?"

"Yes, my family name was Babs. Everyone called me that. When Felicity came, they gave her that name. It sounds silly, but I never wanted anything to do with her. All that noise and disruption!"

Helen's baby was happily gurgling as if to dispute Ronny's description.

"It's quite different when it's your own. Didn't your mother try to involve you in bathing and feeding?" Helen enquired.

"Helen, my parents were socialites and rather distant. You forget I'm English! The hired help brought us up. I don't think my mother really had that much to do with us. The irony is that, when I was only three, my mother published a book called *Woman and Marriage* under the pseudonym of Margaret Stephens. It's a layman's guide to conception, childbirth and child-rearing, and I'm embarrassed to say that I've never read it. It was a huge success and very daring for its day," said Ronny.

Helen stopped. "How fascinating! I didn't know you were the daughter of a famous authoress!"

"Not famous, I assure you, although her book was highly thought of in medical circles and is still in print. I should have read it. For the life of me, I can't remember my mother being involved in the mothering process; she was too busy socialising with my father."

"Where are your parents now, Ronny?"

"They were in Haifa, Palestine, when war was declared. My father's a manager in the oil industry. My mother was evacuated from there to South Africa. I asked her to join me here, but she wasn't keen."

Ronny and Pat had written to her parents with news of her pregnancy, but she imagined that they had no idea as to what had happened to her since. They had not been at her war-restricted wedding in London, and it would be folly to imagine that, even under normal circumstances, her mother would have changed her plans to be with her at this time.

—⊢⊣⊢⊢—

It was after the lunch queue that Ronny heard the barked orders. She watched from a distance as male missionary internees were ordered to gather on the tennis court. Helen, ever optimistic, thought that they might be going to be liberated. Five missionaries who had worked in China were selected and transported away to the Kempeitai military police headquarters (HQ) in Baguio. The Kempeitai had a reputation for extracting information under torture, but other missionaries had previously been taken in for questioning and had returned safely.

Two of the men were returned that evening, but Roland Flory, Herbert Loddigs and Rufus Gray were detained, and concern in the camp escalated. The committee approached Nakamura on their behalf, but the commandant feared the military police and was not prepared to interfere. The mood in the women's dormitory that night was subdued.

When the men had not returned the following day, the whole camp became alarmed. Still Nakamura did nothing.

It was not till the evening that Pam came clattering into the dormitory with news. "Loddigs and Flory are back. I just saw them!" Her voice was shrill with importance.

Ronny was quick to react. "Are they all right?"

"I couldn't see them clearly, but they appeared to be in a bad way. They were being carried into the barracks by internees. They must have been tortured."

A chill went through the room, and even the children were hushed by something intangible in the air.

Pam lowered her voice. "I think the guards were embarrassed by the brutality, as they let Bob get close enough to talk to me. He said that one of them had been beaten up badly and that the other had been water tortured."

"Water tortured?" asked Ronny.

"You know! It's repeated simulated drowning with the man tied down and unable to move. It's barbaric!"

Ronny winced. "Why? What had our guys done?"

"They wanted to know about their Chinese connections."

"Will they be OK?"

"Yes, in time. But Rufus Gray wasn't brought back with them." The implication was frightening. It was a direct threat to one of their own.

"Where's Marian? Does she know?" Many voices asked this question.

"She's at the guardhouse. She says she won't leave until Rufus is returned," stated Pam.

Rufus Gray did not return and the women could offer no comfort to Marian, who had no idea as to her husband's fate. Ronny found her despair hard to watch over the following weeks. She often saw the distraught woman sitting on the ground outside the guard hut, keeping a lonely vigil for hours until the demands of her little son, Billy, drew her away. The mood in camp was bleak.

The third barracks' block was still standing empty, and Ronny was surprised to see sudden activity one morning when a group of Chinese men arrived and started to work on the building. This was followed a few days later by an influx of Chinese prisoners, who walked in carrying all their personal possessions and bedding. They appeared as exhausted from the walk as Ronny and her fellow internees had been a couple of months earlier. The barracks were separated by a wire fence and it was made clear that no contact whatsoever was to be permitted between the two groups.

With the ongoing hatred between the Japanese and Chinese, it was a surprise when Nakamura allowed the camp doctors to check over the new internees and look after their medical needs. Ronny thought Nakamura was a strange man, one full of contradictions, and she never made assumptions as to what he might allow.

—※—※—

Over the weeks, Ronny became resigned to the role of captive. The blur of the Asian faces of their guards had become individuals with distinct features and personalities, and they acquired nicknames reflecting this. The tall, swarthy, mean one became 'Bullyboy'; the one who was so thin and reed-like, bizarrely, became 'Puff'; and the beaming, little one who could not resist smuggling sweets to the children was known as 'Sunny'. Fear of the guards had receded, but their distrust of them had not.

—※—※—

A more relaxed routine had set in, so the events of 15th February 1942 came as a devastating blow. Ronny stood in the small group staring at the notice board on which was posted the news of the fall of Singapore to the Japanese.

One woman wept. "It can't be true. I can't bear it."

"We'll remember this day, when reality dawned." The voice came from a wizened face, with lines like it had been scoured by rivulets.

Ronny thought the owner was getting satisfaction from everyone's distress.

"Oh stop it. I can't believe it's happened! My George told me there were 85,000 of our troops stationed there," declared one woman.

"Yes, that's if you include the Indians and the Aussies," said the wizened woman.

"It's just a story, made up by the Japs." George's woman was adamant.

Another woman intervened. "It's true, unbelievable as it is. The Nips have done it. God help our soldiers."

The wizened face had the last comment. "Face the facts, ladies. We're here for the long haul."

Ronny turned away from the group and all their speculations. Any hopes of rescue from that direction had been put to rest firmly, although many were still convinced that help would come from the troops in Bataan. Ronny tried to ignore the rise and fall of rumour, but was as prone to despair as the next woman. She wished Pat was with her. She missed him, but knew her job was to look after herself and prepare for her approaching labour.

—⟩⟩—⟨⟨—

The mood in camp changed from the apathy of waiting to be saved to the realisation that they needed to make the best of it. Days took on a regulated shape, with a gong sounding for the daily segregated roll call and for lights out in the evening. Exercise classes were established, and, after a few shaky starts, a school was set up for the children. There were plenty of qualified teachers to run it, and it gave children a much-needed structure. Curiously, the subject the Japanese forbade them to teach was history.

Ronny had been reared to be a more-than-competent bridge player, and card games filled many empty hours. Books of any title or subject were a welcome distraction and were handed round with delight. Eleanor turned out to be good at knitting and introduced her to a group of women who kept busy with a variety of handicrafts. Ronny was thankful for her impulse buy of the sewing kit in Baguio.

Her baby was due in the second week in March, and the hospital in Baguio was by then out of bounds for women in labour. The little camp hospital was continually filled with dysentery cases, so was not considered a suitable birthing place. Isabelle Scott had already safely delivered a baby, nicknamed 'John Hay', in a partitioned-off section of the barracks, and she appeared none the worse for it. Ronny could only hope all would be well.

Ronny's group of friends expanded and diversified. A chance meeting in the little jailhouse introduced her to a first-time mum called Betty, a tall, big-boned American with short-cropped red hair, a mass of freckles and a big laugh. Her husband Bernie was also interned, and her son, Bud, was three months old. Ronny loved her quick intelligence.

One of the constant irritations in camp was the self-promoting elite, and it was a favourite topic of conversation with Betty.

"The 'Colonial Club' are the worst. They go back generations in Baguio and have money to spare. Their contacts are always going to bring them food and luxuries, in the belief that they'll be employing them again one day," Betty explained.

Ronny had no support outside the camp, and mused, "I find it strange to think that Nakamura used to mix with the elite. Being interned under him must really grate on them."

"Fancy casually nodding to him over a G'n'T [gin and tonic] at the golf club one minute, then having to bow to him the next."

"Did he ever fill up at your petrol station?"

Betty's husband's most recent enterprise had been to own a Baguio petrol station.

"He must have! I should have put sugar in his tank!" declared Betty.

"That'd be a waste of sugar! At least he speaks colloquial American and has some understanding of us. I know he veers from helpful to bloody-minded, but he's in a difficult position. I hear his family are impoverished now," Ronny stated.

"Well, that's the system. The Imperial Army doesn't financially support army families in wartime. Thank heavens our government doesn't think the same way! Most of these guards are conscripted from local Filipino farming families, so they get family support until they move on. We can be pretty sure the next lot will come here from the front lines, and then there'll be trouble!"

"All the more reason to support Nakamura." Ronny sensed Betty was ready for a scrap.

"Holy Cow, Ron! Why do you champion him? If you scratch the surface, he's just as bad as the rest of them."

"You must admit we've been lucky so far," Ronny countered.

Betty spluttered. "You call starvation lucky? And dysentery? And humiliation? Do you think for one moment Mukaibo didn't mean that about shooting five men and five women for any one escape? I'm still waiting for one of the men to be stupid enough to try to join Walter Cushing's guerrillas in the mountains."

Ronny and Betty were strange bedfellows, but their similar quality of stubbornness made their friendship fun. Ronny's dormitory mattress had become her home, and all these women were her sisters. Living in close proximity meant that emotions ran high and irritation at others' idiosyncrasies was always a skin's scratch away. Rows flared up, tears were shed and died as abruptly. Ronny was aware of her own short fuse and tried to avoid confrontations.

Her legs and back ached most of the time by then, and she felt grossly unattractive. Sometimes she was happy that Pat was not there when she watched the anguish of married women who still went to great lengths to look good for their men. They only had the exasperating hour on the tennis court, where they had to 'keep moving', to communicate with their husbands.

⊢⊣⊢⊣

Ronny had little materially to give her baby, so she was totally overwhelmed when, one day in late February, she found a priceless gift had been left on her mattress. It was a woven basket with stiff frills of white curtain fabric round the edge and finished with a pink bow. At each end was a curve of bamboo, which secured a little mosquito net. The care and consideration that had gone into making this pretty baby carrier was evident. Her throat closed and her eyes blurred at this gesture of friendship, and she knelt in front of it, transfixed.

She turned to Betty who was watching her. "Who did this? Is this your doing?"

"I've no idea where it came from. Isn't it swell?" asked Betty.

"It's absolutely perfect. I don't know what to say." The squalor of her world disappeared and she wiped tears from her cheeks. "Who would have gone to all this trouble? I don't deserve it."

Betty was indignant. "Of course you deserve it. I've seen the little toys and outfits you and your group have made for others. You're a great seamstress, and you've made a lot of moms happy."

Ronny was proud to be part of the group of women who stitched and knitted, and she herself had become the beneficiary of their generosity. "But it's too perfect. Please Betty, who did this?" she asked.

"I truly don't know and I guess we never will. Just enjoy it, Ronny."

"Oh I will. And my baby'll love it. It's a beautiful basket."

She resolved she would do everything in her power to shield her baby from the ugliness that surrounded her.

Six

16th March 1942

80 days in captivity

On the day before St Patrick's Day, the dining room was cleared for action. The committee, in an effort to lift morale, had suggested that they stage a celebration concert. Many in the camp claimed Irish ancestry, however American they might be, and great fun was had by the men and women in their barracks, rehearsing skits and songs. Surprisingly, Nakamura had given his permission for men and women to enjoy the performance together.

Ronny felt strangely restless as she wandered in to watch the last dress rehearsal of *Life Behind Barbed Wire* before the afternoon performance. She had enjoyed helping with the costume making, so was allowed into the big secret area. Eating benches and random wooden boxes were pushed around the edge of the hall for seating, and the normally clinical space was awash with improvised props and nervously excited performers. Musicians, stand-up comedians and singers were all bedecked in impressive home-made costumes as they watched the sketches that poked fun at their daily plight as captives.

Seated next to Pam, Ronny felt wired up, which heightened her sense of hysteria and she laughed and laughed. Everything seemed funny.

Suddenly, she was mortified to find that she had wet herself and struggled to stand in her shame, only to find that the liquid continued to run down her legs.

"Ronny, what's wrong?" asked Pam.

"Oh please, no. Pam, I think I've wet myself. How awful. How embarrassing!" cried Ronny.

Pam was alert instantly. "Just stay still. I think it's more than that. I think your waters have broken and your labour's started."

She called out for help, and Ronny was embarrassed to find herself surrounded by concerned faces. Someone shouted for Dr Allen, and everyone had an opinion as to where to take her for her confinement. She was helped out of the dining area and back to her dormitory, where Pam – full of self-importance – organised a curtained construction to be erected round her mattress to give her some privacy.

Dr Allen arrived, as reassuring as ever. "I just need you to relax here, Ronny. This baby is going to take its own time, and you need to get as much rest as you can."

"Just when I wanted to be part of the party!" Ronny exclaimed.

Beulah Allen laughed. "You've seen most of it, Ronny! And this is a far more important party. We will keep a close eye on you, and then, once the evening meal has been prepared and served, we'll have the kitchen at our disposal."

"The kitchen?"

"That's where there's the most reliable lighting and a fan. We'll be able to have it for the whole night if we need to! Who knows, we might be able to dig up something for you to eat if you feel like it!"

"I don't want you to miss the show!"

"Ronny, we'll be popping in regularly. You won't be alone. We'll take care of you. Just relax as much as you can."

The hours passed slowly.

The contractions came like a ripple of stomach pains, surprising in their stealth, but certainly manageable at this stage. She tried to read a book, and her friends distracted her with conversations over the partition, whilst the pains increased in severity gradually.

The dormitory was abandoned at show time, and Ronny could hear the distant bursts of laughter and high spirits erupting intermittently from the dining room. She managed her contractions as best she could between turning the pages. She was proud to be experiencing the same sensations that were ending her life as a girl and joining her to the realms of mothers before her. She thought about her mother and wondered whether it had felt the same for her. Had her birth pangs been any different? Her mother had been an orphan, so she, too, had managed these moments without maternal support. This job of labour was really a solitary job.

In a pause between contractions, she became aware that someone was moving stealthily about the dormitory. She listened intently. When a young Japanese face appeared above the partition, she did not know who was the most surprised. Nakamura and the guards were expected to attend the show, and this solitary guard was obviously on the prowl whilst all attention was elsewhere. He looked confused and stepped forwards, seeking an explanation for her presence, but a well-timed contraction made communication impossible and, when she looked up again, he had gone.

Eleanor and Pam dropped in during the interval.

"You're doing so well, Ronny. We're all very proud of you," said Eleanor, looking serious.

"What stupid timing this is! I really wanted to see the concert. How's it going?" queried Ronny.

"It's wonderful, and the Japs are finding it as funny as we do. Even the ones who can't understand English are laughing!"

"I'm sorry to be missing it."

Pam was showing her sensible side. "They're going to move you once the kitchen has been cleared up. I see you've plenty of water, but do you want us to bring you something to eat from the chow line?"

"Nice offer, but I don't think I could eat!" Ronny was distracted by her body, and the effort to carry on a conversation was just too much. She was grateful that she had concerned friends, but did not want them to stay. She needed all her energy to look after herself.

Much later, it took two people to lift her off the mattress and support her on her walk to the kitchen. She blinked at the bright lights that were already in place. All the surfaces smelled as if they had been liberally scrubbed with disinfectant. It was a stark stage set, and the only comfort was to be found in the smiling Dr Allen, who welcomed her warmly. Ronny had been told that she would only be allowed to commandeer the kitchen table between the serving of the evening meal and the start of breakfast preparations. She did not want to inconvenience anyone and was very aware of the time restrictions.

Ronny was helped onto the wooden table. The makeshift lighting cast surreal shadows onto the ceiling, and a portable fan that had been commandeered stroked cooling wafts of air across her skin. The sturdy and unyielding boards felt cool and hard under her weight. A light sheet covered her.

As the waves of pain mounted and became closer together, time and events became confused and unreal. There was no significant pain relief, although, miraculously, someone had produced a slug of brandy from a hidden cache, which blurred the sequence of events that night to an even greater degree.

Despite the heat in the kitchen, Ronny became feverish. Cold sweat started to run down her body and she asked for a blanket and for the fan to be deflected away from her. Dr Allen came and went from her line of vision, and she lost all sense of time. Once she thought she saw Dr Nance in the room and, at another stage, she sensed a state of concern between Dr Allen and the nurse, the reason for which she never knew. All her concentration was centred on keeping up with her body as it went at its own rhythm. Ronny was convinced she was in a battle against the clock, and had to push hard, from the first inclination to do so. Her straining was for the benefit of the camp rather than that of her baby. She knew that she had to push this baby out and she believed she had to do it as fast as possible. She did not hear any of the voices that urged her to relax and do otherwise.

It was the longest night in Ronny's life. The hard, wooden table turned into a torture platform, and the pain in the back of her head was unrelenting. There was no cushion to soften the bare wood. Strangely, she later remembered that pain in the back of her head more clearly than the pain of her contractions. The crescendo of waves got steeper and steeper and harder to climb. She remembered sinking her fingernails cruelly into the hand of a helper, as if to pass on some of the agony she was going through. From the start, she had vowed that she was not going to allow herself the luxury of howling out loud, so she was surprised to hear the low, animalistic growl that came from her mouth. The night was endless with the heat, the lights, the cold sweat on her body, the headache and the insurmountable waves of pain.

At last, she felt the overwhelming urge to push, which gripped her whole body so that Ronny disappeared and the urge was a world of its own. Then, finally, the unimaginable relief as her body rid itself of the slithering burden of her first child. She had done it. The fear of the unknown had passed. Dr Allen beamed at her. She was convulsed with trembling as the afterbirth was delivered from her bruised and torn body. None of it mattered. Her tightly wrapped baby was placed in her arms, and she examined the tiny face disbelievingly. Miraculously, her baby had been born just before the kitchen crew arrived and she made her first protesting cry, which echoed in the heart of her mother.

Ronny remembered little else. She was carried out of the kitchen on a makeshift stretcher, her baby in her arms. Even the sharp air of the early morning barely registered, as all she wanted to do was to sleep. She was taken directly to the old barracks' jailhouse where her mattress and belongings awaited her.

Sometime in the morning, she stirred to find a nurse encouraging her to suckle her little daughter, but it was only a hazy recollection when she woke up later in the day.

The jailhouse was narrow and lit only by one small, barred window, but it was a welcome retreat for the small group of mothers and newborn babies. The little building was dark and mercifully cool. The baby basket placed on the mattress beside her was perfect for the little mite. The other mothers were warm, curious and welcoming.

"What's her name?" one of the other ladies asked.

"I've called her Catherine Ann," confirmed Ronny.

"That's a lovely name."

"Yes, but my husband won't like it!" Ronny said ruefully.

"Why ever not?"

"Patrick's daughter is born on St Patrick's Day and I don't call her Patricia! We had only got as far as the name Michael for a boy."

"Is your husband Irish?"

"He considers he is, even though he was born in India! There's a history of Rynds in Ireland, but the closest Pat has come to the Emerald Isle is the Irish rugby songs he likes! I've certainly heard enough of them!"

Ronny spent the first days watching her daughter and learning from the more experienced mothers how to respond to her needs. She marvelled at Catherine's tiny hands and feet; the soft top of her head, where she could gently touch the strong, steady pulse of her life; and her sweet-smelling skin. She was totally absorbed in her new role. Ronny and her baby took to breastfeeding with ease, and she was determined that this would continue for as long as possible. Little Catherine did look a lot like her father, with downy, fair hair; a tip-tilted nose; and blue eyes.

A routine was already in place in the baby house, and Ronny was happy to fit in and be guided by Helen and Betty. The husbands collected the used nappies – or 'diapers' as the American's called them – in a bucket, took them to wash and returned them once dried. It was one of the many kindnesses she experienced that they gladly added Catherine's nappies to their rota. Baby clothes were shared generously and handed down as the babies grew.

With so many hours to fill, conversations in the baby house often dwelled on their families far away. Helen had been talking about her parents, and, in her turn, Ronny tried to paint a picture of hers.

"I adore my father, but it's complicated. He's tall, good-looking and always immaculately dressed. His friends call him Teddy," elaborated Ronny.

"Teddy? Like our president Teddy Roosevelt?" asked Helen.

"Yes, but my father is an Edward, not a Theodore. His greatest passion is music, and he's an accomplished violinist. My mother studied music at the Conservatoire in Leipzig, and she plays the piano beautifully."

"How lovely. They sound well matched and very romantic."

"Yes, but the downside was that we three daughters were supposed to contribute to the musical evenings, which were so important to them. The others were all right, but I failed miserably. It didn't matter what instrument they tried to teach me; it turned out that I'm tone-deaf. My father has a quick temper and thought I did it on purpose."

"Oh Ronny! Surely you couldn't have been *that* bad?"

Ronny pulled a wry smile. "I was, and he was ashamed of me. They used to have all their friends round to their own concerts, and I wasn't even good at turning pages! It really ruined music for me. The more I wanted to please him, the worse it got. When I was older, I disappointed him too because he adores beautiful, well-presented women, and I never came up to his standards."

"Is your mother beautiful? Does she have your great hair colour? What's her name?"

Ronny thought she was lucky to have such a sweet friend. "I think she is. Her name is Caroline, but everyone calls her Elf. She's very strong and independent. She and her two sisters, my aunts, were orphaned, were brought up by their rich uncles and were very well educated."

Helen picked up Carol, who had started to fret for her milk. "How glamorous! Does she make up for your difficulties with your father?"

"She's good at keeping the peace, but she totally adores my father, and he definitely comes first. He has a roving eye, so she makes it her business to be beside him. They are a very charismatic couple who are still living in a golden, pre-war era. They have servants, and, to be honest, I don't think either of them is in touch with the real world. They are both hopeless with money. She is always doing the least expected things, like buying a bunch of unbroken ponies to train or writing the book on marriage rather than minding her own children."

"How about your sisters?"

"My older sister, Joy, is the good and sensible one, and Felicity, being so much younger, always got everything she wanted by seduction. I'm too like my father in character and it never seems to work between us." Ronny watched as the little Carol smiled up at her mother. She was looking forward to Catherine's first smile. "Right now, I need to get a message to Pat that he's now a father. He needs to know that Catherine and I are all right."

—ⸯ—ⸯ—

Eleanor had called round to congratulate Ronny on Catherine's safe arrival.

Ronny was concerned to see how gaunt the other woman was becoming and with a look of fragility that did not bode well. She really wanted to talk to Eric, as she had particular questions to ask, but with the segregation in place, she had to hope that Eleanor might have the knowledge. The name Walter Cushing kept coming up in connection with the guerrillas in the mountains, and she came straight to the point.

"Everyone's talking about Walter Cushing. What do you know about him Ellie?" she asked.

The older woman was totally focused on the baby, and Ronny had to repeat the question.

Eleanor answered, "Eric was talking about him yesterday! He's a fascinating character and he's certainly made his mark on the Imperial Army. Apparently, he's a small, hard-drinking, feisty,

Texan mining engineer. Just one of a kind, I guess. I wonder if Catherine's eyes will stay that colour?"

Ronny refused to be distracted. "Please Ellie, tell me about Cushing."

"Well. Two days after the invasion, Cushing left the mine apparently and started training his Filipino work colleagues to be soldiers. I don't think he had any military training. The next thing we heard was that he'd managed to commandeer thirty American soldiers and their lieutenant who were cut off by the Jap advance."

"I bet the lieutenant wasn't too happy."

"I guess he didn't have much choice, and at least the men were fighting, by ambushing Jap detachments. Eric said that, in January, Cushing and his group killed a convoy of sixty Japs and captured ten trucks of supplies. He once captured a Jap general and his entire staff."

Ronny was sceptical. "All by himself?"

"He's built up a legend for himself and his guerrillas in the last three months."

"Isn't it amazing that they are up there. If we had binoculars, we might catch a glimpse of them." Ronny glanced up to the mountains and wondered if there were binoculars trained on her!

"They wouldn't be that smart if they could be spotted! The Japs would soon roust them." Eleanor was distracted by Catherine's tight grip on her finger.

"Walter Cushing must be a remarkable man to gain such loyalty?"

"He's not your ordinary guerrilla leader, that's for sure. His band of men are out there waiting for the return of our troops and doing as much damage as they can in the meantime."

"It's reassuring to think that they're so close. I'm thankful that none of our men have tried to escape to join them." Ronny had sympathy for active men frustrated by sitting around and doing nothing for the war effort.

"I'm sure the wives remind them of the consequences to the rest of us."

"I imagine that if the guerrillas are too successful, there might be repercussions for us."

"I don't want to think about it, Ronny. I just want it all to go away and be in my own home again."

Ronny looked at her closely. Unless Eleanor managed to find some hidden well in herself, she believed her friend was going to crack under the pressure. As for Cushing, he had become real to her. It was a good feeling that there was this friendly presence out there so close to the camp.

Later, Ronny joined Helen and Betty in the shade on the steps of the baby house as they breastfed their babies. She had become used to the sensation by then, and was proud that she could provide the food and comfort Catherine needed.

Helen was looking forward to Easter. "Nakamura has given permission for us to have an Easter Day service."

"Yes, but you never know whether he will stick to that or renege at the last minute," doubted Ronny.

Betty added, "Well, he enjoyed the St Patrick's Day show, so perhaps he wants to have another party?"

"Didn't I hear that he handed gifts to the performers after the event?" Ronny was curious about what happened that night.

"Yes, but did you hear what he handed out? All the beautiful embroidered tablecloths, napkins and bits from Doreen's wedding chest that had been stolen at Brent. The Japs didn't realise how offensive that was," explained Betty.

"Oh no! I heard nothing about that," Ronny confirmed.

"You had other things on your mind. Of course, as soon as everyone realised where they came from, they returned them to

Doreen. Let's hope she can hang onto them. You never know when they'll raid us again," Betty said.

"I don't think there's anything left to raid!" Ronny held Catherine on her shoulder, gently patted her back and was rewarded by Catherine's satisfying burp.

Helen returned to her subject. "I've been thinking that maybe we could hold the Easter service in a beautiful setting, like behind the barracks overlooking the ravines? I think that view at sunrise would make it really special."

"I'd put money on Nakamura only allowing it to be held on the tennis court, but, hopefully, together with the men," Ronny declared.

"Could you make us an Easter bunny outfit, Ronny?" Betty teased, "You haven't much on your plate at this moment! We could give the kids a treat?"

"How about the new male voice choir having a try out?" suggested Helen. It was easy to find ideas to enhance the daily monotony.

—*—*—

The Easter celebration did happen, on the tennis court as predicted, and the men were allowed to mingle with the women for a couple of hours. Ronny enjoyed showing her baby around to the other families. Filipino staff provided decorated boiled eggs, which were distributed to all, including the guards. The service coincided with the morning routine of the Japanese doing their practice drills, so barked commands and stamped boots intruded, but — for all the distractions — it was still a beautiful service.

SEVEN

———⊦<———⊦<———

9th April 1942

103 days in captivity

The notice on the communal board gave the news that the American divisions at Bataan had surrendered to the Japanese. Ronny stared at it in horror, before stumbling back to the baby house to deliver the blow.

"It's Bataan. They've surrendered," she announced.

Helen paled at the news. "I can't believe it. I thought our boys were holding their own on the peninsula. What's happening at Corregidor?"

"Our troops there are still fighting. There's still hope from that direction." Ronny's words lacked conviction, however hard she tried.

"I thought that, as long as we were holding our own in Bataan, we'd be released. I really believed it."

"Don't cry, Helen. Please don't cry."

They had pinned so much hope on the American troops liberating them, the shock was a hammer blow.

"But how are we to survive? What's going to happen to us?" Helen asked.

Baby Carol started to whimper, and Ronny cuddled her in place of her mother, who was too distracted.

"It's been four months of hell, but we've survived. It's just going to take longer than we'd hoped," said Ronny.

Helen sat with her head in her hands. "I don't think I've the strength to go on, Ronny."

"Our rescue may not be coming from Bataan, but it will come from somewhere!"

"We're going to die here. We're starving slowly and we'll be dead before help gets to us."

"What about Cushing? The guerrillas won't abandon us."

Carol had fallen asleep again and Ronny gently replaced her in the cot.

Helen watched dully. "Oh Ronny, I don't want to hear about Cushing! Your idol and his merry men aren't going to help us. Having a stealth war with the Japs is one thing, but they can't liberate the island. I'm sorry, Ronny. I'm sick and tired of it all."

"I know, but we have to do our bit by looking after ourselves, Helen. We need to keep well for Carol and Catherine," Ronny chided.

Ronny hoped she sounded more upbeat than she felt. That day, it was Helen's turn to despair. Tomorrow, Ronny might be the one in need of positive lies. That was how the friendships in the camp worked.

—✳——✳—

The fall of Bataan depressed everyone and the committee decided, in order to raise morale, to assign compulsory tasks, so that the camp worked better as a unit. Ronny thought it was a good move that the work around camp was divided along lines that were already in place. The manual tasks such as rubbish disposal, woodcutting, vegetable growing, cleaning and building maintenance were allocated. The doctors, a dentist and the nursing jobs were self-evident, as was teaching, sewing, hair cutting and ground maintenance. The most sought-after work was in the kitchen, which covered preparation, cooking and serving. There was a dispensation for inventive men, such as Fabian Ream, who could make anything required with rudimentary equipment, and also for their undercover wireless operator. Everyone would be responsible for some aspect of communal life, and shirking was visible to all. People already provided services in exchange for other services, food or hand-made tools, but this had become organised officially.

———

Betty and Ronny were seated on the ground, watching a group of boys at American football practice. It didn't make much sense to Ronny, but Betty was keeping a weather eye on it as she spoke.

"I think everyone's going to benefit from the new system. It's democracy right under the Jap's noses!" Betty declared.

"I bet the members of the Colonial Club are miffed." Ronny smiled at the thought. Having lived in boarding schools, the unfairness of group dynamics held no surprises.

"The committee's done a swell job. It can't have been easy."

"They've just done what they were voted in to do," Ronny muttered.

"You're funny, Ron. You have a real thing about the committee, don't you?"

"It's bad enough doing what the Japs tell us, without male internees dictating what I can or can't do." Ronny saw that Betty was waiting for a further explanation. "My father expected instant obedience to his commands, so I've been well trained to do what I'm told. But I don't have to like it." She uncrossed her legs hastily as a guard strolled by. Leg crossing was considered immodest and warranted a face slap from the Japanese.

Betty was not distracted. "But you can see we all need direction?"

"I'm happy to do whatever they want me to do, which is more food prep," confirmed Ronny.

"Most people are really happy to do kitchen shifts."

"Yes, but the best details are in the cooking or serving, where people benefit under the counter. Rice sifting doesn't offer that opportunity. It's time for me to be babysitting!"

Within the baby house, they had organised their own system, and Ronny was happy to care for other infants, especially during commingling time on the tennis court, for those who had husbands to meet. The Japanese guards did not understand the behaviour of Western women and took a dim view of mothers abandoning their babies. Occasionally, when guards looked into the hut to find Ronny in sole charge of four babies, there was consternation at this arrangement. One guard even insisted on taking a crying baby from her and carrying it out to the tennis court to present it to its horrified mother.

—⋈ ⋈—

The news that Corregidor had fallen was displayed in May. Sadly, this was verified over the radio concealed in the men's barracks. Conflicting rumours depended on whose intermittent broadcasts were picked up, but this time the internees knew that the American forces had finally and totally surrendered. All hope of an early release vanished, and spirits plummeted.

—⋈ ⋈—

One sultry afternoon, Betty was studying the clouds, and Ronny had cut the legs off her threadbare slacks and was turning them into shorts. Catherine and Bud were asleep on a blanket in the shade.

"Nakamura is paranoid about us getting messages smuggled in inside the food packages. He's been on the rampage since yesterday," said Betty.

"What triggered it?" Ronny asked.

The baby-house internees often seemed to be playing catch-up with camp news.

"Oh, one of the men was spotted opening a typed report hidden in his food package. There was a hell of a rumpus, and Nakamura has insisted that all packages have to be opened and searched. Even loaves of bread are to be cut open and checked!" Betty announced.

"What was in the report?" Ronny bent over her task, satisfied.

"I gather he didn't have time to read it, but – whatever it said – it isn't good news for the camp."

"Nakamura wants to keep us isolated."

"He got it in the neck from the big guns over that note the men sent out saying 'Send food. We're starving.'"

"Well, we are! We haven't had one single Red Cross food package. I'm sure it's against the Geneva Convention." Ronny felt this grievance keenly.

"It would be a disaster if the parcel line and deliveries were stopped." Betty was one of the lucky ones, but, unlike some, she was generous and shared what she received.

Ronny deliberately changed the subject, "Betty, how are you getting along with your women's rights campaign?"

"Don't get me started! Bernie doesn't think there's an issue!" She grimaced.

"Well, your husband wouldn't, would he? It's unbelievable that women don't have a role in camp government. *What self-*

righteous man thought that one up?" Ronny enjoyed stoking Betty's fire.

"You'd think we were in the Dark Ages." Betty was vehement.

"Talking of the Dark Ages, did you hear about Mrs Henderson's books?"

"No."

"Nakamura was furious about the amount of written materials coming into camp, so, when her order came in, he burned the lot of them."

"Holy cow. Burning books! That's criminal!"

"Yes, I'd go crazy with nothing to read. Mrs Henderson's all right, considering she is one of the Colonial Club. She let the books filter round."

The news of the books being burned had upset Betty. She snapped, "You always insist on thinking the best of everyone! You Limeys are so naïve."

Ronny reacted. "It's tough enough here without always assuming the worst."

Betty bit back. "I suppose you even think the guards are OK and *only doing their job?"*

"I'm not getting into this argument. It's silly and a waste of energy." Ronny retorted.

Inevitably, some conversations ended abruptly and in acrimony. No harm was done between friends. They all had days when even a tone of voice could aggravate beyond endurance. The gift of humour and the ability to laugh at themselves was vital, and totally bemused their Japanese guards. Ronny had heard enough about conditions in Santo Tomas and other camps to know that they should consider themselves the lucky ones.

However, just as things appeared to be going smoothly, the carpet was pulled out from under them. Word came down that the internees were going to be moved again. Everyone was unsettled in the baby house, and the distress of the mothers made the babies harder to soothe.

Nakamura confirmed the order, and men were sent on to the new premises to prepare it for habitation. Their next prison was to be Camp Holmes, a former Filipino constabulary campus on the Bontoc Trail, a few miles further north. Ronny spent the next few days anxiously organising Catherine and her possessions. Thankfully, they were to be transported by a procession of open trucks this time.

After four months confined behind barbed wire, Ronny loved every minute of the journey. Perched on her mattress and possessions in the well of the transport, she sheltered her baby in her arms and relished the sight of an apparently normal world. The fragrance of myriad flowers drifted sweetly in the air. The vegetation was vivid green, and quiet paddy fields rose in steps against the blue mountain ranges. The villages they passed through were quiet and sleepy, and she caught glimpses of Filipino farmers and Igorot people still dressed in their beautiful, pink, embroidered costumes, as if their life was unchanging. The season was on the turn, with days of warmth followed by those that heralded the start of the rainy months, but that day was sunny. Ronny enjoyed the sensation of movement that she used to take for granted. She drank it all in and was happy to be in this extraordinarily beautiful landscape rather than the dusty city of Manila. If only Pat were there, sharing this splendid interlude. It was over all too soon.

As they turned through the gateway, she saw that the camp was set in gently sloping grounds, with a backdrop of a pine forest.

The sheer sense of space lifted everyone's spirits. At the top of the slope were the main barracks buildings the men had cleared for three segregated living areas. The men would be in one, and the women and children in another, with the third designated for the Chinese, who would follow the next day. The cottage on the far side of the women's barracks was to be the baby house.

Ronny was entranced. The view from the cottage was stunning, with vistas over the Trinidad Valley all the way to a glimpse of the silver China Sea. The beauty of the location took her breath away, and she turned Catherine's tiny face towards the biggest landscape her six-week-old baby had ever seen. She whispered, "One day, I promise you that you'll be living with your daddy and me somewhere beyond that sea, and you'll be very happy."

The little ex-officers' house consisted of four rooms, which were soon crowded with twelve mothers and their infants. It felt good to get away from the bars on the windows of the old jailhouse. The men had done a good job of cleaning and patching the buildings, but debris was scattered around outside, offering rich pickings for all the internees. The first day there had a distinct feeling of new beginnings, and spirits rose.

—⊬-⊬—

Three weeks after they arrived at Camp Holmes, Ronny was sitting on the grass outside the baby house, feeling the warmth of the late afternoon on her face. The chores of the day were over. Ronny had bathed Catherine in the bright-red fire bucket that they had brought with them from Camp John Hay. Bathing the babies was enjoyed by all those in the baby house, and Helen, Betty and Ronny watched their infants kick their legs on the mat in front of them.

Betty commented, "The guards seem more relaxed here."

"It must be rest and recreation for them, away from the fighting. They'll be changed soon, and we'll have to be careful until we see what the new lot are like," stated Helen.

"The committee's as daunting as the guards!" Ronny made a point of steering clear of them.

Helen insisted, "But they have to be, as we're surrounded by so much inequality! I hate to see the way the Colonial Club waste food when the rest of us are hungry, and they think they're too good for the jobs they're assigned. There are times I'd be happy to give them a good slap."

Ronny laughed. "As a good Christian, you shouldn't be talking about slapping people, Helen!"

"I must have caught it from the Japs! Seriously, I think our committee is pretty amazing," Helen confirmed, "It's no picnic trying to represent us, and deal with the Japs and their directives. I wouldn't swap places with them."

Betty offered, "I hear that they've given the approval for Clarence Mount and his family to have one of the little nipa-palm-roofed houses to themselves."

"It seems unfair. Mount is such a horrid man, why the special treatment?" Ronny queried.

"His wife's no better, but it's really because of the mental state of the child. The dormitories will be breathing a sigh of relief at seeing the back of them," explained Betty.

Ronny held Catherine close, smelling the sweet smell of her wispy, fair hair. The women were deep in thought.

Helen broke the silence. "I'm lucky to have Ed's company. I'm sorry you have to manage on your own, Ronny."

"I'm lucky with our baby group. I've never been one for crowds, so being away from the dormitory suits me well," said Ronny.

Helen agreed. "Yes, I hear the women's dormitory's still too crowded. They had everyone remeasuring the mattress spaces yesterday."

"I wouldn't swap. No more boundary fights!" Betty chuckled as she carried Bud back into the hut.

Helen concentrated on Ronny. "It's so sad you've had no contact with Pat."

"Nakamura sent Ray Hale on an errand to Manila last week, and Ray got word to Pat about Catherine, and Pat sent his love." Thinking about Pat was a waste of time, and Ronny concentrated on living in the present.

Helen, with the sleeping Carol in her arms, clearly had other ideas. "I do admire you. You're a strong woman and have coped so well. How come I never hear you talking about Pat?"

"I guess that's a British thing. I envy you Yanks, as you're far more open about your feelings."

"You Limeys and your stiff upper lips confuse us! Your reticence and English accents often give us the impression you're stuck up. You also seem to use a double language. There's what you say and then there's something going on that you're not saying. It's confusing!" Helen laughed. "Seriously, you don't talk about Pat. How're things between you two? I can't imagine how it must be to be separated from him."

"Pat and I are good, and of course I miss him. He's my family and has been all my life since I was five years old."

"I never understood that tale."

"Pat came to live with my family when he was seven. He was born in India, where his father was a colonel in the Indian Army. His mother died shortly after his birth. The poor woman had lots of babies, but they all died young, except for his sister, who was seventeen years older than him. He doesn't talk about it, but his father wasn't around much, so the Indian house staff pretty much raised him. He was a lonely little boy until he came to live with us."

"Why your family? What was the connection?"

"One of my mother's sisters, Maudie, was a school teacher, and she went to India and ended up employed as Pat's governess.

Maudie was a great 'rescuer'. Perhaps she should have been a missionary like you, Helen. When Pat was seven and needed to go to boarding school back in England, Maudie arranged for him to live with our family during school holidays."

"Poor little boy. It sounds barbaric, boarding school at seven!"

"His father had plans for him to go into the army, following in his footsteps. He was entered for Wellington, which is the British Army school." Ronny explained. "I'm sure it never occurred to the colonel that Pat could have a choice."

"Did you ever meet him?"

"I do remember meeting him as a child. I was fascinated with his monocle. I remember being frightened that his eye would fall out if he removed it! Pat called him 'sir', and never seemed comfortable around him. He married again and to no less than an Italian countess called Margo. Anyway, he died not long after Pat came to us."

"Oh Ronny! You and your stories."

"But it's true. I met Margo lots of times over the years, and she was the only parental presence at our wedding. She scares the life out of me. She's always dressed in black with high, white ruffles at her neck – very much the Italian countess. She has lots of jewellery of the flashy kind and sets of initialled silverware." Ronny recalled her dark, velvet eyes, her impossibly soft skin and the closet smell of her. "I still remember her musky perfume."

"She sounds exotic. How come she was in India?"

"I don't imagine she was. Ouch!" Catherine was pushing her strong, little legs into Ronny's thighs, flexing her limbs. "On home leave in London would be when they met, and I've no idea why she married Colonel Rynd. They were an unlikely pairing. He was so stiff and formal, and she was so flamboyant and Italian! Whatever it was, she finished him off pretty quickly!"

"Ronny!"

"Pat's mother gave birth to countless children in India, which couldn't have been a picnic, and only two survived, then she died herself. And along came Margo who managed to kill Pat's father off within six months of marrying him! I doubt she ever intended to go to India, and she now spends all of her time living in the West End of London in Claridge's hotel!"

"No! How could she afford to live in a hotel like that?"

"Well, perhaps I'm exaggerating about the hotel, but every time we were summoned to London to meet her, it was always at Claridge's! Pat never seemed to receive an inheritance, although his schooling was paid for."

Ronny had kept in touch with Margo over the years, and visited her dutifully when she was in London. Margo had never approved of her own lack of sophistication. 'If she could see me now!' she thought.

Helen continued probing. "How come Pat didn't join the Army if he went to military school?"

"He would have been a disaster as a soldier. His poor eyesight failed him at the final hurdle after all that training. So he had to change direction and ended up working for the Hong Kong Shanghai Bank." Ronny looked around, "And here we are!"

"Isn't there any way Pat could get himself transferred here?"

"I can't imagine the Japs would be remotely interested in allowing him to do that. Why would they? They could be opening up the flood-gates. Camp Holmes is a holiday camp compared to Santo Tomas."

Helen mused. "Well then, perhaps the mountain will have to go to Mahomet!"

With that casual aside, the seed of a plan started to germinate in Ronny.

EIGHT

May 5th 1942
130 days in captivity

Ronny clutched Catherine to her breast and tried to control the violent trembling that travelled through her body. Her eyes were glued to the spectacle in front of her and much as she wished to she could not look away. She felt sick. All the internees had been summoned onto the parade ground and forced to witness the punishment of a Chinese prisoner who had attempted to escape.

The prisoner was named Leung Soon and whispers circulated that he was not in his right mind. He had taken advantage of the new, relaxed atmosphere of Camp Holmes and had walked straight out of the main gate and was picked up heading along the road back to Baguio. Ronny sympathised with the little man's need to return home, he had obviously been desperate and he was now paying the price. She thought about Mukaibo's threat of multiple deaths in retaliation for attempted escapes and selfishly hoped the Japanese would confine any punishment to the Chinese internees.

Mukaibo and Nakamura were standing in the entrance of the guard room, as Leung Soon was dragged onto the parade ground. He was stripped to the waist and his narrow frame and chicken wing shoulders already showed red welts from manhandling. His pale flesh looked vulnerable against the grey-green fabric of the guards' uniforms. Ronny winced as they knocked him down, kicked him with their hobnailed boots and dragged him to a large tree, to be strung up by his hands in full view of everyone.

The beating was the worst savagery Ronny had ever witnessed. She shook with the horror as she watched through her tears whilst the Japanese took turns to beat him with sticks and rifle butts, with no holds barred. She winced with every impact. The sound of his screams fell on the silence of the watchers. When his screams were strangled to a whimper, and he slumped, hanging from the rope unconscious, they threw water over him, revived him, pulled him further upright and continued to attack his helpless body. She was horrified to see that even the guards whom she had started to consider humane took their turns with apparent relish. There was not a flicker on the faces of the watching officers to show any revulsion at the sight.

The repetition continued for nearly an hour, with the cruel beating till the man passed out, the water dousing, the kicking and the hauling of the body up again. Ronny could hear the subdued crying of women and children around her in the crowd, but there was no respite until the Chinese man looked more like a bloodied carcase of meat than a human being.

When the torture stopped finally, Ronny was convinced that Leung Soon was dead. She watched as he was dragged off to the guardhouse, leaving a trail of blood in the dust. The camp was silent. The shock and horror of what they had witnessed awakened a renewed fear and distrust of their captors, which could not be shaken off, and the hours that followed were filled with tears and anguish.

Later the next day, word got round that Leung Soon was still alive, but this did little to relieve the deep despondency that had settled on the camp.

"The Chinese are on the move. They're all packing up," explained Ronny, who had witnessed the activity through the wire and hurried back to tell her friends, who were lazing on the grass in front of the baby house.

Betty sat up, interested. "Why would the Japs release them? That makes no sense, especially after what they did to the little guy for trying to go home."

Ronny suggested, "Helen, do you think it's all to do with the Chinese funeral ceremony we watched the other day?"

Helen nodded. "That poor man; there's got to be a connection. Perhaps he was out of his mind with grief?" she told the others. "It was so sad. It turns out that they are all Christians over there. We know so little about them and would never have known that if we hadn't spotted the cross."

Someone asked, "Is it unusual for Chinese to be Christians?"

"Yes, it was uphill work trying to enlighten them on the mainland. Our Chinese neighbours must have been living here in the Roman Catholic community for a while," said Helen.

Ronny added, "It was a pathetic sight, especially as it was pouring with rain, but the little service had such dignity. Helen and I saw the whole thing. We sheltered under that huge tree as it was teeming down. They had a service with a wooden coffin and flowers on the funeral cart, and then they all trooped out of the gates, soaked to the skin, to bury their friend. It's surprising the Japs allowed it, even if they were escorted by guards."

Betty spluttered, "That's what makes me so mad. It's like trying to keep your feet on shifting sand. There's no logic I can see to anything the Japs do!"

"They're changing the guards soon. It's going to be a completely new crew." Helen had gained this information from her husband Ed.

Ronny was adamant. "Well, that makes sense, after what they forced us to witness. Seeing guards, who had given the children sweets, acting like animals. I'll never forget it. They've destroyed what little rapport we had with them!"

"I agree. Although I don't for one second imagine that they give a fig about how we view them," stated Betty.

Helen was busy inspecting her bare feet, as any cuts or injuries could become infected rapidly. "I'll be glad to see those guards go. Good riddance."

Ronny felt that something had changed irrevocably. Everyone in the camp was feeling weak, both emotionally and physically. Dysentery was going the rounds and this, coupled with malnutrition, meant the doctors feared a tidal wave of serious sickness. The very old and the young were the most vulnerable. It was a long time since anyone had eaten citrus fruit, eggs or milk, and a lack of vitamins led to a lowering of resistance. Ninety per cent of the prisoners were going down with one sickness or another and there was a growing fear of fatalities.

She recalled the conversation she'd had with Dr Beulah Allen when the doctor came round to check on Catherine the previous week.

The then noticeably pregnant doctor had things on her mind and stated, "I'm furious that nothing's being done about the fly situation. Unless the flies are dealt with, we'll continue to be exposed to dysentery epidemics. It's so obvious."

"What can be done? The kitchen staff are pretty good about keeping the surfaces sanitised, but the flies seem to be getting worse and worse. They drive me crazy." Ronny hated brushing them away from Catherine's eyes and mouth constantly, as well as her own.

"The reason they're getting worse is clear, and Nance and his cronies are blind to it! It's the accumulation of garbage. The garbage crew dumps the stuff far too close to the camp, and it's a rich breeding ground. The only way we can check the dysentery is to move the dump and bury it."

"That sounds like good sense. What's the problem?"

"We stand a fair chance of moving the site, as the Japs are complaining about the flies now, but burying it is another matter." Obviously, Dr Allen had been exploring options already.

"Surely the committee could put some men on to it?"

"Oh, Nance thinks it's stretching the men too far. He says they don't have the strength to do the digging. It's crazy thinking! They certainly won't have the strength if they're carried away with dysentery. Preventative action is the answer. It's all very well giving inoculations to the children, but it's glaringly obvious that we need to stop the flies at the source."

Beulah Allen hardly had glanced at Catherine, and Ronny wondered if her visit was as much about letting off steam as doing a check-up on her daughter.

"I support you 100 per cent, and so will all the mothers, I'm sure," verified Ronny.

"I'm taking it up with the committee, but I'm not holding my breath with Dr Nance opposing the idea. I've half a mind to get some strong women together and dig the pit myself. Sorry, Ronny, I'm just thoroughly irritated by the stupidity of it. Let's get back to this little mite here." Beulah's professional stance reasserted itself and she bent over Catherine.

Unlike Ronny, some of the other mothers were unable to breastfeed and had to substitute milk with soya beans that had been cooked down thoroughly until they became a slimy, grey ooze, which was fed through enlarged rubber nipples. The babies took to it with no choice of real milk. All the new mothers were given an extra allowance of food, and Ronny was relatively healthy under the circumstances.

———+—+———

June marked six months of internment and the start of the rainy season. Beulah Allen had managed to get the rubbish moved and buried, and the number of flies had decreased noticeably. Ronny stared glumly out of the door at the heavy downpour that was beating a tattoo on the iron roof of the small hut. She watched it drift in sheets across the mountains, and visualised Cushing and the guerrillas sitting it out in the caves. She imagined them sharing the same feelings of frustration and boredom at the restrictions imposed by the weather.

At three months old, Catherine was doing well and putting on weight. She was a quiet infant and placid like her father, and Ronny had established a good routine with her and could enjoy reasonable nights' sleep. Ronny loved Catherine, but did not display that love naturally like the other mothers. She knew she was more of a cerebral type of person than a tactile one. Surrounded by mothers who talked baby talk constantly to their children, as if it were the best conversation in the world, Ronny was aware that her comments to Catherine were of a more adult nature. She revelled in the feeling of not being physically encumbered with her pre-maternity weight, and with little effort, and little food, she was regaining her former slender shape.

———+—+———

The new guards were not as threatening as Ronny had feared, and life settled down again. The internees were self-governing to some degree, with all the major decisions being made by the committee, and each internee contributing to the work schedule according to his or her profession or capabilities. There were still a few scroungers, and Ronny and Betty could not resist making loud comments whenever they came across them, but these internees seemed impervious to being shamed.

The camp doctors and teachers were keen to keep their skills polished. Several huts had been turned over to education, and the children, teachers and parents were delighted. Books and paper were in very short supply and were shared. The Japanese considered geography, history and maths from a Western viewpoint too dangerous to be taught, so these subjects were covered subversively when the guards were not around. Men from desk-bound professions were happy to take on manual work, such as the rubbish detail or the lumber-cutting group, in order to keep active. Trees on the edge of the camp were cut and shipped to the kitchen for firewood, using the purloined Camp John Hay cart. The women cleaned the camp, washed and repaired clothing, picked over rice and corn, and gardened in an attempt to grow some vegetables.

With the large American contingent in camp, inevitably, the parade ground in front of the barracks became the site for baseball training and matches. No shortage of men and boys volunteered to play every Sunday afternoon. Amazingly, balls, bats and even a catcher's mask were found, and Ronny – who knew nothing about American baseball – never missed the opportunity to cheer from the sidelines. Teams were drawn up from 'Missionaries', 'Miners' and 'Schoolers'. The matches were a welcome relief from the tedious grind of camp life and carried on through many a drenching rain shower. Volleyball was also enjoyed enormously, and there were two teams: the 'Devil Chasers' and the 'Groundhogs'.

The ingenuity of the internees was utilised fully as people improvised to make up for the lack of basic tools. With the rainy season in full flow, someone was running a steady business making the wooden clogs the Filipinos called *bakia* to cope with the mud and puddles. These were made with a wooden base and old bicycle inner tubes for straps. Palm-leaf raincoats were the most recent 'must have' possession.

After six months' internment Ronny and the women were wearing a patchwork assortment of clothing, which was frequently restitched from curtain fabric or old pillowcases. The men's shorts were made of sterner stuff, but many men enjoyed the liberty of loincloths or just G-strings. Beards were sported, and Ronny thought the men looked like pirates in contrast to the clean-shaven guards. The atmosphere in camp became more relaxed and productive, and less energy was spent on rumour-mongering or anticipating their release.

Ronny stopped and watched the nuns disembarking from a lorry on the main plaza. Their dark robes were caked with mud, and the high, stiff headdresses looked bruised by the rain. They appeared dispirited but splendid as they stood out totally incongruously against the ragtag internees. Ronny had been educated in a teaching convent for one brief spell, and she liked nuns, so she edged her way into the group.

Reverend Carl Eschbach, charming as ever, officially welcomed the nuns, along with forty missionaries and their families, whilst Ronny questioned one young nun.

"We had no option but to come in. We could have hidden out in the mountains, but we had no choice once they took Father Nobes into custody," the young woman responded.

Ronny was curious. "But why were they so interested in you? Remote mission groups hardly pose a threat to the Imperial Army."

"It's all to do with the guerrillas north of Bontoc. They're very strong and active, and constantly sabotaging the Japanese.

Over the months, we've seen several Jap convoys trying to pin them down, but, until now, they weren't worried about us. Our mission is suspected of supplying food to Walter Cushing and the guerrillas."

Ronny pricked up her ears, ever happy to hear of her hero.

The nun continued, "Cushing is considered such a force for good amongst the Filipinos that the Japanese will do anything to make life difficult for him. The soldiers took Father Nobes as a hostage to make sure that the Anglicans from all the outlying missions came in. They threatened to execute him if we didn't obey instantly. We were given twenty-four hours to report to Bontoc. Our mission is really remote, so complying was a nightmare!"

"How did you manage to get there in time?"

"With difficulty! The sisters and I are not exactly dressed for trekking! It was a challenging twelve-mile hike, but we had Filipino carriers to help us. They were amazing and turned out in large numbers to help us. I think we presented quite a spectacle, but, with the grace of God, here we are!"

Carl Eschbach's welcome speech ended with, "Of course we'll make you as comfortable as we can. I'm sure you're used to more privacy than we can offer you, but we'll do our best."

Ronny heard one of the head nuns reply.

She said, "I'm afraid our only gifts to you are well-used umbrellas, but at least you only have us Americans to house. Our European sisters were allowed to remain free. Hopefully, we can contribute something to life here."

The nuns were as good as their word. They moved into three little huts next to the hospital and, although the accommodation was basic, it was no worse than the primitive conditions they had experienced in the hills. They contributed to the camp kitchen with supplies sent in from their Filipina sisters and paid for purchases of milk for the infants with money they had smuggled in with them. The nuns enjoyed the company of little children, and a bond developed between them and the residents of the baby house.

————⋈——⋈——

One afternoon, the rain cleared as swiftly as it had started, and Ronny needed some exercise before the next downpour. She had been feeling particularly miserable, and the heavy rain compounded her lowered spirits. She carried Catherine down to the gate at the expected time for the return of the daily truck from Baguio.

The usual crowd had gathered, hoping for packages from their contacts, and Ronny watched them from a distance, feeling lonely. She was desperate for news of Pat, who felt like the only person on this side of the world who cared for her. She normally ignored the package-line ritual, but, for some reason, she subjected herself to this act of masochism that day.

It was a surprise to see Major Mukaibo stepping out of the truck. Normally, he confined himself to the guardhouse whenever he visited them from Baguio. He was obviously on a public relations mission, as he was accompanied by two cameramen, who took up strategic positions to cover his actions. Children were summoned, and he proceeded to hand each child a fistful of sweets. He patted the children's heads, and gave every appearance of being benign and fatherly.

Drawn like a bear to a hive, Ronny edged her way into the excited group and was struck by the stillness of Mukaibo's stance and his remote smile amidst the excited, elbowing throng around him. She had never studied him so closely before, and was surprised at the whiteness of his teeth under his black moustache and the slender precision of him. Was he genuinely fond of children or was this event staged solely for the cameras?

As news of his presence spread around the camp, the children dropped back and the adult internees stepped forwards with their petitions. This also appeared to be carefully staged.

The Japanese government was promoting a movement to allow certain internees to return to their own houses under the supervision of their Filipino house staff. The scheme offered the prospect of fewer mouths to feed in camp. Ronny watched as Mukaibo listened to prisoner requests for release to their own homes and made notes. He was noticeably agreeable to nearly twenty eligible internees who had approached him, and he discussed the pros and cons in his flawless English. Ronny was surprised at how approachable and reasonable he sounded.

The rule in the camp was that only the committee could approach the Japanese hierarchy to negotiate anything to do with individual internees. Ronny had never doubted that the committee men alone were equipped to negotiate any requests, but here, in front of her eyes, she found ordinary prisoners talking to this ogre who controlled their lives! A half-baked, unconsidered thought propelled her forwards and she met the cool appraising eyes of Lt. Mukaibo, Special Section, Imperial Army.

She bowed as deeply from the waist as she could manage with Catherine in her arms. "With great respect, I wish to ask you to allow me and my baby to travel to Manila to the Santo Tomas camp."

He raised his eyebrows at this unscheduled interruption and took his time before responding, "Why would you wish to do that?"

Ronny's heart was in her mouth. "My husband is interned in Santo Tomas. I have no contacts here. My baby and I would be better off with my husband." She bowed again, aware that she was the focus of the crowd's attention.

He looked affronted that she was wasting his time. "Your country and my country are at war. You cannot expect me to be interested in doing anything for your comfort."

She persevered. "With great respect—" only to be cut off by his snapped reply.

"I have no interest in your case!"

He turned his back on her dismissively, and Ronny felt as if his words had slapped her across her face. She was breathless as the anger rose in her. Catherine started to cry as if sensing a seismic change in her mother, and Ronny buried her face in her baby's hair to hide her tears from onlookers.

Ronny was furious with herself for imagining that he was going to respond with generosity. How could she have been so stupid? The cameras were still rolling and she had made a fool of herself. She had given words to a notion that was still in seed form, harboured in her heart. She really had not considered the full implications of moving to Manila, and she had blurted out her request before she had thought it through. Her paper aeroplane had been crushed underfoot before it was even launched! Humiliated, Ronny turned away, grim-faced, and vowed that she would never repeat that mistake.

NINE

———⊁——⊁———

10th July 1942
197 days in captivity

Ronny took comfort in the camaraderie of the baby house. If one or other of the babies was having a bad night, there was no guilt, as every woman had a vested interest in helping the others. It was a lot like boarding school, with intimate secrets shared after lights out.

She enjoyed Betty's company especially.

Betty had been an ample lass who loved to eat and was addicted to coffee, so she moaned endlessly when the coffee ration was so diminished by the end of the week that they were drinking hot water smelling of coffee. She still had to have it! Betty was also an avid smoker and tried unsuccessfully to introduce Ronny to the habit.

They would sit on the ground outside the baby hut, as thick as thieves, and talk about their lives.

"The big passion of my early life was Harry," Ronny disclosed. "I met him in Switzerland when I was teaching at the finishing school near Lausanne. He was everything I wanted from a beau. Harry was doing a business-management course, and was smart, funny and good-looking. We were young and very much in love." She described to Betty his soft, brown hair that fell in a lick over one eye and the mole at the base of his throat, which always reminded her of a little bow tie.

"What became of him, Ron?" questioned Betty.

"The problem was that he was the only son of wealthy tea planters in Jamaica."

"Wow, would that be a problem? It sounds like a lucky strike to me!"

"I didn't have any money apart from what I earned, and Harry didn't mind one bit. We got engaged, and he gave me a beautiful sapphire-and-diamond ring. He wasn't particularly interested in the tea business that he would inherit, but we were both happy to live on the family plantation and were looking forward to it."

"Did you go to his place in Jamaica? I guess it must have been wonderful?"

"No, I never made it. I became ill, really ill. I developed this persistent cough, felt exhausted and started to lose weight. I was running a high temperature every night, which came down every morning, and when I finally went to the doctor, he diagnosed me with tuberculosis [TB]. They put me in a Swiss sanatorium and virtually threw away the key." She remembered feeling desolate and abandoned.

"What do you mean? You got better surely?" Betty rolled another cigarette.

"No, Betty, I didn't get better or worse. They tried all sorts of medicines and treatments without any luck. Every day they wheeled me out onto the balcony in the sun, with only a hand towel to shield my modesty – you can imagine how brown I got – and then they brought me back inside in the evening. Every day

I started with a subnormal temperature and ended up running a fever by the evening."

"Didn't Harry stand by you?"

"Yes, he came round as often as he could. It was a horrid time with no end in sight. I'd been there for four months when his parents came to see me."

"What a lovely surprise. Was that the first time you'd met them? What were they like?"

"Nice enough, I'm sure." She recalled the large, glamorous woman, with her smaller husband, both of whom had trouble meeting her eyes. "But I'd been diagnosed with TB and you know what that means."

"Well, you obviously didn't die."

"No, but TB meant that I wouldn't be able to have children. As Harry was the heir to the plantation, they'd come to ask me to release him from the engagement."

"Oh Ron. I can't believe it. What a nerve! I hope you and Harry sent them off with a flea in their ear."

"Actually, I did what they asked."

"You Limeys are unbelievable!" Betty was at full throttle. "I can't believe you took it lying down, without a fight."

"I was lying down, remember! I didn't have any fight in me and I never saw Harry again."

"What a dismal coward he turned out to be! Oh, you poor thing; you must have been devastated."

It was a distant story for Ronny by then. "We were just too young to stand up to them. I was only in my early twenties, and it felt as if my life was over. The positive side was that I made up my mind that I wasn't going to stay in the sanatorium for the rest of my life. One of the new nurses told me about a doctor in Geneva who had a great reputation for curing people, so when my sister Felicity came out to see me from London, we plotted my escape."

"Wow, good for you."

"It was wonderful to see a familiar face, although Flick couldn't stay for more than a week. We managed to put a secret scheme in place, and organised a taxi to the train and a ticket for me to Geneva. The new nurse was prepared to turn a blind eye, so, one afternoon when she was on duty, I literally ran away." She remembered the exhilaration on the train and the fatigue of her body that had known no exercise for months.

"How brave of you! I wouldn't have had the courage." Betty regarded Ronny with a new respect. "I guess the clinic in Geneva managed to cure you?" She was about to roll another cigarette, but apparently thought better of it.

"Yes, it wasn't TB after all. It was something similar called Malta fever, which you can get by drinking unpasteurised milk from infected cows. It had the same symptoms. Anyway, he cured me!"

"I'm amazed you were misdiagnosed for so long."

"Apparently, the smear test of lung fluid for TB is only accurate half of the time, and, once diagnosed, the guidelines for treatment are rigidly set."

"Did you contact Harry once it was over?" Betty couldn't let it go.

"Oh, I dreamed of doing that. Turning up at the plantation dramatically! Running into his arms! But, no, it wouldn't have been the same and I just had to move on."

"That's so romantic and sad. You've had so many adventures during your life. In comparison I've had it easy!"

They looked at each other, sitting in the dust and sporting patched clothing like a couple of scarecrows, and the incongruity of the remark made them laugh helplessly.

"Time for the haircut time I think!" declared Betty.

Ronny groaned. She had promised to cut Betty's hair. She wasn't very good at it, but, luckily, Betty's hair was so thick and wavy that any mistakes would soon grow out. Despite the obvious advantages of short hair in camp, Ronny had resisted the temptation. Pat always gloried in her long hair, and she kept it as an act of faith that they would be reunited.

Betty settled down to the ritual. "I heard Nellie McKim was called in to see Nakamura this morning."

"I think she is amazing, what with the way she speaks to him. How does she do it?" asked Ronny.

"Her father's an Anglican bishop in Tokyo, and she's a second generation missionary. Being fluent in Japanese is part of it, and she knows their culture inside out. She confronts him in a polite way and gets away with it! I heard she played her part in keeping the European nuns out of internment. Nakamura respects her."

Ronny was curious. "What did Nakamura want this time?"

"He wanted to know about the guerrilla groups near where she lived in Sagada. He believes that if they turn their attention to Camp Holmes, his life is in danger. It's ironic that the commandant is frightened of guerrilla attacks!"

"Do you think the guerrillas are interested in coming here? We're small fish for them. I can't see why they would risk it. Of course, I'm sure they would come if they thought we really were in danger of being wiped out." Ronny held fast to her conviction.

"Oh Ron! Dream on! Cushing has enough on his plate without being concerned about us."

"What did Nellie tell Nakamura?"

"That the guerrillas are spies, not fighters. I don't think he's convinced."

"I heard that we're going to get a new commandant anyway. Personally, I don't think Nakamura's been bad for us. He did ease the commingling rules, and he's allowed us religious services and the regular evening entertainments! Life has been better recently." Ronny considered the back of Betty's head and the patch she had cut shorter than the rest. Fortunately, Betty would not be aware of it.

"Well, Nakamura's been very jumpy since he brought the nuns in. He's considering moving us down to Manila to join everyone at Santo Tomas."

Ronny was startled. "Are you serious?"

"Please don't get your hopes up. I don't think the committee believe it would be a good move and will resist it. The climate in Manila is one of the main objections, as you well know. The heat there is unbearable at times. We're very lucky to be here when you consider the amount of crowding there is at Santo Tomas, without us adding to it. They're already struggling with not enough medical personnel and facilities." She paused mid-flow. "Oh! I'm sorry, Ron; I shouldn't be talking like this in front of you. You must be so worried knowing Pat is there."

"It's all right. I'm not deaf. I'm aware of what's being said."

"If they're having a worse time than we are, it seems crazy to go there." Betty tailed off lamely.

"I don't believe Nakamura is in danger from the guerrillas."

"Yes, and the Jap officers would be worse off in Manila. They certainly wouldn't get the medical attention that our doctors give them. I think Nakamura'd be crazy to give this up. Despite the problems, I imagine you must want to join Pat?"

"It's really hard, Betty. I don't know what to think." And that was the truth.

—⊹—⊹—

The camp internees had a reputation for hard work and self-government, and Nakamura had that to his credit. Ronny attended his final roll call in which he expressed sorrow that the female internees were still behaving in a manner of which he did not approve. Women wearing slacks, like coolies, particularly upset him. He was an enigma, but she was sorry to see him go. She watched him strolling casually round the camp – with his shirt sleeves rolled up, distributing bananas to the children – before driving off.

Ronny thought he had gone, but then witnessed an extraordinary sight. Nakamura had decided to redress the clothing problem as his last gesture. Horn blazing, he drove back in to the compound in a truck which was piled high with a glorious assortment of women's clothes: ball gowns, hats and shoes. Smiling broadly, he jumped down and piled these into the arms of the astonished crowd who had rapidly gathered. The dazzling array of fabrics presented a kaleidoscope of colour and texture that almost hurt the eyes. Black velvet, shining satin, silver lamé and the luxurious swirls of an elegant life so far removed from their current existence. For some it was unbearable. These garments, looted from a parallel universe, appeared to be couture clothes that had simply never been worn. Ronny stood there open-mouthed, watching this pantomime. It was shocking. The clothes were received as a mockery of the women who worked so hard toiling at menial tasks, with bellies distended from malnutrition, and Nakamura smiled his big, delighted smile, totally uncomprehending how flawed his gesture was. Many women were in tears at this evidence of how degraded their lives had become.

All was confusion until the committee stepped in and organised the removal of the clothes and for them to be put into storage. Ronny imagined that a few garments could be adapted, but the majority were as useful as a grasshopper in winter. Official thanks were offered to Nakamura and he remounted the truck and left.

—⊢—⊬—

Nakamura was replaced by Hayakawa Masago, the son of a Japanese businessman and a long-term resident of the Philippines.

He was young, and his whole manner was more relaxed than his predecessor. Hayakawa allowed the many different sects' church services to be held, and these were well attended, even by those who previously had shown no interest in worship, as the internees enjoyed any diversion from the working day. Hayakawa gave permission for the internees to hold a Saturday night programme of lectures, and there were ample presenters and subjects of interest. He allowed more freedom within the confines of the barbed wire, and the rules on commingling were further eased. Ronny was delighted to learn that the women were to be allowed to walk up to the edge of the woods where the trees were cut.

The negative side of their new commandant was that he avoided conflict whenever he could, whether it was from the ever-forceful Nellie McKim, the committee or the higher Japanese authorities. In time, this meant that he became invisible in camp. The committee had to step up their self-governing discipline to avoid a break down in camp morale.

———————

Ronny and her friends were having an excited discussion in the baby house.

"People have been caught stealing from the dining room! It's not fair to the rest of us. Something has to be done," said Ronny.

Betty was one step ahead. "That's why they appointed Don Zimmerman to be the camp judge."

"How will that work?"

"It means that he can dish out punishment to miscreants, which is what happened this morning."

"Betty, how come you always know *everything* first?"

"It's my big ears!" Betty chuckled. "This guy admitted to stealing two yams from the kitchen. He was spotted, but I guess he thought that nothing would be done about it."

"Two yams!" Ronny salivated. "What would I do to have two whole yams to myself! What did Zimmerman do?"

"He's ordered him to spend one week in solitary confinement in the little room next to the men's barracks."

"Good. I think it's important to set an example. This wouldn't have happened with Nakamura." Ronny wrinkled her nose as she detected a change of diaper was needed by Catherine.

"I don't think that Hayakawa's doing his job properly. All he does is to hand down the regulations from military HQ. He never follows through."

"Sometimes that's to our advantage!" interjected Helen, who was thinking about the more relaxed commingling rules.

"Of course it is, but it makes more work for the committee without backup." Betty often championed the committee, despite her women's rights campaign.

"Well, it's nice to be spending more time with Ed, so I'm happy the guards are more relaxed." Helen sighed deeply.

Ronny changed Catherine's diaper decisively. "I don't want to be a killjoy, but people take advantage without guidelines. Yesterday, I saw someone smoking in the kitchen! It was much better when the guards enforced the rules." Ronny had not succumbed to the smoking bug, yet.

"It's tricky, though, when it's raining like this," said Betty.

"You don't smoke in our house, Betty, and we appreciate it." Ronny smiled at her friends, and thought she was lucky to share her life with people whose company she truly enjoyed.

The rain hammered into the sodden earth on a daily basis at that point. The drumming on the tin roof was a background to conversation, with sudden interludes of surprising silence. Occasionally, a destructive storm rushed through camp, making them feel exposed and small against the majestic mountain surroundings. Rain restricted activities, and morale was low.

Ronny had little tolerance of the noise generated by the older children in camp. Some of them had turned feral and were going around in gangs, and by then, in the rainy season, they were driving the adults crazy. The older boys shared the men's barracks, and she heard concern from mothers that the men's card playing and blue language was a bad influence on the kids. Ronny was quick to forgive the Brent boarders who were there without their parents to guide them.

———·—·———

One soggy mid-July morning, Ronny was standing at roll call on the parade ground. The women had formed a rota system so that they could cover for each other, whilst one mother stayed behind to care for the babies. The guards turned a blind eye to this practical solution. Ronny was contemplating the puddles when her attention was sharpened suddenly by the announcement that Noah Sy Sorrel had escaped in the night. She was worried instantly about the implications. Ronny had seen Sorrel's lean, black-bearded, scowling presence about the camp often. Terse with everyone, Sorrel was a loner, shunning adults and children alike, and no one would miss him. The only concern was what punishment would be meted out to the remaining internees.

Confined back in the baby house after dismissal, the friends waited for the arrival of the Japanese hierarchy.

Ronny felt bitter. "What a despicable man Sorrel is. How can he do this to us? He knows what penalties we face if he escapes, and he doesn't care."

Betty agreed. "He's the worst! The men and guards are doing a thorough search whilst we wait for Mukaibo to arrive. He's definitely gone, so it seems rather pointless."

"Hayakawa won't do anything without Mukaibo's backup, and they'll be searching for anyone who helped him escape," added Helen.

Ronny explained. "Why would he need help? It wouldn't be difficult. When Pam and I climbed to the wood perimeter a few days ago in that fine spell, we went right up into that meadow where you can see Baguio in the distance. It's a stunning view and it would be tempting to just keep walking, if it wasn't such a stupid thing to do. He wouldn't have needed an accomplice."

"Mukaibo will try to point the finger at someone to make an example," posited Betty.

"Do you think he'll carry out the reprisal threat?" Helen voiced everyone's thought.

Ronny answered, "Maybe not. I think that they won't do anything against us. At the beginning, they'd no idea how we were going to react, so they had to frighten us, but now they know we're passive prisoners. This is the first major escape, unless you count the Chinaman, and he paid the price with that terrible beating."

Betty was not so sure. "I don't think Hayakawa would want reprisal shootings, but you never know what Mukaibo might do."

An uncertain silence descended on the group.

By the evening, it was clear that, despite a steady flow of men into the guardhouse for questioning, no scapegoats were found. No action was to be taken against the internees on this occasion, and the relief in camp was tangible.

TEN

7th August 1942

220 days in captivity

One afternoon, finding the confines of the baby house too claustrophobic, Ronny decided to walk off her depression. Above the perimeter pines, the clouds were still banked in the sky, but there were patches of bright sunlight between them as she headed for the furthest corner of the camp. She loved the smell of warm turf and, although the grass was still damp, sank down onto a secluded spot behind the little shanties, and turned her face to the sun's rays. Swinging the sleeping Catherine gently round onto her lap, she gazed at Catherine's little face.

She wondered about her daughter. With her blue eyes and blonde hair, she was a pretty little infant, but she was solemn. Ronny was concerned that she wasn't a good enough mother, and sighed. This was not how Ronny had pictured raising her baby. She thought, with irony, about her own mother: the authority on child-rearing, who had showed little interest in spending time with her children. She remembered her mother's laugh, as well as her saying, "Adult interactions are so much more rewarding!" Although she loved Catherine, she recognised that she, too, was happy to hand her daughter over to the teenage girls who were keen to practice motherhood.

Catherine smiled in her sleep, and Ronny's heart melted. She wished that Pat could share this precious time with them.

She sensed rather than heard that someone was standing over her, and blinked up into the wild eyes of Clarence Mount. She had never been this close to him before. He had a reputation for unpleasantness. He towered over her, thrusting his scrubby dark face within inches of hers, and she reeled from the alcohol on his breath.

"Spying on me?" he demanded.

"I'm sorry?" queried Ronny.

"I said, are you spying on me?"

"Why would I do that?"

"What are you doing so close to my place? Are you trying to make trouble for me?" He reached over, gripped her arm and then stopped short as he noticed Catherine for the first time.

"Please let me go!" Ronny cried out as his fingers dug into her arm.

Distracted by the presence of the baby, he hesitated.

"I don't know what you want, but I certainly don't want trouble. I'm sorry if I've offended you." She could hear the tremor in her voice.

He swung his grizzled face back to hers and focused again. "If you know what's good for you, you'll leave my patch alone and make sure that you don't come back."

Catherine woke up and started whimpering, startled by the huge presence.

"And take your mewling brat with you. If I see you again, you'll regret it!" he threatened.

Ronny scrambled to her feet, trembling, as she was frightened by this unexpected attack. She hurried back to her side of the camp, and, as she did so, shock turned to anger.

Her heart was beating wildly as she burst into the hut with the story on her lips. After she had told her tale, she was answered with more stories. As a result, she declared, "The committee needs to do something about Clarence Mount. He's getting worse. There isn't an hour in the day when he's not drunk. I feel sorry for his wife and kid, even though they're as antisocial as he is."

Betty knew the gossip. "I heard he gave Joe Smith a really bad shiner last week. The kitchen crew were enjoying their soup after the main service, and Mount, late as usual, expected to be served. Joe made a comment and the next thing he knew was a punch in the eye that floored him. Something's got to be done. He thinks he's a law unto himself."

"Where does he get the booze from?"

"He'll have his sources amongst the locals, no doubt."

Ronny was still angry. "I thought he was lucky getting special treatment when the committee gave him his own shanty. He should be grateful."

Helen, ever generous, was quick to clarify. "That was because of his kid, who's not right in the head. Mrs Mount's a problem too. I think it was a question of isolating the whole family."

"He's a monster and his drinking could get us into trouble." Ronny was adamant.

"I'm sure Hayakawa must be aware of him. Even in the chow line, the men avoid him. He reeks of whisky," declared Betty.

"He can't be distilling it; he's got to have an outside contact. I wonder if the men who drink now and again get it from him?"

Betty was clear. "There's a big difference between the occasional glass and what he's like. He's an alcoholic and puts everyone at risk. I don't think that's fair."

"Well, I, for one, will avoid him. He really scared me today, and I won't be going anywhere near him again!"

The baby house resembled a Chinese laundry; every surface was covered, as no washing could be hung outside to dry. Ronny and Betty took the opportunity to stretch their limbs when the rain eased off. They carried Catherine and Bud up onto the slope that overlooked the camp, and sat on the grass, contemplating their world. The birds started to call again, and Ronny wished she could identify all the different Pacific Island species. She looked down on the red roof tiles of the two dormitories standing side by side and facing the parade ground. She could see the hospital with its weathered roof tiles, and next to it was the tin roof of the baby house, almost hidden under foliage. There were the cottages that housed the nuns, and the shed where the unsavoury Mount family lived. She saw the flagpole and the guardhouse, with its dominating presence, in the centre. From where she was sitting, she could not see the barbed wire perimeter, but only the pines and the distant, rising mountains set against a heavy sky.

The mountains drew her attention as they always did, and she studied them with care, imagining what life was like for the guerrillas and their leader, Walter Cushing.

"Don't you wonder what the guerrillas are up to?" she asked.

"I can't say I give it much thought." Betty lived firmly in the present.

"I think about it a lot. Cushing could be watching us at this moment. I wonder what he's doing? He could be planning his next assault!"

"Ron, you and your fantasies! He's just a jumped-up, hard-drinking, feisty, Texan miner with a Napoleon complex."

"Well, the Filipinos worship him. They call him the Slaughterer of Japanese. He's killed 500 by his own hand, I've heard." She halted at Betty's laugh and smiled, abashed.

"Yes, he's a regular Robin Hood!"

"Don't laugh, Betty. He's got to be something special. He's taken on this challenge, trained his men and done a lot of damage to the Jap troops."

"Yes, but he's not going to take back the islands. All he can do is continue to be a thorn in their side. I've heard his infantry group has been disbanded since the fall of Bataan."

Ronny ignored that remark. "I've heard that he's now spending time persuading rich Filipinos to buy up black-market ammo left behind by the US Army, to help the cause."

"I grant you that he's one smart guy, but it's his story that's doing the work. He's only a man after all."

"He's a hero! As long as he remains free and fighting, he's keeping the enemy occupied looking for him."

"He's certainly useful until he's dead."

Ronny was shocked. "Dead? He can't die. He's got a job to do, and the luck of the Irish."

"Hey! He's a Texan, *remember?* Don't you try to adopt him!"

Ronny laughed. "The truth is that his father is Canadian, and his mother is Mexican, but don't let that stop you!"

She believed there was hope for them as long as Cushing remained fighting for them in the shadows. Ronny smiled at herself for the power she had given this man so unrealistically.

Sitting on the slope above the camp had been refreshing, but duty called, so Ronny and Betty made their way home. Ronny relinquished Catherine to her friend's care as she headed for her rice-sifting shift in the kitchen.

When she arrived, Pam was bubbling with news. "I've just seen that girl who lost her teeth. What a change in her! She's so happy and smiley now! Dr Walker and Fabian Ream have done an amazing job."

"Slow down, Pam. I haven't a clue what you're talking about!" stated Ronny.

"You remember the pretty teenager who was so miserable after she knocked her front teeth out in a fall? Everyone was worried about her. Well, the dentist and Fabian Ream have made her some false teeth carved out of carabao bone attached to a metal plate, and it's worked wonders! It's so lovely to see her smiling again."

"I'm a big fan of Mr Ream. I love his banana machine on the chow-line counter."

Ream's banana machine was the answer to endless squabbles over the handing out of bananas in the food queue. Size mattered to internees, who were always desperate for food, so Ream had designed this watermill-style construction that stood at the end of the serving counter. Bananas were fed into the revolving wheel by an internee. As the wheel rotated, it delivered one random banana at a time, ensuring any favouritism was eliminated.

Ronny continued, "He's a clever man. And, talking of clever, I think I've found a way to make some money! One member of the Colonial Club approached me in the toilet block, as the skirt I was wearing impressed her. She asked me to remake one of her dresses. It's a straightforward adaptation, and if she likes it, she says there'll be more work."

"My dear, you could be on a roll! I wish I had your talent." Eleanor was genuinely pleased for her.

"It's not talent. It's a necessity from when I was a student. I don't have the ability to design anything from scratch, but I can follow a pattern. I was always short of money, and it was the only way I could keep up with the fashion," Ronny explained.

"You mean your pa kept your allowance short? I always thought you were rich with your posh Limey accent, boarding school and all that!" Pam's raised eyebrow said it all. She rose to her feet to ease her back and rolled her shoulders.

Ronny remained focused on the task. "Oh, I had the boarding-school education at Cheltenham Ladies' College and the elocution lessons, but my parents are hopeless with money. My father's parents were comfortably off, as they owned a mill in Painswick, which is a beautiful, old village in the Cotswolds. It was a small factory employing several people. My father designed and built the house next to it, which is where I grew up. I remember my grandparent's pony and trap. It was an idyllic rural childhood."

"See, I knew you were well heeled! Tea on the lawn. Cricket on the green."

Ronny laughed. "You're not listening! My father inherited the mill, made some bad decisions and went bankrupt. My mother kept hens and ducks, and they grew their own vegetables, but it wasn't enough to keep us afloat."

"Not if you were going to a private school! It all sounds crazy."

"You don't have that British 'keeping up appearances' sort of thing, do you? You Yanks are much more honest. My parents had a county image they didn't want to give up."

"So what did they do, Ronny?"

"Thankfully, my father is a bit of a charmer. He had friends who found a job for him managing an oil field in Romania." Ronny eased her back from too much stooping.

"You are kidding? What qualifications did he have for that?"

"He knew the right people. My older sister and I were abandoned in school in England and went out there to visit in the summer holidays. My parents never really knew how much things cost, so in the short holidays when I stayed with school friends, I was embarrassed by my lack of clothes. One lovely mother showed me how to cut out and sew from paper patterns, and I've never looked back!"

Eleanor said, "Well, good for you. I think it's great that you can earn some pesos from those lazy creatures. If I wasn't so useless at sewing, I'd join you. I'll see that the word is spread around."

Ronny had nothing but contempt for her new clients. She felt it was poetic justice that, although she did the work they required, she charged them as high a rate as she dared, asked for too much fabric from them and then shamelessly made children's clothes from the leftovers. Her clients had ample food and supplies, and Ronny, with only her wits to fall back on, was determined to survive. Eleanor was as good as her word, and Ronny earned enough to buy eggs and other necessities for Catherine and herself.

———✠———✠———

The entire camp gathered together to attend Rufus Gray's memorial service. There had never been any account of what had happened to Rufus once he had been swallowed up by the military police. Mukaibo had denied all knowledge consistently, but, a few days previously, Hayakawa had received formal notification of Rufus's death, dated almost six months previously. To his credit, he had informed Marian immediately. She was told that Rufus had died in hospital, having refused to eat, but there was no doubt in anyone's mind that he had died under torture. He was only twenty-six years old.

The service was held on top of the hill overlooking the camp, facing the view of the freedom of the sea – a freedom that had been denied Rufus forever. The rain had cleared, but the clouds were still low and heavy as they sang 'Lead Kindly Light', accompanied by the occasional muffled sob. Ronny was impressed with Marian's ramrod-straight back and quiet composure as she held her eleven-month-old son, Billy, in her arms. It was a brief but intense ceremony, and it enabled Marian to move forward.

—⊬— ⊬—

Thoughts of escape always hovered, but the reality was that the Philippine Islands, surrounded by water, were their own prison. Caucasian escapees would stand out a mile, and disguise was impossible. The men could dream of escape to the mountains, and Ronny imagined that many did, but it had to remain a fantasy as the repercussions on the camp of any escape would be massive.

One night in October, the outside world intruded directly into theirs. In the early hours, Ronny sat bolt upright on her mattress as she registered that something was not right. Everyone in the baby house had been roused at the same time. The sound of what later became known to be a second shot came from the road below the barracks and, without considering the implications, she rushed to the window to look out. It was still dark with only an indication of creeping early morning light, but the guardhouse was already illuminated starkly, and she saw figures in front of it.

Hayakawa and Nellie McKim were in a deep conversation. Nellie, with her intimate knowledge of the language and psyche of the Japanese, obviously had been summoned already. Ronny watched the woman run back towards the main buildings, and opened the door to waylay her.

Nellie shouted, *"Put on warm clothes. Dark ones. And go straight to the women's barracks. All of you! Now!"*

There was panic as startled infants were swept up and wrapped against the cold of the night, and the mothers scrambled across the damp grass to join the body of the camp. Without question, there were guerrillas on the road below the wire, and Ronny was sure Cushing and his soldiers were amongst them.

The unusual sight of men and women crowded together in the dormitory met her eyes as she made her way to sit on Eleanor's mattress. The American woman was happy to see her, especially as Eric was isolated in the hospital with dysentery.

"Do you think this is it? Do you think our troops are here?" Eleanor looked as brittle as ever, but there was a savage gleam of excitement in her eyes.

Ronny replied, "I don't know, Ellie, but I think it's more likely to be the guerrillas. We would have heard if the Allied troops had landed."

"Guerrillas? Perhaps once they've liberated us, they'll send a signal to our troops to come back?"

Although Ronny had her own fantasies about Cushing, she would not get drawn in to the other woman's unrealistic optimism. There would be nothing to be gained by releasing a camp load of ill-equipped, sickly, civilian internees to join forces with the guerrillas. She humoured Eleanor as best she could, but wondered if her friend was becoming unstable.

The unmistakable crack of gunfire punctured the night in intermittent patches, as guards and guerrillas crept through the vegetation outside the camp. From the windows, everyone was watching for the sudden flashes illuminating the side of the hills. There were pauses when everything went quiet. Then, just as the internees were tiring of straining their eyes into the impenetrable dark, a sharp bark and accompanying flash would happen again from another position. There was no way to recognise either set of adversaries, and it was exhausting to try to speculate continually. Finally, the excitement petered out completely, and the rest of the night was spent in dozing and desultory conversation with no further gunshots heard. Ronny shared Eleanor's bed throughout the long night, and was stiff and weary in the morning. Catherine needed changing, and Ronny wanted to return to the baby house.

After roll call, the internees were allowed to go back to their regular camp duties, and the morning was abuzz with rumours. Ronny caught sight of a very weary Nellie McKim crossing the compound, and stopped her.

"Can you tell me what was happening last night?" Ronny asked.

"I can't tell you much, Ronny! It was guerrillas, of course, but you already know that," confirmed Nellie.

Ronny's next question was close to her heart. "Did the Japs capture anyone?"

"No, they all got away. The Japs sustained a few injuries, but nothing to concern them. They were trying to take out the Trinidad Bridge, and it looks as if they did a pretty good job."

Ronny tried to recall the bridge. "That's the one just below us, isn't it? No wonder the Japs were alarmed!"

"They're trucking in more troops, but they have to go the long way round now."

Truckloads of Japanese soldiers arrived later that morning, but the guerrillas had faded back into the mountains. Ronny loved this disappearing act. A solitary plane flew over, the first Ronny had seen since arriving at Camp Holmes, and the sound of it intruded in this world where birdsong was the constant backdrop of their lives. After nearly ten months of captivity, it was hard to remember what normal life had felt like. News of the war raging across the world did seep in, but it was always viewed with suspicion and a feeling of impotence.

Ronny just concentrated on coping with Catherine, who had learned to sit up, pull herself up and stand. She longed for Pat's company, and the familiar sound, smell and feel of him. He was a good man, a beloved old friend and the father of her child, and she wanted to be with him. She believed that he would make a lovely, patient father, and it was cruel that this was being denied him.

Eleven

4th December 1942

343 days in captivity

Ronny was still buttoning her blouse as she left the hut and headed for the parade ground. The barked orders of the guards indicated something serious was up. Infants were permitted to stay in the house, and Helen was the lucky one who stayed with them.

Clarence Mount had been caught red-handed smuggling whisky into camp and they had been summoned to bear witness to his punishment. The guards had been aware for some time that alcohol was coming in, and it was the belligerent and unpleasant man himself who had given the game away. Originally, Hayakawa thought it was arriving in the package line, but, when they found nothing, the Japanese turned their attention to the perimeter fence at night. They were looking for collection points and hiding places, and they found a hidden cache before long. Mount had an arrangement with a local Filipino farmer, and Mount had been picked up outside the wire retrieving his contraband. Smugly Ronny felt that he deserved to be caught and punished.

The rain had cleared that morning, but a gloom remained as they watched Mount being dragged to the punishment tree in front of the guard house. A tall man, he struggled uselessly against the smaller guards, cursing loudly. The first blow to the back of his legs came as a shock, delivered with a baseball bat and his cry slammed into Ronny as he toppled forward. As before, the Japanese guards tied the prisoner's hands above his head, threw the rope over the bough, and hauled him up helplessly to standing. The guards took turns in the savage attack that followed. The screams of the man, the grunt of the guards, and the unrelenting deliberate pulverising of flesh sickened her. She could smell the blood on the dust and no matter how she tried to avert her eyes, she could not escape the impact. Ronny's dislike for Mount didn't lessen the revulsion at the damage being inflicted on his defenceless body. No one deserved such barbaric treatment. Mount was a sick man, an outcast because of the drinking, but he did not deserve this. Like him or not, Mount was one of them so the beating felt personal.

Forbidden to move but unable to bear any more, she looked around at her fellow internees. Several of the men were wincing at each blow and having been Mount's clients, she imagined they felt guilty by implication. Commandant Hayakawa stood alone, concentrating on the punishment. The relaxing of the regulations that he had allowed was inconsistent with the savagery with which he lashed back at his prisoners.

She saw Mrs Mount, isolated as always, her face devoid of expression. She gave no indication that her husband's pain had affected her even when finally the bloody mess of his body was allowed to slump in the dust, apparently dead. Ronny watched the woman turn on her heels and head towards her shack whilst several men, led by Dr Nance, carried Mount to the hospital.

Ronny was convinced she had seen Mount's execution and it hurt her more deeply than the original beating of the Chinese man. When she later learned that he had survived, she was relieved.

Ronny became desperate for the end of the perpetual grey veil of rain which lowered even the most optimistic of personalities. One of the boffins measured twelve inches of rainfall in one day. The view of her restorative mountains was hidden and her world was a sea of grey green mud, which echoed the colours of the uniforms of the guards. Ronny's spirits were low, imprisoned by nature as well as by the Japanese.

Dysentery had claimed the lives of one or two of the most vulnerable. Helen had a spell in the hospital and shortly afterwards it was Ronny's turn to suffer stomach cramps, the like of which she had never experienced before. In a state of collapse she was carried to the hospital where the doctor administered a large dose of castor oil, followed by a total fast, with only strong tea to drink. The next twenty four hours were really unpleasant, but survive them she did. When the worst had passed she was allowed a small amount of soft Filipino rice porridge and mashed banana. She found Pam had succumbed at the same time, so on mattresses side by side, they slowly regained their strength.

In the long hours of recovery Ronny learned all about Pam's small town American past, with its stifling church-going-all-seeing community.

Pam could chat endlessly. "Bob was my escape route, he came from out of town. He was a salesman and, poor chap, once I saw him he didn't stand a chance! He was my exit ticket and I wasn't going to let him go!"

"But I know you love him! You make out you're so tough, but I know you're a softie inside."

"Sure, I love the goof, but, between you and me, married life has been a bit of a let-down! I never dreamed that his job in the lumber business would bring him here. It's such a different world from the home I left behind and right now I'd do anything to be in that stifling little town again!"

Hours of conversation between the beds showed Ronny a different side of Pam. Behind the brassy exterior, the young woman had a great sadness that she had not conceived and the dashing Bob had proved a bit of a disappointment. Ronny reciprocated by telling her the story of her second fiancé, Bonzo.

"Bonzo! What sort of a name is that? It sounds like a dog's name!" exclaimed Pam.

Ronny laughed. "Oh, Bonzo was far from that! He was wild and exciting and utterly charming."

"Where did you meet him?"

"In London. Just before war was declared, I worked as a PE teacher in a South London borough school. It was a chance meeting on a bus, and he swept me off my feet, literally! I was trying to get on a bus when it started moving, and he grabbed me and didn't let go!"

"Wow. That sounds romantic."

"Yes, he was very special and lightened up depressing London, that's for sure." She remembered his dark-brown hair and brown eyes that were always sparkling as if he found the world inexplicably amusing. He teased her constantly for her serious attitude to life, and she, who was not used to being teased, adored him. "He was a navigator in the Royal Air Force and was on call constantly. That was the way he lived life, on the edge, and he liked it that way."

"I'd love to have met someone like that! Bob is so predictable; he always was."

"Being in love is not all it's cracked up to be!" Ronny sounded old even to herself. "We were forced to change plans endlessly to meet. We got out of London as often as we could, and we stayed at the small hotel my cousin ran in Sussex. Pat met Bonzo there once, but they couldn't stand each other. Bonzo proposed, and we became engaged almost as a lucky token against an uncertain future."

"How wonderful. I hope he gave you a big ring. Did you meet his parents?"

"Yes, he gave me a ring, a pretty opal. I went to Colchester to visit his parents and his two younger sisters. The parents were tall and good-looking, and worshipped him. They were very arty. I remember the house was full of sculptures and orange walls, and they all seemed to talk at once."

"I never liked Bob's mom and dad. Did Bonzo's folks try to put you at ease?"

"No, what happened was that Bonzo held centre stage. I don't think he even noticed that I was getting quieter. He just bathed in their admiration, and I ceased to exist! I turned into a handbag when I was with them!"

"What did you do?"

"To try to even things up, I took him to meet my stepmother Margo, at Claridge's of course! Margo was surprised I'd been capable of landing such a charming young man. She took to Bonzo instantly, so I disappeared in her company too! Margo flirted outrageously with my fiancé!"

Pam, who knew about the exotic Countess Margo, said, "Well, she was Italian! That's what they do, isn't it? I bet Bonzo loved it."

"Yes, he encouraged her shamelessly. He thought it was amusing and laughed about it, but I didn't think it was so funny."

"Gorgeous as he was, it sounds as if you had your hands full with him."

"He definitely wasn't marriage material, but I adored him. He showed me a different way of life and was never serious about anything, not even me, really!"

"What happened, Ronny? How come you married Pat?" Pam was impatient.

"I was called out of class one day to be told on the telephone that his plane had gone down over the North Sea. His luck had run out. I'd only known him six months."

"Oh, how terrible! I can't imagine what that would be like. What a shock!"

"I was devastated. It's easy, with hindsight, to see the relationship was doomed. It wouldn't have survived in peace time, but I was totally knocked sideways."

"Oh Ronny. How sad. What a terrible thing this war is. All these young men dying, and no end to this madness."

· A silence descended on the two women, each deep in their own thoughts.

They were interrupted by the arrival of Dr Haughwout on his rounds, accompanied by a fluttering nurse. The doctor was a research scientist, reportedly never happier than when examining stools. It was the illness that interested him and not the patients, and his cure was dire. It wasn't long before they were left alone again.

Ronny said quietly, "The nurse told me this morning that Harold Palmer died after his appendix operation."

"Oh no! His wife and daughter are in my dormitory. They're lovely people. I thought he was supposed to be on the mend?"

"Apparently, there were complications. In other circumstances, he would have been saved, and the nurse was pretty angry about it."

"What a waste of a life." Pam sounded bleak.

"What a waste of so many lives. The futility of this war makes me furious!"

Pam broke into Ronny's thoughts. "Was it after Bonzo that you got together properly with Pat?"

"Pat heard about Bonzo's death and stepped right up. He was great, Pam."

"And?"

"His proposal was a surprise. I was over thirty, had been engaged twice, and I wanted some stability, a family life and children. I felt as if I was running out of time. The one man who'd always been there for me was Pat. I'd never looked at him in a romantic way, as he was already part of my family. I wasn't sure about it, but he was persistent."

"So he wore you down at last." Pam did like happy endings.

"I do love him, and I badly needed a port in the storm. We make a good team."

At that moment the nurse arrived, armed with a small portion of soft porridge to fortify the two women.

—※—※—

Sometime after her recovery, Ronny was wandering back after her shift shelling peanuts in the camp kitchen, with Catherine slung in a papoose on her hip, when the excitement of a rapidly gathering crowd distracted her. Two Imperial Army trucks had arrived and dumped loads of trunks and baggage on the ground in front of the guardhouse. Ronny joined the throng to be greeted by a scene of open trunks and a kaleidoscope of garments and possessions strewn over the damp ground. There were dresses, trousers, shoes, undergarments, hats, children's wear and the occasional fur coat. Tension was high as men and women dived in, looking for lost possessions as they recognised their own suitcases left behind on the march from Brent.

Ronny watched spellbound as, in desperation to reclaim their clothes, men and women elbowed and shoved each other. Many recognised their own containers, only to find that there were other peoples' clothes in them as the soldiers had pushed all the left-behind debris into whatever container they could. The crowd pushed forwards, eyeing this haphazard process of reclamation, and, suddenly, the dam broke. It became a free for

all. Ronny, with no reservations, joined the throng. Here was
bounty for the taking, and she was not going to hang back whilst
others benefitted.

The guards stood by amused, as disputes broke out and chaos
ensued. The universal compulsion to loot took hold. Ronny,
mindful of Catherine on her hip, scavenged round the outside of
the mass, and found a pair of shoes to her liking and grabbed a
couple of dresses. She wanted something for herself and, at that
instant, did not care if the owners were her friends. She avoided
a scuffle between a normally self-effacing woman and a man
twice her size over a coat. It was shocking to see the teeth-bared
nature of both parties unmasked, and Ronny sidestepped them
and dived onto some infant outfits she saw discarded in the mud.
These were obviously meant for her!

As the adrenalin slowed, Ronny made her way back to
the baby house. Dogged with a mixture of shame and the
pleasure of gain, she dragged her heels. She was overtaken by
an overburdened Betty, her colouring high in her cheeks and her
eyes sparkling.

"Wow, what a bun fight! I've no idea what I've got! I just
grabbed everything I could," Betty declared.

"Where's Bud?" asked Ronny.

"I left him with Helen, so I'll share these with her. Did you
find anything you wanted?"

"Yes, I managed to get a couple of things, but I feel bad about
it now."

"Did you see that fight?" Betty was unstoppable. "I reckon
that woman may have lost some hair! There were some very
unhappy bunnies there! What've you got?"

"These shoes and dresses, which will be perfect – that is, if
nobody claims them – and I grabbed things for Catherine. I hope
I won't have to give them back." Ronny was feeling a mixture of
emotions: triumphant at what she had scavenged, ashamed at

taking others' possessions and cross that she had not taken more. She was feeling worse by the minute.

"Well, I'm not giving anything back! People have so much that they shouldn't begrudge us a few things."

"The committee would have organised it in a more civilised way, but they were taken by surprise. Do you think the Nips did it that way deliberately?"

"Do you mean in the scheme of degrading us? No, I think they just don't think that way. Looting's the same the world over. Everyone takes advantage if they have the opportunity, so don't tell me otherwise."

"I imagine the Nips already took what they wanted." Ronny tried to justify her actions, but she could not quite convince herself.

"I'll enjoy wearing something different. I just hope that I don't run into the original owner." Betty stood firm.

"Actually, I don't think this morning's done us any good as a community. I know I'd be furious if I saw someone wearing my favourite dress." Ronny was by then feeling really bad.

"Most of the stuff had already been claimed when the fun started. You worry too much, Ron. It'll be fine, and I have to admit that I enjoyed myself. Come on. Let's get this stuff into the house. It's going to rain any second."

Betty was impervious to embarrassment and would brazen out any situation, but Ronny was full of regret. She had learned many skills in camp. She could make milk out of rice and roots, and wash clothes without soap. She had gained a vocabulary of American swearwords and had learned how to kill vermin. In addition, she had added looting to her survival techniques, and she knew Pat would have disapproved. He would have been dismayed at her lack of moral fibre this afternoon!

Life in camp was improving. In an attempt to regulate the black market, a community store was set up by the committee. With the pesos Ronny earned, she could purchase necessities from it. There was a shortage of milk, so the committee bought some goats, which turned out to be a mixed blessing. Some earned their keep, but several only provided sustenance once they were in the cooking pot. Chickens and two pigs were bought, as were bags of seeds, with the idea of creating vegetable gardens. All these attempts at providing sustenance gave the internees something positive to focus upon.

Expectations of release had been shelved, and Ronny concentrated on the life they had. That day, she planned a new venture.

"Look what I've got!" Ronny held out her eating bowl, which was piled high with beans for planting. "I got it from the store, and we're going to plant them!"

Betty looked up from her book and pulled a face. "Planting's your bag of beans, not mine!"

Bud was playing quietly at her feet.

"Come on, Betty, stir your stumps. Who knows, they may be magic and will take us to another level!" speculated Ronny.

"I never took you to be a gardener, Ron," Betty responded.

"I'm not! My father was an avid rose grower and spent more time talking to his roses than us. But we'll be able to eat these!" Ronny was set on a plan of action and would not be denied.

"Well, what sort of beans are they?"

"I've no idea, but we'll find out in due course. Come on, I'm not taking no for an answer!"

Betty succumbed with a sigh. She knew Ronny would not leave her in peace.

They set off, infants on hips, up the steep slope to the area designated for gardening. Ronny had never paid any attention to the allotment, so was surprised to find a well-established square of well-turned and watered earth, already showing the tips of vegetation coming up. The area was cordoned off with netting to keep away animals. A layer of carabao manure covered the beds.

"I wonder how they manage to keep children from eating these goodies?" Ronny mused, thinking of her childhood days of scrumping apples and other forbidden produce.

"The kids aren't allowed to come up here, which is a shame, as it could teach them the pleasure of gardening." Ronny checked her friend's face to see if this was meant as a joke.

Putting Catherine down, she found a small area of unturned ground and planted her share of the beans. She watered it with a conveniently full can she found and promptly forgot about the harvest yet to come. A slender yellow snake sunning itself in the long grass close to the allotment had distracted her. Her heart stopped in an instinctive reaction, and she backed away from the plot and scooped Catherine up. She did not know whether the snake was dangerous, she just had a gut-wrenching aversion, which could not be denied.

"Come on, Betty," she said. "It's time to go. I think Catherine needs changing." Ronny concealed her haste to leave the spot.

It was a pleasant walk back in the late afternoon sun, and they were in a relaxed frame of mind as they entered the baby house.

Ronny and Betty knew immediately that something was wrong. They had interrupted their friends in mid-discussion, and the pause was pregnant. They all looked at Ronny, their faces grim. Whatever the topic had been, she was implicated.

"What is it? What's happened?" she asked.

Helen moved towards her, and Ronny sat down on the bench whilst the others bunched up to give her room. There was awkwardness and a shuffling of eyes, which made the tension unbearable.

Ronny demanded an answer, "Come on, please. You've got to tell me. Has someone died?"

There was silence.

"Someone has died! Oh no! Please tell me," Ronny pleaded. She feared something had happened to Pat. Her stomach dropped. Pat was ill. Pat was dead. She gripped the bench and stared around the group.

The courageous Pam said, "There's news about Walter Cushing."

"Walter?" Ronny's immediate response was of relief. Pat was OK. It wasn't going to be her Pat. Then the name sunk in. Walter? The news was about her guerrilla hero and, judging from the faces surrounding her, the news was bad.

Helen said in a small voice, "He's been killed, Ronny. The Japs caught him in an ambush in Isabela province. He was so severely wounded that he couldn't escape. He shot himself rather than surrender. I'm so sorry."

"But he can't have!" Ronny gasped, knowing instantly that he could have and had. So he was just a man after all. Ronny felt wiped out.

People were speaking, verifying the news. This iconic figure – half fact, half fiction – had been her talisman, and, suddenly, he was gone. In her imagination, she could see the bullets pounding into his jerking flesh in some distant glade and then his last gesture of defiance as he lifted his Colt 45 to his head. It was over. There was no imagined rescue left, and life would have to continue on without it.

Later that evening, she lay in bed, but sleep would not come. Shafts of moonlight threw bands across the sleeping bodies, and she felt totally and sharply awake. She listened to the rhythmic breathing of the other women, and thought about her response to the news of Cushing's death and her immediate fear that it was Pat that had come to harm. Pat was her reality and always had been. It was with Pat that she needed to be. Ten months was too long. Somehow, she had to be reunited with her husband and the father of her child.

TWELVE

---++---++---

13th December 1942
352 days in captivity

The shock jarred her as Ronny almost tripped headlong over something sticking out across the pathway.

"Hey! That hurt!" yelped a voice.

"I'm so sorry. I didn't see you," she responded as she steadied herself and studied the shapely legs stretched out from under the baby house. Somebody was lying on her back, full length on the ground, scrabbling under the floorboards.

"What are you doing?" asked Ronny.

"It's my job detail." The voice was melodious and very English. The owner hauled herself out and extended to her full height, stretching her back. "I have to gather all the hair between the cracks. The pest control people decided it's a haven for spiders and bugs."

"But that's ridiculous. Not the bugs, but giving the job to someone of your height. It's plain silly. I'd complain if I was you." Ronny was indignant.

"Someone has to do it. But I've finished now. My name's Iris. Are you all right?" the woman replied.

"I'm fine. I'm sorry I banged into you."

The dark-haired and attractive woman surprised her again. "Do you fancy a walk?"

Ronny was happy to agree. Iris Herklots was bringing up her three children – Peter, Jeremy and Stella – alone in camp, with no idea as to where her husband was.

Iris explained, "We lived in Hong Kong, where Geoffrey was a reader in biology at the university. When the Japanese invasion of China threatened us, ex-pat wives and children were evacuated to Australia. The British government believed that Hong Kong would be held to siege, and Geoffrey was seconded to organise the vital firewood the Chinese use for cooking."

"Then how did you end up here?" Ronny quizzed.

"We didn't go to Australia. Geoffrey had worked here, and thought it would be a more convenient and secure base for the family. I got a secretarial job at the Chinese language school here."

"Was your husband in Hong Kong when they were invaded?"

"Yes. We did have two lovely visits from him before the invasion. He was busy working to feed the city, organising the preparation of fish oil and salted fish. He's ingenious and invented hard biscuits that are from the ground residue of peanuts after the oil was extracted."

Ronny liked the sound of Iris's husband. "He sounds like a resourceful person. We could use him here!"

"I miss him enormously and the children do too. We've heard nothing since he last returned to Hong Kong." Iris paused and added, "Someone told me he could have been sent to a camp in Japan."

"Oh no! I'm so sorry."

—✳—✳—

The two English women – one tall and dark, and the other shorter and auburn-haired – made their strolls a regular event. They shared histories, hopes and fears. Iris was actually physically frail with a recurring gastric ulcer, which she managed to self-medicate stoically. Ronny was full of admiration for her.

One afternoon, the two women wandered up to the small meadow behind the wood shop that had been fenced to form a farmyard. They examined the new influx of animals that graced the camp. There were pigs, chickens, goats and even two ducks that the guards had bought in, to the delight of the children. Ronny thought this abundance of livestock would mean an increase in the amount of food they were receiving, but, sadly, this was not the case. The trickle of new internees had swelled the numbers in camp to over 500, and they could not be catered for. Supplies purchased in the Philippines had become very expensive, and the Japanese were not prepared to increase the internee food allowance.

Iris was downcast. "I hear the committee can only buy less than a pound of sugar per head, each month now. They say that cooking lard's going to be rationed too, which is going to affect my business." The enterprising Iris cooked up the local sweet potatoes called *camotes* to sell chips to fellow internees. The bachelors in particular could not resist them. "I don't know what I'm going to do without that income. The children need it desperately."

"I won't try to grow beans any more. Someone stole them as soon as they looked tempting. We're still better off than those on the run. Did you hear about the four American fellows with the little girl who arrived last month? They were from the Itogen mine and had been hiding in the mountains," said Ronny.

"Yes, I remember; they were in a shocking state. The Igorots betrayed them, and the Japs shot two of the American women whilst they were trying to escape. One of the husbands was a Filipino doctor."

"I can't imagine what it must have been like for them. They were so thankful to be interned with us."

Iris agreed, "They'd spent the last weeks in a prison in the lowlands, so this seems like heaven to them. Did you see those poor men who were trucked in a couple of weeks ago? They'd really been knocked about."

Ronny shuddered at the recollection. "Yes, they looked half-dead. Apparently, the Japs had held them for quite a while in the mountains. They'd obviously been tortured. I saw one man had a terrible open wound."

"They weren't military either! They're American civilians."

"It's amazing they managed to hide away for so long. I imagine the problem was the Filipinos hiding and feeding them. I've nothing but respect for the locals; the pressure on them must be enormous. It was different in the beginning, but these people have been hiding out there for nearly a year."

"I agree, Ronny. With such a food shortage and the rewards that the Nips have been offering, it's hardly surprising if they handed them in. What a sad world we live in."

A year had passed since Ronny had made that holiday trip up to Baguio, and they were approaching Christmas again.

In the baby house, Helen laughed. "Have you seen who's arrived to look after us over Christmas?"

"Father Christmas himself?" Ronny was not enthused.

"No, but it's just as bizarre! They've bought in the Filipino constabulary to cover for the guards' holiday."

"Why should the guards have leave? How many are Christians?"

"Oh Ronny, just come and see!"

At Helen's urging, the two ladies left the baby house.

Out on the parade ground, the sun was merciless as Ronny watched a ragtag selection of the local constabulary going through their paces. Under the barked orders of the Japanese, the unenthusiastic group were being drilled, but their relaxed and casual approach to life in general was clearly upsetting the guard. Ronny wondered if the Japanese could possibly instil discipline in these unmilitary, likeable islanders.

It was fun to stand and watch the floor show, and a small group gathered. The next drill was even more bizarre, as the officers lined them up, looking towards the break in the mountains, where the sun always rose. Ronny could not help smiling as they tried to teach them the Japanese traditional bow, straight-legged and from the waist, all in unison.

Christmas in Camp Holmes was an emotional day. Ronny gasped on entering the dining room, which was decorated with pine branches and an assortment of home-made Christmas decorations. Extra food had been acquired by the committee, and dawn broke to a feast of bacon and eggs. The smell of the pine wafted towards her in competition with the smell of bacon, and she salivated at this once-familiar smell as she joined the excited and chattering line to be served. Nine-month-old Catherine chuckled in delight at the woollen teddy that Ronny had made for her and stared, round-eyed, at all the brightly coloured baubles that hung from the greenery.

Later, there were gifts for the children from a rather dishevelled Santa Claus, his scarlet, padded uniform contrasting with a very moth-eaten grey wig and whiskers of improbable ringlets. Ronny smiled to see the children's enthusiasm, as she had been part of this real effort to make it a special day for everyone. The school put on a nativity play with the usual star-struck Mary and Joseph, three kings, assorted animals, and a host of distracted angels. Hayakawa had agreed that the guards would not have their rifles on display, and even the Japanese appeared to enjoy the event enormously.

In the afternoon, the main gate was opened and vetted visitors were allowed in. Former gardeners, amahs and housekeepers all visited, and gifts were distributed after inspection.

Putting on her renovated blue-and-white polka-dot dress, which softened her slim outline, Ronny felt feminine and special. Pam lent her a lipstick. Small wall mirrors had recently made their way into the women's quarters, and no expense of effort had been spared that day. Two baby-house mothers had generously volunteered to give the other women the chance to attend the Christmas evening dinner.

When they were all ready, the ladies left the baby house and went to the dining room.

Ronny compared the last Christmas, which had been so fraught with anxiety, with this one, which was held in the embrace of a group who were bound together so intimately. She studied the faces of those sitting near her and marvelled at the richness of new friends that the last year had brought. She was seated next to Pam, with her solid husband Bob on the far side. Pam had cut her mid-brown hair stylishly short, finally deleting all traces of the brassy blonde. She looked pretty, and Ronny complimented her.

Further down the table, Helen leaned across the table towards her husband, Ed. Her dark hair was swept up stylishly for this occasion. Ronny was struck by the serenity of the couple, who were deep in conversation and momentarily unaware of the demands of their environment. Iris was seated further off, along with her children, and Ronny reflected that Iris was eye catching and special, and would have been in any environment. On Ronny's other side, the effervescent Betty was chortling with her husband Bernie, their American twang cutting across the room as they recounted some shared joke in unison. Eric and Eleanor were seated separately from the group, and the cast-iron bond between them was tangible.

Hayakawa had allowed the purchase of special food, and there was pork, roasted sweet potatoes and other vegetables, cookies, and candies for all. It was a feast indeed, and Ronny gorged herself.

The evening ended with a carol service. Everyone sang with gusto, including a handful of the watchful guards. The day stood out as an unreal jewel in the year of grim hardship.

—⊬—⊬—

The start of the second year of internment was a watershed for Ronny. Half-baked ideas consolidated themselves, and she found herself considering seriously the idea of joining Pat in the Santo Tomas camp. She pondered the pros and cons of making such a move endlessly, and became reclusive and withdrawn. She needed to talk it over, but, although Betty and Helen were her closest baby-house friends, she was wary of seeking their opinion. Leaving them felt like betrayal. Ronny chose her special English friend to talk to, and picked a time when she found herself alone with Iris on a weevil-sifting stint in the kitchen.

Ronny took the plunge. "I'm glad I've got you to myself. I wanted to ask your advice."

"I'm happy to listen, but I can't guarantee I've got any worthwhile answers to give. What is it?" Iris enquired.

"I've been thinking such a lot about trying to get down to Manila to join Pat."

"Of course you're missing Pat. I understand that all too well. If it were possible to go there, have you considered the implications?"

"I do nothing but consider them! I know we're lucky to be here. I heard Ray Hale say that, in Manila, they call us the 'holiday camp.'"

"How did he describe life down there?"

"He said it was like a town with shops and entertainment. But he also said it was terribly overcrowded as there are about 3,000 internees. It's humid and polluted in comparison to here, and the disease and death toll is higher. It sounded pretty grim."

Iris took her time. "So Pat is the sole reason for you considering transferring there?"

"I'm not a city person, Iris, and it sounds as if that camp has all the worst aspects of city life without any of our advantages. Here, we have fresh air to breathe, we have this amazing view to feed ourselves with, and more chance of fighting illness and staying well. We're really better off here." Ronny found tears welling up in her eyes, which she blinked away.

Iris picked up her struggle instinctively. "I understand."

Both women were silent.

"It's just not fair. You don't even know where Geoffrey is. At least I know where Pat is, but I've no idea as to how he's coping. If only he were here, I could just sit this out like everyone else," elaborated Ronny.

"Oh Ronny, if only we had a crystal ball! No, perhaps not! It would be terrible to see Geoffrey in pain and not be able to do anything about it," Iris responded.

"I remember what Marian Gray went through, knowing but not knowing. I think it was a relief to her when Rufus was officially dead. We just have to hope that Geoffrey and Pat are all right."

Iris said quietly, "In a strange way, I feel that I would know if he was dead. I can't explain it. Do you feel that?"

"I'm not sure." She thought about her response to the death of Walter Cushing. "Pat would never do anything rash or stupid, but he's not a practical man, and that's the most important thing for survival."

"He'll have friends who are looking out for him."

"I imagine so." Ronny was doubtful. "But we didn't have time to make friends in Manila before the invasion."

"Yes, but look at you. How many people did you know before internment? And now you have a network of friends for life."

Ronny smiled. "It's easier for me. I'm more sociable than Pat is. He's shy. I do the talking and socialising for both of us."

"He'll be fine, Ronny. This experience has taught us to cut away all the superficial rubbish, and we know each other for who we really are. It'll be the same for him."

"He is special, Iris. He's patient and solid and funny at times. Did I tell you how good he is at chess? He's won lots of tournaments, and we make a great bridge partnership."

"There you are then. Of course he'll have friends to support him. You just need to work out what's best for you and Catherine."

"Perhaps I'm just wasting time thinking about it, but I can't help it."

"Listen. I'm sure you'll reach the right decision. Give me a hug. I think we both need it."

Saying it out loud had eased the burden a little, and Ronny was able to concentrate on the job in hand, which was to safeguard the communal food from weevils for one more day.

In February, dysentery returned to the camp. The plague of flies had reappeared and, despite Fabian Ream's bamboo-and-netting fly swatters, they just kept coming. The hospital was so full of seriously ill patients that they overflowed, and part of the women's dormitory had to be commandeered to house them. The commandant allowed an extra shipment of the disinfectant Lysol to be released, and there followed a frenzy of scrubbing.

The baby house went into siege mode, and a trough of the disinfectant was set up at the doorway as an added safeguard. Ronny feared the babies would not have the resilience to survive the epidemic. She still breast fed Catherine, despite the emergence of her little teeth, which made Ronny wince at times. Concerned that Catherine's diet lacked calcium, she scavenged the discarded eggshells from the bins behind the guardhouse. Pounding these up small she tried to feed these to the toddler, who rejected them stubbornly, so Ronny swallowed the grit herself in the hope that it would enrich her milk.

Ronny watched through the window as two guards were making their inspection rounds. Rather than barging in, they stopped at the doors, adjusted surgical masks over their faces and risked a token peek into the interior.

"I've never seen the Nips so jumpy. I hate the way they wear those masks whenever they come near us, as if we were the vermin responsible," stated Ronny.

Betty was preparing the formula for Bud's bottle with extra care and concentration. "I'm scared, Ronny. I simply couldn't bear it if anything happened to Bud." Betty was, for once, truly depressed.

Ronny struggled to reassure her. "You'll both be fine. We're taking every precaution with the men doing all the errands for us. This is the safest place to be." Ronny watched the two retreating figures. "We've learned a lot from the Nips about treating illness. Remember how we used to laugh at them for wearing those woollen belly bands round their stomachs when they had diarrhoea. Now we're all doing it! And switching to rice water instead of milk seems to work. None of us are allowed to enter the guardhouse any more, not that I ever have."

"Nellie and the committee are pressing for inoculations against typhoid, dysentery and cholera to be sent in. They're suggesting that we inoculate the guards too. Please, God, that it won't take the death of a kid to get them to agree." There was panic in Betty's voice.

"Bud and Catherine look fine to me, but I wish that we could do something about these flies."

"They're worse than they've ever been. The water supply is on the blink again, and now we've no soap. There's no sugar or fat. Just when you think it can't get worse, it does! I just can't take it." Betty was distraught.

A hug was all the consolation that Ronny could manage. She had nothing to give her friend. Or had she? "I can think of one positive! We now have Philippine-made toilet paper, after all these months of wiping our backsides on Japanese newsprint."

"Oh, that disgusting newsprint, with the photos of the emperor cut out by some poor guard! I can't believe the trouble they went to so we didn't wipe ourselves on the emperor's face!" Betty hooted with laughter, and Ronny, relieved, joined in.

Betty's laughter would be one of the things she would miss the most if she managed to get to Santo Tomas, and she had no idea how she was going to tell her friend what was on her mind. The thought of leaving Betty brought tears to her eyes, so she got busy sorting her laundry.

The epidemic lasted about three weeks and there were no fatalities in the baby house.

<hr />

Feathery ground mimosa covered the slope Ronny was sitting on. This little plant, native to that part of the world, was able to curl up its leaves instantly when touched or stroked. It offered endless delight to Catherine and held her attention almost as much as the farm animals. The little girl was happy to just sit quietly and watch the world go by, unlike the bouncy Bud, who had the makings of an intrepid explorer, much to Betty's secret pride.

They were seated on the mimosa slope together when Betty voiced her thoughts. "Ron, when are you going to talk to me?"

"What do you mean?" Ronny asked.

"You've been doing that Limey thing for weeks now. You've gone all quiet and withdrawn into yourself. You're grumpy too."

"You mean more than my usual early morning stuff?" Ronny was not a morning person at the best of times.

"Come on, Ron. Don't try and laugh it off. Are you going to tell me what's going on?"

Ronny struggled. "I was thinking about the father and little boy who arrived last night. I hear they'd been hiding out in the mountains for more than a year, but the wife was diabetic and she ran out of insulin. They had to give themselves up to get the medical supplies."

"I didn't see the wife, but the other two looked in bad shape."

"The Japs held them in a mine up there and refused to let them come in, so she died."

"How barbaric! It makes me mad to hear about the waste of life."

"All our lives are being wasted, Betty, whilst we're sitting waiting to live them again. I can't go on doing this. There's no rescue round the corner. Catherine changes from day to day, and she's never known her father." She took a deep breath and ignored her somersaulting stomach. "I need to get Catherine and myself to Manila. I need to be with Pat, somehow."

"Is that all? I thought it was something serious!"

Ronny stared at her. "I'm serious, Betty. I mean to make it happen! I feel so torn about leaving you all now. This is my home, and you're my family, but I know I've got to get down there and be with him."

Betty gave her a hug. "We love you too, no matter how mad you are!"

"I know I'm lucky to be here. Sometimes I think I'm mad to even consider leaving."

"Why have you then?"

"It's Pat, of course. He's been part of my life for as long as I can remember. He's a good man, but vulnerable, and I've always felt responsible for him. I need him to survive this, and I think he'll do better with me at his side. Does that sound very complicated?" she ended lamely.

"No, it sounds like love to me."

Catherine had tired of the mimosa-stroking game and wanted the attention of her mother.

Ronny half-heartedly played with her, but her mind was focused on her friend. "Oh, Betty. I'll miss you so much."

"I'll miss you too, but I have my man here, so who am I to stop you from going? How are you going to make it happen?"

Ronny was overwhelmed with gratitude at her friend's response. She had been feeling so disloyal and, as it was out in the open, she could now concentrate on the logistics of getting down to Manila.

"What've you done so far? Have you put in a request to the committee?" Betty enquired.

"No, Betty. I suppose that's the only way to go?" Ronny asked.

"You're funny. You've a real thing about them, haven't you? Carl Eschbach is the most approachable one, so why don't you make an appointment with him?"

"But he reminds me of my father! He's exactly the same physical type." Ronny caught Betty's suppressed smile. "Yes! How old am I? It's pathetic!"

"You and authority figures! Just because your father disapproved of you, doesn't mean Eschbach will. Gee, Ron, he's only a few years older than you! I sometimes think you'd prefer to confront Hayakawa directly."

"I'm not that stupid! Hayakawa really scares me."

"No, that wouldn't be smart. If you are going to get to Manila, the only way is through the committee."

Ronny sighed deeply. This time she would go through the official channels and she would not contemplate defeat. She allowed herself the luxury of imagining the reunion with Pat. She visualised his excitement when he met her off the transport and the emotion on his face when he met his little miracle daughter. They would face the hostile world together and would make it through this war. Ronny was convinced she was on her way.

Thirteen

10th March 1943

440 days in captivity

Ronny studied the man seated on the grass beside her. Carl Eschbach was tall and slim with sandy hair and grey eyes that were resting patiently on her. He did indeed remind her of her father, who had always challenged the course of her life, the choice of faraway jobs and even her final choice of Pat as a husband. Dealing with this committee member was a choice that she would have avoided in any other circumstance.

Carl Eschbach broke the silence. "I don't think we've actually spoken before, have we? Isn't it odd that we can live in such close proximity and yet we've never talked?"

"No. I'm not one of your congregation, Reverend. Thank you for giving me your time," replied Ronny.

"May I call you Ronny?" Carl said smoothly, and his eyes wrinkled up at the corners in a genuine smile. "How may I help you today?"

They were seated on the grassy slope outside the dining area, and the sounds of someone playing the piano haltingly reached her ears. This gift to the camp, doubtless spoils of war, had been presented by the old commandant Nakamura. The piano was a joy in the hands of veterans, but a jarring discordant note for those overhearing learners, as it was at this moment. The fumbling repetitions floating over the grass distracted her and threatened her mission.

"I want to put forward a request to the commandant. I need permission for me and my baby to move to Santo Tomas to be with my husband." Her heart was beating so hard she was sure he could hear it.

"Are you sure you and Catherine would benefit from being with Pat?" Apparently, he knew all about her, whilst she had assumed she lived under the committee radar. "You look surprised! Did you think we weren't aware of your situation? Before considering your request, I need to be sure that you've given this considerable thought. Life in Manila is very different from how it is here."

"I can assure you that I do know that it'll be tougher, but I should be by Pat's side. Catherine and I need to be with him, and he needs us."

The grey eyes never left her face. "I understand you approached Mukaibo a while back and he turned you down."

Her face burned with shame at the recollection of the Japanese man's rebuttal. "I realise it was a mistake to talk to Mukaibo directly. It was a spur of the moment thing, which I know wasn't smart. Would you be prepared to talk to Hayakawa on my behalf?"

"As you know, there are no guarantees with the Japs. There's a limit to the amount of requests that we dare put forward, and negotiations take time. We have to be cautious and sure of our ground. We have a list of requests to put forward, so we have to prioritise what we consider to be the most urgent."

"Are you saying my request for a transfer is low priority?"

"Ronny, I know it's important to you. You've obviously wanted this for some time, but there are other internee transfers that I must consider a higher priority than yours."

Ronny was stung. "What could be more important than reuniting a family, if it's possible?"

"Quite right!"

"I know there are people who are really ill or have other claims, but, surely, my baby and I have ample grounds? Who are these people whose needs are more important?"

Carl paused. "I'm going to tell you something in confidence. Even the people involved don't know we've been negotiating for them. We don't want them to know in case of disappointment, but we've been working for some time for their transfer." He considered her carefully. "Ronny, this is a secret to be kept. Are you prepared to do that?"

"Yes," she agreed reluctantly; she felt she had no choice.

"We're negotiating the transfer of the Brent boarding pupils to be reunited with their parents in Santo Tomas."

Tears sprang to her eyes and she knew immediately that their claim was greater than hers. The boys and girls had been stranded without their families for well over a year and, of course, they must be reunited with their loved ones if it was remotely possible.

"I understand." Her voice came out low, and she wanted to flee. She had already started imagining the reunion with Pat, but because these ideas had been dashed she just wanted the interview to end. She was bitterly disappointed and angry that she had allowed her dreams to take wings. She growled her excuses hastily, needing time to herself to come to terms with her disappointment.

In the next few days, Ronny concentrated on Catherine and tried to appreciate the advantages of life in this particular camp. As a distraction, Ronny cast around to find a diversion at which to throw herself. Her encounters with the all-male committee had left her feeling frustrated and negative, so word that the camp's suffrage movement was recruiting beckoned her.

Dr Beulah Allen led the group, and greeted Ronny with tired courtesy when Ronny arrived to see her. "What exposure have you had to the movement before this?"

"None, I have to confess. It didn't seem to be an issue in my family," said Ronny.

"Your mother and sisters did what your father wanted, without question?" The woman raised her eyebrows.

Ronny explained, "No, it wasn't like that. My mother was always independent. She was orphaned young, and she and her sisters were brought up by uncles. She took herself off and studied piano at the Conservatoire in Leipzig. My father respected her and certainly couldn't have stopped her doing whatever she wanted. My mother never seemed aware of obstacles in her path."

"She sounds as if she had a privileged upbringing. She wasn't interested in politics?"

"I think she was confused by the women's movement, as she'd always just taken what she wanted. She didn't see the feminist cause as an issue. With her example, I grew up only dimly aware of the battles going on between the sexes."

Beulah Allen pointed out, "Did you know that the movement in your home country originated in 1832, but it took British women till 1928 to get the law passed for equal votes for the sexes?"

"That's extraordinary! I didn't realise it took so long!"

"It was a hard-won fight in both our countries. But what good has it done us here? In this supposedly democratically run camp, we're still being blocked by men in 1943! Only men have the right to vote for the committee, which of course is all men. I may be the chair of the women's committee, but we have no say and are totally ignored for the most part. We've got to get the right for women to be included in the vote for the selection of the general committee."

"I gather that Dr Nance is always being voted back into the chair."

"Nance is a dyed-in-the-wool chauvinist. We're actually making some progress. Seventy-one women have now signed a petition demanding that we can conduct a poll. It's too long for me to recite, but the gist of it is 'Do you favour women's suffrage to allow them the right to vote for the entire membership of the general committee?'"

This was what Ronny needed and she readied herself to do battle.

⸻

A few days later, Betty confirmed that the poll had got the go ahead, so Ronny, who had never canvassed before, focused wholeheartedly on the crusade, to distract herself from her failed attempt to join Pat. She soon discovered that a suffragette poll, in a Japanese prisoner-of-war (POW) camp, would be met by indifference. Shocked and angered by the apathy she encountered, she worked tirelessly, finding energy she thought she had lost over the many months of malnutrition. By late March, both men and women had been polled and, much to the exhilaration of the women campaigners, the yes vote carried the day.

Ronny and her friends were over the moon. She and Betty, high on success, were dancing a jig on the grass when Beulah Allen approached. One look at her face stilled them.

Beulah was struggling. "I can't believe it! The committee say the vote isn't valid!"

"What? They can't do that! We have the numbers!" cried Ronny.

"They say that eighty-three women have voted against the resolution, so they will disregard it! They say it has been a personal crusade by me against Nance, so they're going to disregard the vote."

"A personal crusade? That's crazy!"

"They accused me of creating a rift in camp, and stated that voting rights was just a side issue. The committee intends to disregard the poll completely."

Ronny was furious. "No! That's so wrong! *That's so unfair!*" Despite her best efforts, nothing had changed, and this felt like a reflection of her life. Her anger towards the committee was compounded, and overwhelmed any previous respect that she may have had for them.

It was a beautiful, misty morning that promised to be scorching by noon. Ronny listened to the birdsong as she stood at roll call, with Catherine on her hip, but was distracted by Carl Eschbach signalling to her across the tennis court. She studiedly ignored him. She had nothing to say to him.

However, as they disbursed he blocked her path, saying, "Ronny! Stop!"

She had no choice.

He explained, "We have a date for the transfer of the Brent boarders. It will be tomorrow. I wanted you to know before you heard it from others."

"Thank you. How kind of you." She knew she sounded stiff.

"I put in a request that you accompany the boys and girls on the journey. We did our best, but Hayakawa wouldn't consider it. I'm sorry, Ronny."

Ronny stared at him, colour draining from her face. He had put in a request for her? He had tried to get her on that transport? She wished he had not told her. It confused her, and she felt her frustration bubbling up and buzzing in her head. The transfer was for tomorrow, and she would be left behind. She felt impotent and sick. She could not accept that her chance had passed her by and she was supposed to stand aside and accept it. She turned on her heels.

Aware of the restraining hand on her arm, Ronny flung herself free, and ran back to the baby house. Betty was standing outside it, and, after one look at her friend's face, she recognised Ronny's determination, and took Catherine from her, setting her free to stride towards whatever destiny awaited her.

Ronny knew she was putting herself at risk of universal disapproval, but the impetus of her need propelled her forwards. Approaching the guardhouse, she had little time to take in the startled expression of the guard who stood outside. Blocking her path, he forced his gun across her chest. He was the same height as her and his face was familiar, and they stared at each other in mutual shock.

"I wish to see the commandant. I wish to see Major Hayakawa," demanded Ronny.

"No. You no appointment," said the guard.

"I must see Major Hayakawa."

"You no committee. You go back."

The gun pressed firmer into her chest, pushing her back, and she strove to keep her balance. Regardless she raised her voice. "I want to see the commandant."

Ronny was aware that she was attracting attention from other internees and tried to ignore them. This was a meeting she had to have, and she was not going to be deterred. The guard shouted something over his shoulder and the door swung open as another guard joined him, frowning at her. She didn't understand the words he spewed out, but the menace was clear. Long minutes crawled past as she stood her ground.

Miraculously, she heard the voice of Nellie McKim behind her. Nellie had been summoned at the run and, despite her heaving chest, she projected the courtesy to the uncertain guards that she always did. The exchange in Japanese went on and Ronny would not move. Thankfully, her rescuer did not ask her to explain herself. At last, Nellie's presence deflated the tension, and one of the guards turned back into the guardhouse for instructions. Ronny continued to brace herself. She was not turning back.

When they were ushered through the guardhouse into the inner sanctum, she found a room devoid of character. It was furnished sparsely and it was immaculate. The fan whirred overhead. Despite her anxiety, Ronny noted how pristine and orderly the Japanese room was in comparison to the clutter of the internee quarters. There was one branch of jasmine on the desk behind which the commandant was sitting over a neat pile of papers. The two women bowed deeply in unison to Hayakawa, and she saw the man at close quarters for the first time. He was small, moustached and neat as expected, and his eyes were hooded.

Nellie turned to Ronny, the tension lines between her brows evident, as she waited to translate her request. Ronny knew she was way out of line and was putting Nellie's relationship with the Japanese in jeopardy, but there was no irritation in the other woman's manner.

"I have come to humbly request that I should escort the Brent schoolchildren on their transfer to Manila. I wish to take my baby and rejoin my husband, who is interned in Santo Tomas," entreated Ronny.

There was silence.

Ronny continued, "A request that I escort the children was submitted to you through the committee. I would humbly ask you to reconsider your order for the children to make this journey alone."

Hayakawa did not even look up.

"I understand that this transfer has been approved by the Imperial Army and would humbly suggest that it is not fitting that the children travel unescorted on such a long journey," concluded Ronny.

Hayakawa spoke in Japanese, despite the well-known fact that he spoke good English. "Mr Ray Hale will be driving the vehicle and there will be an escort of a guard. That will be sufficient."

"With respect, Commandant, the driver must concentrate on the road, especially after the damage that the enemies of your army have inflicted on the route. It is imperative that the children are delivered safely whilst they are under your care. They will need an adult who can communicate with them to be responsible for them," Ronny cajoled.

Ronny followed Nellie's lead by bowing between each interpreted sentence, as it was imperative that humbleness be displayed. The interview had taken on a dream-like quality, and Hayakawa still did not raise his eyes from his paperwork.

"I will consider your request and let you know," he stated.

An initial rush of excitement, followed as quickly by doubt that she had achieved anything, overwhelmed Ronny. She had risked a great deal this morning by getting into Hayakawa's office, and she was determined that she would not see Catherine again until she had achieved her goal. She was convinced that neither the Japanese nor the committee would allow her to get this close again.

Ronny did not follow as Nellie bowed and retreated. Her heart was pounding and she was sick with fear, but she would not follow suit. "The children will leave tomorrow and the escort decision has to be made now in order that I can prepare myself and my baby for travel. With respect, I will wait here for your decision." There, she had done it.

As Nellie's eyes widened in shock, Ronny took a step back to the wall and sank to the floor, cross-legged, waiting for whatever fate awaited her. She would not allow herself to consider the peril that she had placed herself in. An image of the public beatings she had witnessed rose unwittingly to mind, but she thrust it away and waited for whatever was to follow.

Nellie was dismissed with a curt wave of the hand, and she felt Hayakawa's eyes on her as he considered her intrusion.

To her surprise, the guards were not summoned and silence followed Nellie's departure, broken only by the humming of the overhead fan. Hayakawa, inscrutable as ever, continued with his paperwork, and Ronny straightened her back against the wall to ease it and prepared for a long wait on the hard wooden floor. There was no going back, and she could imagine the consternation that her actions would be creating in the camp and Carl Eschbach's disapproval. She had broken the rules, and she imagined that she may have made other negotiations more difficult for the committee. On having time to reflect, she decided that – having survived the first confrontation with the guard, thanks to Nellie's intervention – she was unlikely to be physically hurt. She could certainly be humiliated and perhaps be punished by a spell in solitary, but did not think her actions would result in punishment for the camp in general.

The clock on the wall behind Hayakawa's desk ticked lazily and two hours limped by. Guards came and went, delivering documents to the commandant, who grunted his orders and continued to ignore her. Several flies became embedded in the glue strip above the Japanese desk and, after a frantic struggle, gave up their hours of life, and still Ronny sat on the hard floor. She was used to physical discomfort, but she was anxious about what was happening in the outside world. She thought about Catherine. She trusted Betty implicitly to care for her child.

Time dragged on. With neat precision, the commandant took an occasional sip of water from the upturned glass of the decanter that stood on his desk, and Ronny willed herself not to watch.

As the hours passed, not once did Hayakawa acknowledge her presence. Finally, he pushed his chair back, locked his papers in his desk drawer, pulled the overhead cord to still the fan and left the room without a glance. Ronny was a little surprised that her presence was considered of so little consequence that she was left to continue her vigil on her own.

As the temperature rose in the burning midday sun, the room became stale and stifling, and Ronny's thirst became a torment. She started to question her sanity at placing herself in this insane standoff. It was the result of her impetuous stupidity, and it was madness to think that she could benefit. The Japanese would not give in and lose face, especially to a woman. Without the fan to circulate the air, the sweat was running down her in rivulets. It ran into her eyes and she tasted the salt on her lips. Her back ached unbearably. Her buttocks felt bruised as she tried to shift her weight.

Four hours passed.

Trying to ease her legs, she rubbed them one at a time to increase the blood flow, but dared not grant herself the luxury of standing up. If she stood, she knew she would not be able to stop herself from reaching for the water, and then the impetus to leave this tomb of her own making could not be denied. Her dress stuck to her body, and she knew humiliation, as her breasts began to leak, which was an indication that it was past feeding time. She could do nothing about the spreading stain. A headache, brought on by dehydration, became insistent and dominated her thoughts. The reason she was in this room became confused in her mind, but she never doubted that this was where she had to be. She had to achieve something terribly important to her. She knew that she must not reach for the water, and she had to concentrate on her breath-by-breath survival.

Ronny never knew how many hours passed before the door swung open and she looked up into Hayakawa's face. The expression in his eyes was undecipherable, but she thought she saw disgust mixed with something else. With her rat's tail hair, scarlet face, and pool of sweat and milk-stained chest, she knew she must have looked like the debris of humanity in his ordered office. She was past caring.

"You are a persistent woman, Mrs Rynd. Get back to your child and organise your things. I have decided to allow you to escort the children to Manila tomorrow," he announced.

The pain in her back was excruciating and her legs refused to move, so she was assisted to her feet by the guards, who – with surprising kindness – helped her walk back to spend her last night in the baby house.

Fourteen

1st April 1943
462 days in captivity

A surprising number of people were gathered in the early morning to say farewell to the Brent pupils. Ronny recognised all eight of the young people who had been adopted by the community and would be reunited with their parents. Close bonds had formed under difficult circumstances, so emotions ran high and there were tears on all sides.

It had been a turbulent night with the checking and rechecking of possessions. Intense conversations with friends had gone on late, and Ronny kept Catherine's routine as normal as possible. She had intended to exit quietly, but was touched by how many of her friends turned out to wish her a safe journey. She looked at the dear face of Helen, who showed her habitual care and concern. Iris was quiet and serious. Betty and Pam made no attempt at being adult, and tears streamed unchecked down their cheeks. Eric had turned up, although Eleanor was nowhere to be seen. They had all gathered for her, and Ronny had never felt so loved.

A lunch package and a quantity of water containers were provided by the kitchen. The open army truck was piled with bedrolls and treasured possessions, and they would have to ride on top.

It was time to go, and Ronny braced herself for the emotional hugs all round. Handing Catherine into the truck, by then padded with everyone's paraphernalia, she was the last one to scramble on board. Ray Hale was at the wheel. It seemed apt that it was he who had taken the news to Pat that he had a daughter and it had become his role to deliver her to him. The one guard, armed with his rifle, settled casually in the other seat in the cabin. Ronny was going to be the only authority in the back as the group of young internees were not considered an escape risk.

The faces that surrounded her matched the list the committee had given her. Donald Marshall was seated next to his sister Coleen, who was fussing over him as usual. Past her, Ronny saw the pretty and eager faces of Ann Miller and Margaret Morris. The twelve-year-old Patricia Briggs was there and seemed anxious in comparison to Neville Stopford, aged nine, who was treating the day as a great adventure. The group was completed by the inseparable eighteen-year-olds, Henry Parfet and Norman Oss, known informally as Bud and Buck. These young people were her responsibility for the 155-mile journey. Ronny busied herself and warded off tears as the lorry started to move. They were a subdued lot as the vehicle turned left out of their old home and started the drive to the lowlands.

The early morning air was brisk, and they were glad of warm clothing. Ronny advised the teenage girls to cover their hair with handkerchiefs, as the dust from the parched road would soon be coating them. Catherine had been silent and Ronny carried her favourite toys to amuse her, hoping the novelty of the changing scenery and feeling of motion would be sufficient distraction on the journey.

The city of Baguio was quiet, and they were the object of curiosity as they passed. Negotiating the open market, one of the boys recognised a friendly face and started to call out, which brought about a menacing rebuke from the guard immediately. This was not to be a pleasure trip. As they left town, they turned onto the Kennon trail and started the treacherous journey down from the mountains.

The road twisted severely, and the truck slid on hairpin bends, jolting its passengers from side to side precariously. With no rail along the sides of the truck, and with the group seated on top of their bedding rolls, falling off became a real possibility.

Interludes of straight roads gave Ronny the opportunity to reflect on the previous day, but it already seemed unreal. She preferred to enjoy the beauty of the vibrant landscape, and the green, brown and yellow of the paddy fields. They passed villages with Igorot peasants living their domestic lives amidst scatterings of dogs, poultry and livestock. They encountered groups of Filipino farmers pushing hand carts laboriously back up the trail, weighed down with rice for market. They overtook horse-drawn carts and had to pull over for military vehicles loaded with Japanese soldiers.

The softer vistas of the mountain range they were leaving looked benign in contrast to the terrifying ravines that dropped sharply away from the snaking road. Overtaking or negotiating oncoming trucks demanded squeezing to the side of the road and praying. Two of the girls were white-lipped and frightened, but Ronny had confidence in Ray, who had driven this route many times before. They were certainly vulnerable to pot holes and loose stones. Catherine was in a safe nest in the bedding, but if the truck overturned on one of these bends, the consequences would be horrifying.

After two hours, the novelty had worn off, and the teenagers were becoming irritable. The sun cleared the last of the fragrant mist and promised another day of relentless glare. The road was shaded by high trees and vegetation, but Ronny knew that, as they descended into the lowland plains, they would be exposed to the direct sun and the worst it could do. She made sure that each girl and boy drank water at regular intervals and, above all, hung on tight.

As they covered the miles, she knew the families in Santo Tomas would be expecting them. She smiled imagining the excitement of Pat as he waited and hoped that she would not look too battered at their moment of reunion. Catherine, who was then dozing, would win her father's heart instantly.

Ronny was distracted.

"Mrs Rynd, I think Donald's going to be sick." Coleen had interpreted the sweat beading on her brother's forehead and his pallor.

"Bang on the cab roof. Hang on, Donald, we're going to have a break," Ronny replied.

The lad did indeed look ill, and Ray took long minutes to pull up. The guard watched closely as they all lowered themselves over the tailgate to stretch their legs.

Forbidden to wander into the trees, they took turns relieving themselves by the side of the truck. Ronny was pleased at the group's lack of prissiness. These young people had been trained by camp life, where practicality and the common good came first, and she was proud of the way they behaved that morning. The pain in her back needed easing, and she walked up and down whilst breastfeeding Catherine.

Everyone felt better for the break, and they pressed on in their descent to the plains of the south. The thick canopy overhead gave way to scrub and the gentle cooling breeze petered out to become a warm, dust-laden wind. The group stripped down to lighter clothing as the heat intensified. At the bottom of the trail, the road straightened out and Ronny became concerned at their exposure to the relentless midday sun. She erected a light sheet tent above Catherine in her well, and there was room for one of the girls at a time to share it. She blessed the mothering talents of Margaret and Ann as they entertained her daughter.

Ray called another halt at a banana grove near Binalonan for lunch. One sniff at the wrapped fish was enough to tell Ronny that the heat had done its worst, and she insisted the group only ate the rice balls that accompanied it. Food poisoning would not be welcome on their journey. Ray persuaded the guard to cut down a hand of bananas with his bayonet, which was shared quickly.

The land smelled differently as they continued south. The scented flowers of the highlands gave way to a flat and drab countryside, and it was a test of the calibre of the little group that they kept their spirits up. They sang songs and roundelays, and played I-Spy and word games from Ronny's repertoire.

"Mrs Rynd, where did you get these games? They're good fun!" declared Ann Miller, who was seated next to her.

"I used to work on a cruise liner, so part of my job was keeping everyone entertained. Cruises sound wonderful, but it's quite boring for passengers at times, so I had to have ideas up my sleeve," confirmed Ronny.

"I've always wanted to be a teacher."

"I'm sure you'll be a natural. I started out as a PE teacher."

"Were you scared the first time you stood up in front of class?" Ann leaned closer to be heard.

"My first job was at a finishing school in Switzerland. I was supposed to teach girls who were only a little younger than me and far more sophisticated! They were rich Americans and wore loads of clunky jewellery, which wasn't a good idea in a gymnasium!"

"How did you manage?"

"Without breakfast! That's how! I used to skip breakfast so I'd be bad tempered!"

"Mrs Rynd! You're a hoot!"

Ronny was not sure she had been called a hoot before. Encouraged, she continued, "I had another problem. When I went for the job interview everyone assumed I could ski! They'd never asked me, and I'd never skied in my life. Then, that first week, I found out they'd put me in charge of girls who were advanced skiers!"

"What did you do? Did you come clean?"

"I didn't dare and tried to fake it! I went up the mountain in the ski lift with the girls and watched them as they strapped on their skis pretending to check, but really following their example. It felt all right when I stood up and managed to walk with the skis. Then they started to go downhill, and I followed them. I thought that I'd got away with it, but almost immediately they turned one way and I kept on going until I crashed!" She laughed at the recollection of seeing their astonishment as they helped her to her feet! "The girls were wonderful and never let on. They taught me to ski every afternoon, and the school never found out. I loved those girls, despite their jewellery."

"I think skiing sounds fun."

Ronny and Ann soberly contemplated the concept of snow, which was so far from their current reality. Their clothes were sticking to their bodies, and they were grimy with sweat and dust. Ronny shifted from position to position as she tried to alleviate the pain in her back, and Catherine became fractious and it took all Ronny's resolve not to snap at her.

Extreme fatigue became an issue, and there was a frightening moment when the youngest girl, Patricia, gave way to it suddenly – thankfully, nodding off into the truck rather than out – so Ronny demanded another stop to reorganise themselves. A nest was made so that the young wards could take turns dozing, sheltered by the light sheet that covered Catherine. Ronny kept watch, determined that the boarders would be returned safely to their parents.

It was late afternoon before they reached the outskirts of Manila. Shanty villages blended into each other, and rice fields and paddocks gave way to the sleepy urban sprawl. It was only when they had penetrated the built up areas that changes were evident. The thriving, throbbing, cosmopolitan city life was gone and in its place there was an air of neglect. Craters in the highways had been patched crudely, and tall buildings had been reduced to rubble. A feeling of desolation and dusty spaces abounded where once busy, cheerful little shops had thrived. The Filipinos on the streets were watchful and unsmiling, and Japanese soldiers were much in evidence. Bicycles abounded where once taxis held sway. From her lofty vantage point, Ronny viewed the strange world that bore little relation to the bustling metropolis she had left behind sixteen months ago.

Exhaustion gave way to anticipation. Everyone made an attempt to freshen up, to cover their sunburned and sore state. Even the more sophisticated teenagers were elated to catch the first glimpse of the tall elevated cross that marked the Santo Tomas University campus.

When they turned finally into the spacious road that fronted the university grounds, Ronny's first surprise was to see the beautiful, ornate railings that ran along the front of the campus had been covered. *Sawali* reed matting obscured the camp from the street. A newly erected guardhouse stood by the entrance gates, and Japanese soldiers with fixed bayonets and set faces stepped forwards to halt the vehicle. The paperwork inspection took an age, after which the gates were opened to a different world.

The lorry swept in through the wrought-iron gates and past the lawns, which then resembled a picnic area with groups of people stretched out on the grass in the late afternoon. The three main blocks of buildings and attached annexes miraculously had survived any bombing and stood proud. The travellers could not contain their excitement. They drove up the leafy drive to the plaza in front of the main block, towards the milling mass awaiting them, and all strained to find their loved ones in the throng.

Ronny was worried for the safety of the group as they leaned over the sides towards welcoming arms. The mass of bodies pressed against the lorry, rocking it, as it came to a halt. One young person and then another was recognised and claimed with tears of joy. Eager hands helped them down, then grabbed their belongings. Emotional mothers thanked her for her help, but it was all a blur as she, in her turn, tried to find the one face in the crowd that meant so much to her. Holding Catherine close, she sat stranded on her bedroll whilst the crowd dwindled and the hubbub dispersed. Finally, Ronny allowed herself to be helped down, but on the ground she found it even harder to search for Pat. Her legs were weak, and the pain in her back was crippling.

Kind strangers gave her blank looks when she asked for Patrick Rynd. Obviously, there was to be no warm welcome for her. Pat's name did not even register with these strangers. The enormity of this camp of 4,000 souls, where people were merely numbers, sank in.

Ronny and Catherine were ushered to a bench in the shade and given welcome drinks whilst enquiries were made. The open transport stood abandoned; it was her last link with her old world. And the un-thanked Ray had disappeared. Catherine was interested in these new sights, but Ronny was alarmed at this lack of knowledge of Pat. Was he even here in Santo Tomas? Her impetuous behaviour had brought her here and just then she felt totally abandoned. Tears of emotional exhaustion rose in her eyes.

Officialdom kicked in, and they were escorted to the camp offices, where they were allocated billeting in a women's dormitory. American personnel were in charge of vetting their papers, with the nominal supervision of the Japanese. The process was done with efficiency and professional courtesy, but she would have swapped it unreservedly for the more slapdash-but-genuine reception she would have received in Baguio. She turned to follow the stylish American woman with shocking-pink lips, when a voice halted her.

"We've found Mr Rynd. He's in the hospital. He's fine. We've told him you're here," the person explained.

The relief was overwhelming. She had done it! She had made this happen and her path to reuniting her family had become clear.

———✂——✂——

The dormitory room in the annex was light and functional, but it had not been designed to house twenty-three individuals. The walls were covered with a light-green utility paint, and the patched-together curtains did little to give the room any sense of home. Ronny felt a pang of regret for the homely little baby house she had left behind. Dormitory living was going to be a very different experience. She understood that she was lucky to have been assigned space next to the wall, with a hook for her mosquito net, and her mattress and belongings were delivered promptly.

The women relaxing in the room were a mixed bunch of professional singles and those separated from their husbands, and there were raised eyebrows immediately when they became aware of Catherine's presence. It was obvious that an infant would not be welcomed warmly. Ronny could only hope that this placement would be short term.

'Pink lips' told Ronny that it would not be possible to visit Pat in the hospital. Her fantasy of a wonderful welcome had disappeared, and she consoled herself that after a night's sleep she could present herself and Catherine, looking less bedraggled. She had waited this long, so she could wait another day.

Bone-weary from the journey, she wanted peace, but was bombarded with questions: "What's it like in the hills? I bet Baguio is lovely. Did you have your own shanties? Why were you brought here?" and most tellingly, "Why have they put you in with us?"

She answered as well as she could and was relieved when this barrage was interrupted by the arrival of a young woman with a daughter. She would not be the only mother and child, thankfully!

Anna was from Pennsylvania, and had an open, intelligent and freckled face with brown hair and quick, greenish eyes. Her nine-year-old daughter, Daisy, was a miniature version of her mother. They had the same light laugh. Anna's husband, Marvin, was also in the camp. The recognition of kindred spirits was cemented when the young woman invited her to join her in the chow line for the evening meal. Ronny dug out her serviceable food container and was amused to see glances were cast at it, in order to assess the newcomer depending on the quality of receptacle. Nothing had changed from her old camp!

Daisy held Catherine's hand as they wove past the washing troughs and clothes lines to queue on the grass for the meal on offer. There appeared to be four lines converging on the kitchen. The queues were understandably long and she was interested to see that many had brought little folding chairs with them.

Whilst Daisy entertained Catherine, Anna filled Ronny in. "What we have here is a small town. We have shops run by the

Filipinos, including the equivalent of Manila's Harrods. We have cafés, a couple of restaurants and all the fun of the fair for those who have the money. We have a hospital, a school, a dentist, entertainment and religion; you name it. All we don't have is privacy and freedom."

"How does it work? I don't see many guards about."

"We have two commandants, Kuroda and Kodaki, who are jointly in charge of the camp. They have to approve any request or decision, but within that framework we're totally self-governing. We've our own police force, our own patrols, our own courts and a prison."

Daisy had wandered close to her mother and chanted an endless list of the committees that were operating in camp, which she had been taught in school. "Committee on Order, Committee on Internal Regulation, Department of Patrols, Finance and Supplies Committee, Family-Aid Committee…"

"That's great, Daisy. Well done. Of course, we all have assigned jobs for the community as well as the ordinary day-to-day tasks of living. I guess Camp Holmes was run in a similar way," supposed Anna.

"Yes, but we weren't as sophisticated as you seem to be. We had a committee who managed all the financial things. It took a couple of months, but, finally, the Nips agreed to pay us a per capita allowance, which the committee managed on our behalf. We survived with barter and earning money from those who had continuing means sent in from Baguio," said Ronny.

"That's how it's done here, supplemented by the Red Cross and agencies such as that."

"The Red Cross only made one shipment to us in all the months I was there."

"I imagine they didn't get past us! Sorry, Ronny! We have a Finance and Supplies Committee with Fay Bailey as treasurer.

He has a full-time job managing all the money for us. We're lucky that way."

"From what little I've seen, you Yanks seem to be running the show. It's confusing. Are the Japanese soldiers just a token presence? You must outnumber them by thousands. Why don't the internees just walk out?"

"We have a problem with too many people actually wanting to be interned, and I am not just talking about the Filipino families of internees. The committee members who go into town on a regular basis with their passes tell us life in Manila is no better outside than it is in here."

"Do you get news of what's going on in the outside world? They were paranoid about us getting any information about the war in Camp Holmes."

"Oh, they're paranoid about that here too. Everything has to be negotiated with the Nips, and if there are violations of their orders, enforcement is ruthless. There have been executions."

"Executions? Internees executed? Here?" Ronny dropped her voice instinctively and glanced around.

Daisy had wandered off with Catherine, and was showing off her new living toy.

"Not on the premises," Anna confirmed, "But two young Brits and an Australian escaped in the early months, and were recaptured and shot."

"Shot? We had to witness beatings but no one was shot in our presence."

Ronny was cut off by a shout of, "*Hot stuff!*" as a young man with a large pan of something steaming, held chest-high, pushed through the line to the front counter. The smell of the food distracted her.

"If there's so much interaction with the outside, do you have a problem with money and shortages? We had to fight for every penny from the Nips in Baguio. It was handled by the all-male committee, and we women didn't have any say," stated Ronny.

Anna responded, "Sure. The chauvinist thing goes on here too! The committee earns its keep with endless negotiating with the commandant, and it never ends because of inflation. Prices have gone bonkers outside, and there's less that's affordable every week. Luckily, we have a Relief and Welfare Department to help the internees who have nothing. Many internees are wealthy and have a constant supply of food delivered here. We call it the package line. Then there are the rest of us, who rely on this chow line. That's life. There'll always be privileges for those with the means to pay, and that includes the committee members themselves sadly."

"It sounds as if it's a picnic for some here."

"I guess it all evens out. Those who've always lived in luxury are in a state of shock, as they've got to fit in with us mere mortals. They do things they never did before, like clean, cook and look after their own children. We ordinary people have lost less, except we're hungrier."

"That's an interesting way of looking at it!"

Ronny had her new meal ticket stamped and accepted the food from white-jacketed youths behind the counter. The smell had been drawing them in, but once they had found space in the adjoining dining area she found the rice with a hint of vegetables and meat was the same as she had been used to at Camp Holmes. She was too tired to eat. Tomorrow was a new day, and tomorrow she would see Pat.

---✦---✦---

FIFTEEN

2nd April 1943

463 days in captivity

The murmuring from the movement of twenty-three restless women and other unfamiliar sounds, together with her anticipated reunion, had made it a difficult night. Ronny had been told that Pat was suffering from dysentery, but would be released from the hospital for a few hours on compassionate grounds. It had been sixteen months since he saw her off at Tutuban railway station, with a smile on his face, confident of being reunited the following week.

The weather had turned overnight, and it was cool and overcast. It was still early, but Ronny's heart raced with anticipation. Seeking a diversion for the hours ahead, she wanted to explore the campus and get a first-hand impression of her new surroundings. Catherine, who was used to communal living, was sleeping peacefully, but across the crowded dormitory she could see Anna was awake, with Daisy on the mattress beside her. They communicated wordlessly that Anna would see to

Catherine whilst Ronny went for a walk. Stepping into a pair of shorts, Ronny was stopped by frantic gestures from her new friend. Miming, Anna told her that shorts were not allowed! She wondered if this came from Japanese regulations or the appropriate committee, and then scolded herself for bringing her prejudices with her.

Once out of the claustrophobic room, Ronny inhaled deeply and made her way to the adjoining block, where she gloried in an early and plentiful shower, luxuriating in the unending water. Her hair was clean, her skin was scrubbed and she put on her favourite blue polka-dot dress. She felt alive again. The morning air felt good, and she had a spring in her step as she set out to explore.

The university, founded in 1611, was known as the oldest university in Asia, but was referred to jokingly as 'the oldest university in America', and covered nearly sixty acres of spacious grounds. The strong, grey façade of the main buildings, built in the 1920s, were grandiose and imposing in a way that only Spanish religious architecture could be. They were designed as a staggering show of Spanish Catholic superiority and sophistication to the Filipinos. The campus was enclosed by high stone walls at the back, and with the ornate, gated iron railings in front. Three separate main blocks – the central one containing sixty large classrooms, numerous offices and spacious foyers – housed internees. Her dormitory was situated in the annex at the rear. Sports fields, a three-hole golf course and a swimming pool must have made it a manicured haven for the students, but, that day, it resembled the confusion of a shanty town. The spacious grounds, by then overgrown, were still beautifully green with trees and flowering bushes, but the lawns resembled an untended wasteland between the sea of encroaching shanties. This once-splendid establishment housed about 4,000 internees, and it was to be her home too.

Ronny took off her shoes. The damp grass was refreshing under her feet. Despite the early hour, the men on rubbish duty were already in operation, chatting and joking quietly whilst picking up the litter left on the lawns from the previous day. She avoided the shanty areas, so as not to disturb anyone, and threaded her way past closed-up sheds advertising shops and cafés. She passed rows of troughs for washing clothes and the drying areas next to the education block that then served as dormitories. The commandant's office stood centrally, as if to monitor the surge of American life surrounding it. The large campus had been an obvious choice for the Americans to house the internees, and had been immediately approved by the Japanese. The Dominican fathers, who previously ran the university, remained on the grounds in their monastery and garden, within the complex. Ronny wondered about their state of mind from watching the ever-increasing shanty town enveloping what had once been their beautiful seat of learning.

As Ronny's meandering led her to the entrance of a huge gymnasium near the fathers' retreat, a stale smell assaulted her nostrils. The door was wide open, and she saw a sea of white mosquito-net sails hanging over hundreds of closely lined up beds in various states of occupation and disarray. She was repulsed and embarrassed to have stumbled on this version of life that no one could be proud of. She was met with hostile stares from men in dirty shorts and singlets taking their first smoke of the day. She imagined that these were men who had not the means to organise shanty accommodation or negotiate to live in the smaller dormitories. Most, she assumed, would be older ex-patriots who had married into local families and were struggling to look after themselves whilst their wives remained outside. Ronny hoped that Pat was not based here. She cursed herself for not having been more aware of the territory before wandering in aimlessly and giving offence.

Retracing her steps back to the annex, she passed close to the kitchen, where clanking pans rang out and somebody's voice rose in a curse.

———✳— ✳———

Ronny held Catherine by the hand as she walked into the plaza, and she saw Pat before he saw her. She stood rooted to the spot, hardly breathing, and looked at him as a stranger would. She enjoyed the advantage of taking him in before he could make a judgement on her.

Pat had always had a softly rounded appearance since he was a child. The planes of his face had always been gentle and unremarkable, with a high forehead with soft, brown hair, and a bottom lip that was full and sometimes petulant-looking. His most remarkable feature was hidden behind the round, owl-like lenses of his glasses, and it was only when this barricade was removed that his fine, grey eyes fringed with dark, curling lashes were revealed. Ronny had been jealous of those eyelashes, which put her own straight, non-descript ones in the shade. She remembered his endearing habit of pushing his glasses onto his forehead when he read small print. From the boy of their united childhood, Pat had grown into a large man, not obese but untoned. The Pat that Ronny saw just then was not the man she had left behind. He appeared to have grown in stature, or had she just forgotten? She realised that she had not remembered his actual physical presence – more Pat as a concept, dimly recalled – not the reality of this man as flesh and blood. The glasses still sat on the distinctive, short, tip-tilted nose, but the moustache that he used to shape lovingly was gone. The soft roundness of his features had been shed, and, for the first time ever, she saw the distinct lines of his high cheek bones and jutting jaw line. Where had her husband gone? She had never seen this handsome Pat before.

She knew she, too, had changed from when he last saw her, and the addition of Catherine was not the only difference. She was not the same young woman, and it would be marked on her body and her face. Unconsciously, she fluffed up her auburn hair, which, being unpinned, cascaded down to its full length over her shoulders. Her lipstick was in place, and she was ready for him.

As he turned and saw her, the huge smile said it all, and any reservations were forgotten. He covered the distance in strides, and the intensity of the bear hug almost cracked her ribs. They did not speak, and he knelt down in the dust and gazed at the little mite who looked so like him. There were tears in his eyes and a hesitant, "Hello there!" to his daughter.

Catherine stared at him.

He sat on the ground, not making any move towards her, waiting for her to get used to him.

Ronny squatted down too. "Say hello to Daddy, Catherine. This is your daddy, he loves you very much, and we're going to have a lovely time together." She smiled at him over the child's head, and the initial awkwardness passed.

He said, "I'm so sorry I wasn't here to meet you. I can't believe you made it."

"It doesn't matter. You're here now. But perhaps I wouldn't have recognised you!"

Pat laughed. "Oh, you mean the new slimline version! You know me, I've always preferred the cerebral type of exercise, but there's not much call for that here."

"Don't tell me you're becoming a sporting hero?"

"It's the hard, manual work, my dear! Nothing less!"

"Well, whatever you've been doing, it suits you! But you haven't given up chess and bridge, have you?" She looked searchingly at her husband.

Pat was an outstanding bridge and chess player, with a prodigious memory for cards and moves, coupled with the patience of a saint and a dogged persistence that wore many an opponent down.

He confirmed, "No, Ronny, of course not! I'm still the same me. I just cannot believe that you're here. You look wonderful. And here's our beautiful baby! I dreamed of it for so long, and you've made it happen. I can't tell you how grateful I am. Only you could have made this happen."

She smiled and hugged him, and both turned their attention to the tangible proof of their marriage, who sat quietly on the turf between them.

The afternoon was spent talking non-stop, recapping histories and playing with Catherine. Ronny knew that she had a mantle to pick up, but nothing was going to happen that day to mar this interlude between reality and reality. No plans were made and no promises given. They lived totally for the moment, amidst a cast of literally thousands milling around them. Pat showed her around the camp, and introduced her and Catherine, with obvious pride, to an assortment of people. She re-met George and Joy Stewart, and their young children: Judy and Jimmy. George also worked for the bank in Manila, and the family welcomed her warmly.

Pat showed her the shanty communities of traditional huts made from bamboo and native nipa-palm trees. The shanties came in all shapes and sizes, and were connected by paths winding between papayas, maize and banana trees. Off the ground due to being built on stilts in the native fashion, they were deliberately exposed on two sides so that privacy was impossible. This camp requirement was enforced even in the more sophisticated homes that contained windows, porches and basic cooking facilities. Many shanties sported gardens and appeared well furnished, with brightly coloured flowers trained up the bamboo poles to overflow onto the thatched roofs. The fragrance from the flowering bushes reminded her of Camp Holmes.

The moment came when Catherine slipped her hand into her father's, and he took it without comment – and Ronny sensed that they were bonded for life.

Ronny and Pat fitted back together naturally as if into an interrupted conversation, but she was also aware of being on her best behaviour. She wanted to look good for her husband as well as the community he was introducing her to. This new version of Pat took a little getting used to, and she found herself examining him more closely than she ever had before. Santo Tomas was his domain, and she was the outsider with a lot to learn.

A tiny incident rang warning bells when Pat was introducing her to a group of internee friends, who welcomed her warmly after the initial surprise. One was a woman in a blue dress that matched her eyes. It was a small gesture, easily overlooked, but it quickened her senses immediately. The woman, whilst chatting, casually and almost instinctively, brushed a token of vegetation from Pat's shirt. Ronny alone noticed the gesture that spoke of familiarity and ownership. To Ronny, it was a signal that she was the interloper in a society already formed. She knew Pat would have missed the signal, but she made a mental note that this was one woman who would not be included in their group of friends.

Exchanging their differing experiences was scattered with potholes and had to be negotiated by degrees.

Pat said, "I was picked up in the street by the Nips. I'll never forget it. I was walking back from the bank after a very fraught day, and there was the squeal of tires and a car came to a halt beside me. There were shouts and I was bundled into the car before I could think straight. It was just like in the movies."

"Didn't you know they were interning people?" Ronny enquired.

"Oh yes. Santo Tomas camp was well established, and it was only a matter of time."

"I assume that you were prepared with a suitcase and everything?"

"They wouldn't let me go to the flat. I'd put some things together, but they never gave me the chance to get them."

"Have you tried?" The words were out before she could bite them back.

"They weren't letting anyone back into their buildings. In fact, I haven't seen the flat since going to work that morning."

Ronny was shocked. "What about our special treasures? My painting from Haifa? Are they safe in storage?"

"I told you, Ronny, it happened so suddenly. I didn't have time to put anything in storage."

She stared at him, breathing hard.

Pat continued, unaware of her shock, "I did get some useful stuff from there, three months after being interned. One of the chaps who went into Manila on committee work called round for me. He said the flat was still unoccupied, and he just grabbed whatever he thought would be helpful. He didn't have much time, and I was lucky that he could do it at all. He's left the key with neighbours, and they said they'd keep an eye on it. He certainly couldn't organise storage."

Ronny glowered at him. How could anyone who was so meticulous with other people's possessions, be so cavalier about his own? It was unforgivable. With the clear notice of their inevitable imprisonment, she would have made a better job of it! Swallowing hard, she promised herself she was not going to let her disappointment spoil her first day back with him. Their shared pleasure of Catherine filled any awkward gaps.

Pat avoided the gymnasium, and she did not tell him of her morning's experience. There were to be secrets already. As she had suspected instinctively as soon as she saw the place, Pat admitted to living there. He told her he kept his belongings beneath the iron bed, the stench of mass living was gross, and he was not prepared to show her his domain. It was the haven of most of the older men, who did not invite inspections, and she was left in no doubt reading his little evasions, that his was a pretty grim existence.

Ronny had carefully memorised messages from Baguio internees that she needed to pass on. They sought out an appropriate committee member, who took endless notes, but Ronny had a good memory and was pretty sure she had forgotten nothing.

———

In one of the makeshift, little cafés later, the conversation with Pat inevitably came back to their predicament.

Ronny said, "I don't understand why the Nips haven't decided to release us. We must be a drain on their resources."

Pat took his time replying. "Yes, it's an issue that I don't think the Imperial Army have given much thought to. In the early days, they had no intention of feeding us, whichever camp we were in, and we would have starved here without Red Cross intervention."

"We were lucky to have internees with contacts in Baguio, and they got permission to bring in supplies, until they ran out. Then they were forced to pay us a food allowance. The Red Cross didn't get anything to us till a month ago."

"The Finance and Supplies Committee here does all the negotiating with the Japanese for a per capita allowance." Pat dealt in facts.

"But why hold us? We're not in Japan. We aren't military. We must present a financial burden for them, when it's obvious that they're having a problem feeding themselves."

"It's an interesting issue. The Japanese have an entirely different motivation for this war to the Nazis. They're not on a crusade to rid the world of inferior races. They may have contempt for us, but they're not driven to exterminate us."

Ronny realised how much she had missed male logic in conversations. "No, but they hold life cheap, so I don't ever feel secure. We must have some value to them or they would've got rid of us by now."

Pat affirmed, "I imagine we do have value to them. We're war booty. We could be put to work as slaves, or sold, after whatever wealth we had was confiscated."

"We could be used to trade against their own POWs."

"Or used as human shields, which may well be our fate if the Yanks come back. It's obvious that they don't have an overall policy for handling prisoners. We've enough examples here in the Philippines of the mixed approaches in the different camps. I think we're lucky that Santo Tomas is under Japanese civilian administration."

"I didn't realise that there was a difference between them and the military."

"Oh yes. Heaven help us if their military take over this camp. We're lucky to be civilian internees. The stories about what our military POWs are suffering under the Japanese are horrendous." Pat put his banker's hat back on. "Isn't it the same old story of overextending? The Japs have POWs everywhere: China, Burma, Borneo and heaven knows where else. It must be one big budget nightmare."

"Well, I believe that we're being held in retaliation for the bad treatment of the Japanese Americans in the US."

"I wouldn't spread that version around! We British are definitely a minority group here, and you wouldn't be popular."

"No, I didn't mean it like that! In Baguio, I had lots of American friends. No, it was something that they considered to be a likelihood."

"One thing we know for certain is that there's no second guessing what's in our conquerors' minds. I shall just celebrate you being here, my dear. That's enough for me today."

Ronny had forgotten that Pat was only out on a half-day release and had to return to the hospital. He was still weak from the dysentery, and the adrenaline boost of the last few hours had given way to extreme fatigue. They were content to call it a day. Pat needed to get stronger, and Ronny needed to settle in and find a way to make it work for the three of them.

Catherine and Daisy were in bed, and the muted conversation between Ronny and Anna that evening took a different tack. They were seated on the grass within earshot of the dormitory, and Anna was enjoying her last cigarette.

"I notice you don't have segregation of the sexes like we had in Baguio?" asked Ronny.

"There's segregation to a degree, there's the curfew at night, and you're not allowed to spend time with anyone of the opposite sex away from the well-lit area after dark. The Nips are rigid about relationships, and the committee backs them up. We have the Morality Squad, which keeps an eye on things!" enlightened Anna.

"*The Morality Squad?* Are you serious?"

Anna shrugged. "I'm afraid so, and they're certainly zealous. No one's allowed to sleep in the shanties which have to be open for inspection at all times."

"How can the Japs monitor everyone's behaviour with the thousands that are here?"

"The monitoring is done by the Morality Squad. If you think for one moment that you are going to be able to resume intimate relations with Pat, forget it! PWOP here is bad news."

"PWOP?"

Anna laughed. "Pregnant without permission! In January, the Japs sentenced four men to thirty days in jail as their wives had become pregnant. The poor women were banished to the Hospico de San Jose for the rest of their confinement!"

"How can they justify that?"

"Well, I guess they think we will breed like rabbits with nothing else to do! Actually, the reality is that when you're hungry and ill, sex is the last thing on your mind. Marvin told me the other day that, although he loves me, I'd be no competition for a juicy hamburger with Thousand Island dressing! And I feel the same way!"

Ronny turned in, comforted by knowing that she would find her role in this community, new friends would be made and different challenges resolved. She replayed the day in her mind, and she reran the conversations until, exhausted, she fell into a deep sleep.

Sixteen

5th April 1943

466 days in captivity

The dormitory monitor was a tired-looking American with the soul of a cactus. Beatrice was friends with no one. It had not taken Ronny long to find out that the rules and regulations in Santo Tomas were oppressive. Two days after her arrival, when the room was unusually quiet, she sought out the woman, who was open to conversation for once.

Beatrice explained in her dry voice, "It has to be like this. Unless there's a very strong internee government, the Japs will take over at the drop of a hat."

"I can see that, but do we have to be so regimented?" queried Ronny.

"I think we do. Our own police force will always be more lenient than the Japs, and the Discipline Committee can act quickly with any punishment. A term in our jail is infinitely better than a spell in Fort Santiago."

"Fort Santiago?"

Beatrice's glance made her feel foolish. "It's the old Spanish dungeons in the Intramuros district, inside the walls of the old city. The Japanese do unspeakable things there, and the detention cells they built are even worse than the dungeons. They are wringing wet with damp, being on the bank of the Pasig River. The cells are only ten feet square, and they squeeze in as many men as they can. The prisoners can't lie down, a gasoline can serves as the toilet, which is always overflowing, and the stench is unbearable. They're starved and unwashed, and tortured during interrogations. Some never make it out." This was a long speech for Beatrice, and she broke off.

Ronny was sure she was talking about someone close to home, but the woman did not invite sympathy.

A silence followed. Ronny broke it by responding, "I've witnessed public beatings at Camp Holmes, and you're right that it's far better that we control our own and don't give the Nips any reason to interfere."

"The commandant has threatened collective punishment if the Discipline Committee doesn't enforce internee discipline. We have to make sure the Japs never have grounds to intervene."

"What's the most common discipline problem?"

"Smuggled booze. It's just plain stupid what lengths some folk will go to in order to get it. Lucky for me, it's not a problem in this dormitory."

"Beatrice." Ronny looked for an opening. "I did a lot of sewing in the last camp and wondered if it was possible for me to do the same here. It's where my skills lie. Whom should I talk to?"

The woman snapped back into role. "Me. You don't get to choose your jobs here, and I'm waiting to hear what the Work Committee have assigned you. Work hours are compulsory, and Catherine will be looked after at the 'play base.'"

Ronny later learned they were well organised with regard to sewing, with a small factory operation of sewing machines provided by the Red Cross, with which standardised clothing was made. She had no option but to accept her work detail of sluicing down certain walkways with disinfectant and a large brush. Ironically, Pat's detail was burying the accumulated rubbish in hand-dug trenches, and Ronny thought Beulah Allen would have approved. The care of Catherine whilst she worked was answered by the big play base constructed behind the annex. This was a nipa-palm-thatched pavilion that the little children played in, under the care of a watchful staff.

—⊁⋅⊁—

The first few weeks passed quickly, but Ronny struggled to get used to the overcrowding. There were always people in her line of vision, and the furthest she could see always ended at the containing wall and its obscuring matting. She missed the changing seasons reflected in the surrounding landscape and even her daydreams about guerrilla activities. She chafed at the constant evidence that she was a prisoner. Even the sounds within the camp, from the gramophone records that blared constantly from the loudspeakers to the hubbub of ordinary human interactions, could not be escaped. She tried to find a way to assimilate it all and not let resentment grow at what she had left behind. It had been her choice to come here, and she had not changed her mind. But where was the birdsong? Where was the view?

—⊁⋅⊁—

Ronny and Pat were seated on the grass near the main drive early one evening. The air was still heavy with heat as they awaited an announcement from the commandant over the loudspeaker. Something was about to happen. The American guards had been ordered away from the main gate, the parcel line had been stopped, and no communication or visits had been permitted. The two Japanese stores on the campus had been closed since midday, and the Filipino medical staff had been ordered out. A military guard had been thrown round the entire camp, so something serious was about to happen. Like the reprimanding jerk of a lead, it was days similar to these that reminded the prisoners of how powerless they were.

Ronny was not unduly concerned. Pat had been released from hospital, and she loved having him to talk to. They spent time together as often as they could. He was quiet and infinitely patient with Catherine. Ronny watched as father and child delighted in wordless communication as they played finger games together.

She broke the silence. "I don't get it."

"What don't you get, my dear?" he asked.

"How you can be so good with Catherine when you didn't even know your own mother? And your father didn't set you any example!" Ronny was genuinely perplexed.

"My father was a product of the Indian Army and a busy man. He did the best he could under the circumstances. I'm sure he chose with care the Indian ayah who looked after me."

"I'm pretty sure it was more than one ayah! It would have been a succession of them until you were seven."

"It was not so different for you, I imagine. Thank goodness for Auntie Maudie. My governess and saviour! I'll always be grateful for her intervention."

"She is rather special, isn't she? It's hard to believe she's my mother's sister. A gutsy lady to be working in India on her own! They broke the mould when they made her."

"I'll never forget the first time I saw her. I was about five. She was such a contrast to my ayahs. That white skin, the long nose and the twinkly, blue eyes." His voice was warm with recollection.

"She's a sweetie. Do you think she originally went to India as a hopeful bride?"

"Well, that was certainly not unusual in those days, but it still took courage!"

"It's ironic that she didn't find a husband for herself, but she found me one! I'm so relieved she's safely in England now. With hindsight, do you think she put pressure on your father to send you back home?"

"No. He had my life all mapped out, and it included English boarding school. England is automatically 'home' for you, but it certainly wasn't for me. The contrast was shocking. The sights, the smells, the colours and the cold! It was a huge change for a seven-year-old."

"I remember you being very quiet, but, of course, the enormity of your adjustment escaped me. And then you had to go immediately to boarding school. I do think you're extraordinary, Pat, and I do love how you are with Catherine. You didn't learn that from my parents either."

Ronny turned on her tummy and idly watched a bunch of old men from the gymnasium laughing at some pooled joke. For this particular group of elders, creating stories passed their leisure time congenially, but their notorious mischief-making had the power to disrupt the mood in camp. Rumours were the tides of the camp; they rose and fell on a daily basis. Whispers had been circulating for about a week that the entire camp was going to be moved to a new location; something was certainly afoot, and the atmosphere was tense with anticipation.

The loudspeaker crackled.

Ronny heard the carefully worded pronouncement, which was read twice so that there could be no misunderstanding. In essence, due to the ever-increasing demand of enemy nationals to be interned, it had been decided to move the entire camp to a new permanent location. Los Banos was the destination of choice, which was described as an ideal health resort noted for its hot springs, where there would be plenty of fresh food and clean air. It was promoted as Japanese concern for the internees' welfare.

"But I've just got here! We can't be on the move." Ronny was shocked. Readjusting to another alien world was beyond contemplating.

Pat clarified, "I've heard of Los Banos. It's the campus of the University of the Philippines College of Agriculture, about sixty kilometres away. Some chaps from the bank went there once and said that it was nice. It's quite a small campus, so there would have to be a lot of work done before everyone could be accommodated."

"It's reassuring to know it's a real place."

"What do you mean?"

"Oh Pat. Don't you ever wonder just what the purpose of all this is? Where will it end? There're 4,000 of us and, according to that bulletin, there're another 2,000 battering down the door to get in. Wouldn't it be easier for the Nips to just get rid of us? They're certainly quite capable of doing it."

"The world wouldn't allow it to happen."

"You can be so naïve! Did the world do anything about the massacre of all the millions of Chinese? The Japs blatantly ignore the Geneva Convention and say it doesn't apply. Don't you wonder why they don't exterminate us? We're just a drag on their resources."

"My dear! No! I do not think this is a ruse to massacre us. I think this is a genuine attempt to find a solution to an obvious problem."

"But what about the stories we hear of how they're treating our troops?"

"And that's what they are: stories. We've no proof of anything."

"Of course we have proof! You forget that I saw the beatings in Baguio. I've seen the evidence of torture when prisoners came in. You choose to put your head in the sand. I won't!" She was angry, and this was getting personal, so it was time to put some distance between them and take Catherine to bed.

The proposed move had unsettled them both, and Ronny regretted her outburst. Pat would think the best of every situation, and she should have known better than to have shared her fears with him.

———————

The talk in the dormitory that evening was about the relocation. This was reinforced by a request from the appropriate committee for 800 male volunteers to go in an advance party to Los Banos to work on the site prior to the move. Their luggage was to be ready for transportation in three days, and they were to be ready to leave the day after. Everyone was shocked at the speed of this decision.

Ronny and Anna were huddled together, their voices low, as the dormitory settled for the night.

"Pat won't volunteer. He might have done once as an alternative to living in the gymnasium, before I came. He certainly won't now," confirmed Ronny.

"I think Marvin will," declared Anna.

"Oh no, Anna! What makes you think that?"

"Marvin is a doer. He's worked in the lumber industry all his life. The thing he finds hardest is being idle. He's been chafing at the bit to have a real, physical project, and it's been tough watching him being so frustrated."

Ronny was shocked. "You mean you would support him going?"

"I love him, Ronny. It's been awful to see him so down. He needs to do this for his sanity."

"You're much more generous than me. I don't know how you can let him leave you alone with Daisy." She looked at Anna with wonder.

"He needs this opportunity to get back in touch with the old Marvin, and I have to support him. Anyway, it won't be for too long, and then we'll join him."

Ronny was not convinced. "I'm not sure about it, Anna. All that talk of hot springs, fresh meat, vegetables and new buildings sounded like weasel words to me."

"Weasel words?"

"Seductive half-truths that you can't quite get hold of. Los Banos sounds too good to be true."

"Well, at least it'll be in the country, away from the city."

"That certainly sounds good. I do miss the fresh air and views."

"If Marvin goes, he'll do a good job, and then we can start a new life there. You, Pat and Catherine will come too. It's got to be better than here."

The two women talked it over, and Ronny was persuaded that perhaps, in time, this move might not be so bad. The lure of the country seduced her imagination, and she slept that night with images of a kinder existence.

She woke to the news that only 280 of the men needed had volunteered, so the committee overseeing this was going to be forced to draft the remaining 500 that the Japanese had demanded. The committee had been given one day to make up the list. Single men who were physically fit would undoubtedly be enlisted, and some husbands would inevitably be forced to part from their families.

Ronny's day was spent normally, but anxiety underlay all activities.

Another troubled night passed, and, when she awoke, she found that the final list had been posted on the bulletin boards earlier that morning. Pat's name was on it.

Pat looked shaken when he met her, and Ronny looked at him in disbelief.

"There has to be a mistake!" she gasped. "*You didn't volunteer?*"

"How can you ask that, my dear?" he replied.

"No, of course you didn't. Forgive me. It was just the shock."

"They just need single men to fill the quota."

"You're no longer single! I'm here with our baby."

"I'm sure that's what every married couple will be saying. I've no idea how they came up with the list in such a short time."

"But they can't possibly want you. Why did they pick you? You can't work!" The minute she said it she felt his grey eyes on her and realised her mistake. She had offended him and backtracked. "What I meant is that you're not the navvy kind. Surely they want muscle if it's going to be construction work?" The Pat she knew was a practical liability, and construction of any kind was not where his talents lay.

"I'm so sorry, Ronny. I can't bear to think about leaving you both. You've been through so much to get here, and this is how I repay you…" He tailed off, numb with the pain of it.

"Oh Pat!"

"I've been so happy and had such plans, and it all seemed so hopeful. You don't deserve this."

"It's a mistake. They obviously think you're single. We haven't got much time to put it right."

"Ronny, it's done. I am as horrified as you are, but we have to accept it. We just have to trust that we'll be together in Los Banos when they bring you over."

"No, it's not done. I won't accept it. How can we get your name removed? Can't you prove you're not fit?" She eyed her husband's new, leaner shape dubiously. He was by then, at age thirty-eight, fitter than he had ever been.

"On the way here, I passed the hospital offices, and there's a queue right across the grass. There're not going to be any dispensations given on health grounds."

"What about your eyesight? If the army turned you down because of that, surely we can use it to our advantage? Can we pretend you've lost your glasses?"

"Nice try, Ronny, but they've a whole pile of replacement glasses in the clinic. I know because I broke these once, and they replaced them immediately."

There was a heavy silence between them, each was deep in their own thoughts.

Ronny's instinct was to go on the attack, and she swung into action. "I'm going to fight this, Pat. You've a responsibility to Catherine and me now, and they've got to take that into consideration. We must go to the committee overseeing this. They don't know your situation's changed. You're just a number to them, and they need to know that they've made a mistake."

"Ronny! Don't you think everybody's trying to do the same thing? The Japanese envisaged trouble. That's why the deadlines are so close and we're living cordoned off by troops. I'm sorry for the committee members for being forced to make a selection," declared Pat.

"We've no time for sympathy, Pat. We've got to talk to someone to sort this out."

"I don't know any of the committee members in person, so I've no idea who to ask."

"Well, let's start with your room monitor. Come on, let's find him. We need to do something right now."

The gymnasium monitor, an elderly man, was sitting sunbathing outside his realm. Ronny got the impression that he had already dealt with several similar conversations that morning, but the sight of Catherine sleeping on Pat's neck must have triggered sympathy, because he became forthcoming. An ad hoc committee had made up the list, and the monitor knew one name, Peter Cain, and suggested they speak to him directly.

—⊬-⊬—

Cain was hard to track down, and the morning was spent chasing from one location to another. Ronny would not admit the possibility of defeat, and, finally, they tracked the man down to one of the smaller coffee stalls. He sat there unaccompanied, and they allowed their chosen saviour some solitary coffee space before approaching him. Ronny would have launched into a full attack, but Pat insisted that he would do all the talking. She was left outside with Catherine to watch from a distance.

She could not see Cain clearly, but got the impression that he was a slender, whippet-like man with high temples. She noticed his habit of leaning forwards to look fully into Pat's face when he was conversing. The talking seemed to go on forever, and she could not judge if this was good or bad. She had little confidence that Pat would drive the negotiations in the way she would, as he was too accepting of other's points of view and too courteous to challenge them. She wished she had approached the man herself.

Catherine became crotchety and wanted her father.

Finally, Ronny saw the men rise, and was surprised when they came out of the shack together and walked straight across to her. She steeled herself.

"Mr Cain, this is Ronny and Catherine," introduced Pat.

"Please, call me Peter. Well, Ronny, your husband has made a very good case for exclusion from the group, and I'm pretty confident that there's a sound reason to remove him from the list. I'll put his case forward as soon as I get back to the office," Cain offered.

She stared at the man and then at her husband, who had wrought this change in their fortunes. All she could do was to blurt out, "Thank you; oh, thank you!"

"You're welcome," replied Cain. "How could I do otherwise after what your husband had to say? Pat's given me a very persuasive argument. I must dash, as this all needs to be finalised by tonight."

"How will we know if he's in the clear?" enquired Ronny. Doubt had seeped in. Perhaps this man had an overinflated sense of his own importance and Pat would still be on the list tomorrow.

Peter Cain leaned in towards Ronny's face and said clearly, "Ronny, you have my word that I'll do everything in my power to remove Pat's name. I don't envisage a problem, but if there is, I'll contact you before the final list gets posted."

And she believed him.

Cain walked away, and as they watched him leave, she could not contain herself.

"What did you say? How did you manage it?" she questioned.

Pat smiled gently. "It doesn't matter how I did it, my dear, as long as it worked, and I'm as sure as I can be that we've succeeded, O ye of little faith!" He gave her a mocking squeeze.

No matter how she pressed him, he would say no more, and she eyed him with a greater respect. His way would never be her way, but his way had worked on this occasion.

Cain was as good as his word, and Pat's name was not on the revised list posted that evening. Anna's Marvin had volunteered, as she had predicted.

—⊁--⊁—

Two days later, on 14th May, Ronny witnessed the contingent for Los Banos leaving at first light. A total of 798 men and twelve army nurses were transported out in lorries. They were told it would not be long before the work on the new camp would enable those left behind to join them. Perhaps the proposed move to Los Banos would be for the best after all.

SEVENTEEN

—⊬—⊬—

15th May 1943

506 days in captivity

An animated Pat stood in the doorway of the dormitory, insisting that Ronny should accompany him. She had no desire to do so. Unsettled after the departure of the internees to Los Banos the previous day, and with Catherine occupied at the play base, all Ronny wanted was to relax with a distracting book.

"I'm really not in the mood, Pat. Can't you find someone else to take on your walk?" asked Ronny.

"I'm not taking no for an answer, girl! It will cheer you up. Trust me!" Pat declared.

"I'd really like to finish my chapter in peace. What's so special that it can't wait till tomorrow?"

"I'm going to stand here till you come, Ronny. I'm not leaving!"

Pat stood, his arms crossed, as her roommates negotiated a way round him. They cast irritated looks in her direction.

She gave in. "You can be a real pain. This had better be worth it!"

Reluctantly, she allowed Pat to guide her down the drive that led from the main building directly towards the gate in the back wall. They then branched off to the right on a track behind the isolation hospital, threading through shanty area B10, which ran parallel to the rear wall. This area, commonly called Garden Court, was the pride and joy of Santo Tomas, and the bamboo-and-matting houses were obviously tended with domestic pride. They passed men and women pottering in well-manicured flowerbeds, and, bizarrely, Ronny was reminded of beach huts and their owners' pride as witnessed on family visits to the beach at Bournemouth. Seaside England took some conjuring to mind in this vibrant backdrop, and Ronny came to an abrupt halt. She felt homesick and was no longer prepared to participate in Pat's mystery tour.

She took a stand. "This is ridiculous, Pat. Where are we going?"

"You'll see! Bear with me," he cajoled.

"I'm sorry, but I'm not in the mood." She stood stock still, immovable as a stubborn donkey.

"I want to surprise you, poppet! I've some great news, and I can't wait to show you. It's not far now. Please indulge me."

She wouldn't play his game.

"Oh, all right, but you've spoiled the surprise!" He turned her to face him, his hands on her shoulders, and smiled down at her. "I've bought a home for us. A chap was leaving for Los Banos, and I've bought us a shanty!"

Shocked, tears sprang to Ronny's eyes.

She squeaked, "You wonderful man!" as she flung herself into a big hug. "How did you manage that? Where is it?"

"Come on, and you'll see! The fellow gave me a good deal. I guess he had no option! Now we'll have our own place to call home," he stated.

Ronny gazed around in anticipation. She gripped Pat's hand eagerly and allowed herself to be led further through the little community. As they approached each manicured plot, Ronny wondered if this was to be theirs.

But Pat pressed on till they came to the little creek that divided the Garden Court area from B9, which was better known as Jungletown. Crossing over the swiftly moving snake of water meant balancing on a thick bamboo pole that acted as a bridge. Here, the huts were constructed from nipa-palm fronds and were less regimented. Scrambles of flowers filled the afternoon air with perfume, and the community had an air of improvisation. The huts varied from the well-tended to the shambolic, and an abundance of banana trees covered their walls with a dappling of shade. The narrow path wound between the shanty dwellings, and she thought she heard birdsong in the trees. She breathed deeply, as if she were back on the mountainside.

They came to a halt in front of a small, square hut, with a pitched roof and large window spaces on two sides. It looked ill-kempt and forlorn. The window-lid shutters were propped open by stout bamboo poles, and, like all local native dwellings, the hut stood elevated on stilts with a ramp to the front door. No one had bothered to plant a garden around it, and, like a mongrel in a dog pound, it begged to be rescued. Ronny always sided with the underdog, and rescue it she would. Laughing in their eagerness, they stepped up the ramp, through the door and into the interior.

The small room had been stripped bare by someone in a hurry, leaving a trail of debris. The only items of furniture remaining were a small earthenware stove for cooking; a little, square table; and two chairs. The roof and walls – covered with woven, split-bamboo, *sawali* matting – looked secure enough, though only the next heavy rain would tell. The well-ordered shanties they had passed could not have been as endearing as this daytime home that craved attention and love, and Ronny was thrilled.

She declared, "I'm going to make a garden here."

"A garden? When did you show any interest in gardening?" queried Pat.

She ignored him. "It does look as if anything will grow here."

Their closest neighbours had blue morning glories literally smothering the roof.

"Food. We'll grow food, lots of it. And we'll keep it all for ourselves." Pat was looking very pleased with himself. "You're going to have to learn to cook with that thing, woman. Keep me in a style to which I'm not accustomed!"

Ronny was no cook, as both of them knew. Her lifestyle had never required her to learn.

"I can try!" she offered. "It can't be difficult. I'll be swapping boiled-rat recipes before you know it. Just watch me!" She looked at the stove with an air of bravado.

"And the table's perfect for bridge foursomes. What a shame we're limited to day time only."

Ronny hugged him. "This is wonderful, Pat. Thank you, my dear; you've made me terribly happy."

Wandering round the tiny cabin, they beamed at each other.

Ronny asked, "Do you think this is our very own banana tree? It definitely looks part of the building." The slender tree was leaning on the roof, and she could see a maturing hand of stubby bananas just out of reach.

It was time to pick up Catherine, and Ronny's mind overflowed with ideas for their shanty. She picked a handful of tiny flowers and placed them in a discarded old tin on the table, and promised their house that she'd be back the following day to start caring for it.

—✠—✠—

Ronny saw the value of Pat's quick thinking, as the camp found itself flooded with 819 new internees the day after the exodus. Most were elderly men, many of whom were acutely ill or disabled. Three had active tuberculosis. Additional bed space was needed in the camp hospital, and the children's ward and many others were forced to shift around to accommodate the infirm, who could only live on the ground floor.

It was not until a few days later that Ronny acknowledged there had been a subtle but considerable shift of mood in the camp. The boisterous good spirits of the younger men who had gone to Los Banos were lost forever, as elderly men predominated by then. Many were veterans of the Spanish-American war, with families in the city, and they expressed great bitterness at being separated from them. Everyone suffered accordingly.

Restoring the shanty was a distracting delight. Ronny swept out all the previous dirt, and disinfected every surface thoroughly. The space under the floorboards had been a dumping ground, and she cleared it out by lying flat on the ground. It reminded her of Iris and her underfloor cleaning job, and she remembered telling her dishevelled friend that she looked like 'the wild woman of Borneo', which was one of her mother's favourite expressions. Ronny missed her old friends very much and often held imaginary conversations with them. The memory of Betty's big laugh always brought a lump to her throat.

Her shanty neighbours were all welcoming, but she sensed they were reserving judgement. The community shacks leaned so close together, and, as they were denied the privacy of closed doors and shutters, it made folks wary of one another. As in the dormitories, it took little to trigger irritation. There were squabbles over the ownership of banana trees, and complaints about noise or the disposal of rubbish, which could escalate rapidly out of proportion.

Over the weeks, Pat turned out to be a whizz at borrowing the tools she needed, and even managed to find some tiny tins of paint and a brush. Ronny spent happy hours painting the table and chairs. With her imagination running loose, she painted an assortment of imaginary flowers growing up the legs. Any casual onlooker would consider her obsessive, but Pat made admiring noises and left her to her own devices. Her garden project was started by digging out a flower bed on either side of the little house.

Lost in her own world, she was surprised the first time she had a visit from one of the Japanese guards. He came striding straight up the ramp into the room without hesitation and shouted at her. She had made the error of closing a window shutter to block the sun from her eyes. The vigilant young guard made it clear that she had transgressed. Life under the microscope of too-near neighbours and guards did little to dampen her enthusiasm.

Ronny was contemplating the idea of painting a simulated carpet on the floorboards, when Pat halted her with news.

"Because of the overcrowding, the Japs have given permission for men to sleep in the shanties," he explained.

"That's fantastic! How wonderful for you," she said.

Ronny gave him a hug to suppress her instant envy. She knew that life in the gymnasium was barely tolerable and she must be happy for him, but it was hard to be magnanimous. She resented her own dormitory life, with its petty bickering and unpleasant atmosphere. Catherine was still the only infant in the room, and the restrictions this placed on the other women made her clearly unwelcome. Ronny was also the only European, and the only woman whose husband was present in camp, so conversations often excluded her. Perhaps she was not as tolerant as she might have been, but she felt disliked and responded by spending as little time as she could in the dormitory. Anna and Daisy were the only two whose company she enjoyed.

She managed to say, "You deserve it, Pat," and hugged him again for good measure.

"It would be perfect if only you were allowed to stay as well," he declared.

"It's a nice thought, but I doubt the Nips will ever allow it!"

—⊬— —⊬—

The following day, Pat and George carried Pat's bedding roll and possessions over in a commandeered wheelbarrow. They arrived laughing, after a precarious journey fraught with mishaps, and Ronny was proud to be able to offer them some watery celebratory coffee, heated on the little stove.

She instantly recognised the ornate chess set that she had given him on their honeymoon. This must have been given priority on the hasty mercy mission of his friend. It reminded her of warm evenings in the little flat in Manila. She could not help the pang of resentment as Pat's gain reminded her of her losses, and she found herself frowning at the offending gift she had chosen for him with such care. Oblivious to her conflict, Pat set up the board with such pleasure that Ronny felt guilty. The beautiful pieces took pride of place on their table, and their little house became their home.

One of the heaviest rainfalls heralded Pat's first night there. The commandant, Kuroda, had given permission to close the shanty shutters, and, miraculously, the roof of the hut did not leak.

Pat told Ronny how thoroughly he had enjoyed being on his own, listening to the downpour. "When that ceased, the frogs made just as much noise celebrating! I didn't sleep a wink! I shall have to construct earplugs if I'm to survive." His pleased expression belied his complaint.

The wet weather had set in, and rain was a constant background to their new routine. Ronny took Catherine to the hut when she was not working and carried the food back from the chow line to eat there. Catherine was becoming a more confident little person, understanding about fifty words by then and communicating well with words of her own invention. Ronny's back limited picking her up, so she was relieved that she walked independently, if slightly bandy-legged. Catherine's favourite nesting place was in the crook of Pat's neck. He called Catherine 'Twopence' for no explainable reason, and she noticed that he had subversively added Patricia to her choice of Catherine Ann on official documents.

Ronny joined the bridge group, and, in the late afternoons, it was a pleasure to get back to playing with her old partner, sharing the card language and secret codes they used since childhood.

—⊬—⊬—

The nightly curfew marked Ronny's return to the dormitory, and her conversations with Anna often went on late into the night.

One night, Ronny was celebrating. "They've lifted the ban! I can go back to wearing shorts now, just because the price of fabric went up!"

Anna was more serious. "I'm glad you can think of one positive from the escalating prices! I know the Finance and Supplies Committee is having a tough time with Kuroda, negotiating a raise in the per capita allowance. Even the Nips are struggling to keep up with inflation."

"Kuroda seems to speak excellent English."

"He should do! He was a top Shanghai businessman. But it must be a real worry for him that food is becoming so scarce."

"It's certainly stopped my cooking efforts in their tracks! I daren't risk ruining precious ingredients! Not at the price they are!"

That raised a chuckle from Anna. "That's your excuse?"

—⊬––⊬—

Every day, the queue to receive goods from outside was eyed with envy by those without that support. Ronny believed that she belonged to the section of internees who had nothing, but was aware that, as her husband was the owner of a shanty, she was perceived as privileged. Pat must have had the means to have afforded the purchase, but, as was his nature, he was secretive about money. They both had been brought up in the school that dismissed buying things on tic, but Ronny's principles were not as rigid as Pat's, and she struggled. Many in camp borrowed endlessly against the uncertain future. She was surrounded by a different attitude and started to nag him.

Pat was immovable. "I can't do it. I can't borrow without the sure knowledge that I'll be in a position to pay it back."

"But, isn't that what the whole camp is doing? The Finance and Supplies Committee is constantly borrowing from the Red Cross, with no guarantees at all," she wheedled.

"The whole business is a mess, and I don't envy those who will have to sort it out once we're liberated."

Ronny frowned at him. "If we don't die of starvation in the meantime. I thought I was used to being hungry, but I can't bear seeing – and, worst of all, smelling – the cooking going on. They don't attempt to hide it. I dread going past some of the shanties. It's the smell of what you're missing that's the worst."

"You poor dear. I know it's tough."

"Doesn't it make you angry? It's bad enough that we have to live like this, but the fact that some people are making no sacrifices is too much to bear."

"They are making sacrifices. If they haven't the humanity to share their good fortune, then nothing can be done. It's life, Ronny, and there'll always be divisions. We are actually well off here."

She looked at him in amazement. "How can you say that? We've no quality of life!"

"Just look at what we have. I'm here with my family, thanks to you. We have our own personal space. We aren't in hospital or detention. Yes, we're hungry, but we're surviving. We have Catherine. We have each other. It could be worse."

Ronny's voice was low but intense. "I don't know how you manage to think the best of everything. I'm livid at the unfairness of it all. I just want a normal life. I want it for Catherine. I had such plans for our nursery, but here we are, with a little pretend house that I'm not even allowed to sleep in!"

"Ronny we're healthy compared to so many. I know it's hard, but we really are the luckier ones."

"I'm tired of trying. I just can't be nice all the time."

As if to reinforce her statement some neighbours strolled past the windows, and she turned her back as Pat waved to them.

It was time for a walk to ease her irritation, and Ronny set off at her usual pace – half jog, half walk – concentrating more on quietening her stretched nerves than taking in her surroundings.

She was passing the plaza when she was arrested by the sight of a group of nearly 100 internees who had just arrived from Iloilo. They seemed in good spirits after their sea journey. In no hurry, she flopped on the grass for a breather. Watching the group waiting to be housed, she was struck by their close sense of community, and it made her wonder what had led to this fusion. She studied them and listened to the conversations within the group.

An indefinable quality about one man made him stand out from the crowd, and her gaze was drawn to him. He was average in height and extraordinarily thin, with piercing, blue eyes and an attractive smile. It was obvious he was respected within the group. He spoke quietly and with an air of reflection, which made the more-vocal others give credence to whatever he had to say. Ronny watched him and found herself wondering about his history. It was fun to speculate, even though she doubted that she would ever run into him again.

—⊹—⊹—

The late June rains set in with a vengeance, and the whole camp became a mire of mud and dripping foliage. It was unremitting. The nights were cool, but the shanty became damper by the day without the hot sun to dry it off. A musty smell started to rise from the ground, and there was no opportunity for Ronny to work on the sodden earth of her proposed garden. A silence descended on the community as endless, grey day followed endless, grey day.

One evening, Ronny was waiting in the shanty for the return of Pat and Catherine from an expedition to find *sawali* matting with which to patch the roof, which was threatening a leak. They were later than usual, and she sat listening to the croak of a frog and the gentle drip of water into the puddle that had formed beneath 'their' banana tree. The air was holding its breath with the threat of another downpour, and Ronny was at peace. She had been sitting silently, with the darkening sky making it impossible for her to sew, and her hands were idle in her lap.

Deep in thought, she became aware of another presence in the room. The man from Iloilo had entered their space as quietly as a ghost, and both of them were surprised by the presence of each other.

"I'm so sorry to have startled you. I'll come back later," he said.

"No, please. You're welcome. Are you looking for Pat?" Ronny enquired.

"In a way." He half-gestured to the table with the chess set. "It's my move."

"Oh." Ronny glanced at the ornate board and saw that there had indeed been a game in progress. How typical of Pat not to have mentioned the ongoing match right under her nose. She flushed. "Of course. Do please sit down. He'll be back soon. I'm Ronny. I don't think we've met," she ended lamely.

They shook hands. The man's name was Reginald Winter Verney. He was English and he appeared to be totally at home in their shanty. He drew up Pat's chair and concentrated on the board.

Ronny knew she should leave the man alone to concentrate, but found it impossible. "I saw your group arrive. Forgive my ignorance, but where exactly is Iloilo?" She broke into his thoughts.

"It's on the island of Panay, one of the Visayan Islands, about 350 miles from Manila. We weren't captured by the Japs until April 1942, so we had more time at liberty," he told her.

"How do you find this camp after your island one? It takes some getting used to, doesn't it? I found it difficult to adjust, as I was interned in Baguio before coming here."

He still hadn't made his move. "I certainly enjoy the extra food, but it's hard to feel that you're master of your own ship here."

"Did you feel more vulnerable on the island?"

"Vulnerable?" The blue eyes flicked up from the board.

"I imagine you were more accountable due to being a smaller group? It's easier to hide here."

He turned and stared at her as if seeing her for the first time. "Why would I want to hide?" He appeared wary of Ronny's attempt to draw him out.

"I'm sorry. I don't know you at all and I was thinking along my own lines." She tried to change the subject. "Please tell me about Iloilo. What was it like there? I've seen so little of the Philippines. I never got the chance to explore."

"Well, I lived in Jaro, which is a lovely district of Iloilo town. It's full of Spanish colonial architecture, much like parts of Baguio. Panay was a beautiful island and we had a good life there before the invasion."

"What were you doing so far from home?" she persisted.

"I could ask you the same question! It seems to me that there are some who travel and some who don't. I do." Reg's direct gaze was disconcerting.

"No, seriously, what's your profession?" This was beginning to feel like hard work, but she pressed on.

"I'm an accountant, and accountancy is a boring business – much like banking – but at least you can travel. What did you do apart from marrying a banker?"

He had turned the conversation. He presented a challenge, and she liked challenges. She was convinced he had an interesting story to tell, and he was not going to fob her off. However, Pat and Catherine arrived at that moment, and the conversation immediately turned serious.

Reg shared some news. "The Japanese have promised independence to the Filipinos by the end of the year. Premier Tojo has assured them of it."

"I don't understand the implications," stated Ronny.

Reg turned to Ronny to explain. "It's all to do with the contrived perception that the Japanese have liberated the Philippines from the Yanks. The Americans must be seen to have let the Filipinos down and to have deserted them. By offering the Filipinos their independence and their liberation, the Japanese become the good guys."

"Tojo was over here last month," reminded Ronny.

Pat interrupted with a different slant, "I'm pretty convinced this is a double-edged sword for our loyal friends. I think the first demand the Imperial Army will be making in exchange for liberation is the establishment of compulsory conscription. Under the Japanese, of course."

"I think it's more complicated than that, but I'd agree the only people to gain will be the Japs themselves," confirmed Reg.

Pat responded, "Where will that leave us?"

Pat and Reg were settling down to a lengthy discussion, and Ronny had to tear herself away. It was time to take Catherine back to the dormitory for the night. She always found this a wrench and resented enormously the Japanese regulation of dormitory living for the women. Good conversations were something to be treasured, and she left the men reluctantly, making her way back through the twilight with ill grace.

EIGHTEEN

3rd July 1943

549 days in captivity

Anna had volunteered to babysit, and Ronny, her hair tied up in a high ponytail for coolness, sat on the lawn with Pat. Films on the portable screen were a fortnightly event, which drew crowds who would bring their own chairs or sit on the lawn. The film scheduled was *Vivacious Lady* starring Ginger Rogers, but they had to endure two Japanese propaganda shorts first and chatted quietly through them.

Pat eyed the assembled crowd. "Promise me tonight's film will be better than that last one in Japanese. I didn't understand a word of it."

Ronny countered, "I don't know why you went! The bridge game was far more entertaining, and you'd have been welcome."

"Yes, but it was all women. You know I'm not happy without another man to hold my hand. It's much more fun when we have a mixed foursome, like with the Stewarts."

The sky had cleared and was studded with stars after a day of heavy showers. Rain was threatened again for later.

Pat looked up. "I can see the Scorpion and that might be the Southern Cross over there."

"Can you really pick them out? I'm impressed! You couldn't do that six months ago. I'm glad something's sticking from the lectures!" exclaimed Ronny.

Internees gave talks on a variety of subjects, and these were well-attended events.

Pat glanced at some threatening clouds. "Let's hope the rain holds off. I hear there are problems at Los Banos. Apparently, there's still no electricity in the buildings, open privies and a shortage of reliable water. It's starting to look as if the transfer was a big mistake."

"That's tough on the volunteers. Their places here are already taken by newcomers, so I imagine they won't be able to come back. I've heard there's a problem getting people to leave the hospital now!" Ronny stated.

"What do you mean?"

"One of the nurses told me that some people in the hospital are paying money to remain there, like it was a hotel! There's not enough space any more for the really ill. The unbelievable selfishness of people! Two women, who both have cancer and not long to live, can't get beds. It's wicked if they can't be made comfortable in their last weeks."

"No, it's not right. I'm sure the appropriate committee will sort it out. I heard the hospital is running out of anaesthetic, which means many operations can't be performed."

"All the more reason to stay healthy!"

A sudden squall of rain passed over, with heavy and warm drops plopping on the crown of Ronny's head. After a rustle of consternation, some internees rose to their feet and left. The threatened intrusion swept on, but Ronny and Pat decided to ignore it and stay put.

Ronny breathed deeply; she loved the fresh smell of rain. "These rain squalls never seem to end. Everyone's talking about the possibility of flooding. Were there floods last year?"

"To a degree," confirmed Pat. "It's something to do with the university being built on a flood plain, and the combination of high tides and heavy rains. We were all right in the gymnasium, although it was pretty close one time. Getting to the main building occasionally meant wading!"

Ronny had visions of snakes and unmentionables hidden under the murky water. "Ugh! I don't like the sound of that!"

"You and your imagination, poppet! Touch wood, our shanty seems to be staying dry, but I've heard that Jungletown is prone to flooding."

"Shush now. Here comes Ginger!"

Escaping to the glamour of Ginger on the silver screen took her away from the grim squalor of camp life. Miraculously, the rain held off, and Ronny had a smile on her face until Pat escorted her back to her hated dormitory. The shanty was where her heart lay, and, as she spent every hour available there, she knew she had allowed a distance to come between Anna and herself. Anna was a treasure, and she resolved to change that.

—✶──✶—

It started with a casual statement from the room monitor: Beatrice of the sour face. Post from Britain had arrived, and there was something for Ronny.

She stared at the familiar handwriting. It was 24th July 1943, but the postmark on the envelope was August 1942. Shocked, she stuffed the envelope, unopened, into her skirt pocket, intending looking at it only when she had the opportunity to read it alone. A sense of dread overtook her. Dread of news that she did not want to hear and dread of the conjuring up of memories of her old life in solid, familiar London that she had barricaded up carefully. She did not want this letter from her sister. She could not bear to open it and yet she could not deny her desire to do just that. Her hand trembled as she felt the wedge of paper through the fabric of her skirt, and she felt sick.

She waited until she was in the shanty and then she waited again. Irritated by Catherine's demands, she snapped at her. Even when Pat, with a puzzled look, took the little girl out for a walk, she still couldn't open it. The solitude she had craved scared her. She could not face this letter alone and hurried after them.

The letter remained in her pocket unopened for nearly three weeks.

Initially, she had been aware of it constantly as it nagged to be read, but then time lengthened when she forgot about it. Its shout became a whisper and finally diminished to a token nudge from the deep pocket of her skirt. This was until one day she returned to the shanty after gardening and found Catherine examining the blue envelope before handing it to her father.

Ronny met Pat's grey eyes as he blinked at the implication of what was in his hands. He frowned at it and then at her. "It's Felicity! I'd know that writing anywhere! But you haven't opened it?"

"I can't. I just can't." She felt sick.

"It's from Flick," he repeated.

Then further knowledge sunk in to Pat. She could see it in his eyes.

"You must have had this for weeks!" he declared.

"I couldn't open it. I couldn't bear to see what she'd written," explained Ronny.

Pat flushed. "And what about me? Didn't I have a choice?"

"She's *my* sister." She averted her eyes.

"And she's my family too! Didn't you think I should have been included in this decision of yours?"

"I'm sorry. The letter was addressed to me. I didn't think—"

"*You didn't think? This is our life! It's not all about you all the time.*"

Pat's voice had risen to a level that Ronny had rarely heard before, and Catherine stood frozen in horror. The child's bottom lip came out, and she started to wail.

"Now look what you've done." She reached towards the child and tried to cuddle the rigid form.

"No, Ronny, I suggest you take a look at what you're doing." He had dropped his voice low and the meaning was deadly clear. He was furious. "You never once thought of me in all this, did you? I've been deprived of our family just as much as you. It's all about you. It always is." The letter was still in Pat's hands, and he let it fall to the ground in a gesture of disgust.

Ronny's anger flared up, anger at herself as well as anger at Pat for pointing out what was obvious. She could not find the words to fill the silence.

Pat did. "This letter is for us to deal with together."

"I'm sorry." She meant it this time. She was in the wrong and was unable to summon anger to justify it. "I just couldn't face it."

She stared at him, unable to stop the trembling in her voice and the mist threatening her eyes. Catherine wriggled from her grasp and reached out for her father who enveloped her in a hug. Ronny felt alone, tired and chastened. Pat was right. She had not taken his feelings into consideration.

He concentrated on pacifying his little daughter and the child's tears subsided.

"Please open it." Ronny's voice came from far away. Whatever emotional damage was in the letter, whatever death or bad news, it bore no relation to the damage that she had just done to her relationship with Pat. "I can't open it. Please open it for me. For us," she corrected.

He relinquished Catherine, stood up and walked over to the window. In that long-familiar gesture, he pushed his glasses onto his head and prised open the envelope carefully. She wrapped her arms tightly around herself, both holding her emotions in and creating a solid barrier as protection from any onslaught.

She waited, watching his face, as he read slowly.

He handed it to her without a word and, when she hesitated, the old Pat stepped forwards to protect her. "Don't worry, Ronny. There's nothing to upset you. Just Flick trying to cheer us up, and not being sure how. The censor's had little to do, as she's said little. Nothing seems to have changed in London. There's nothing to be frightened of."

The familiar writing did indeed include nothing of importance or the can of worms that Ronny had dreaded. Her relief was immense and she felt deeply ashamed.

—✳— ✳—

The first Ronny heard of repatriation was from Anna and Susie in the dormitory one afternoon. She would always associate it with the slap she received immediately before hearing the news. She had been dashing to retrieve her towel from the dormitory after her work shift. Sometimes the lingering smell from floor cleaning was unobtrusive, but she had been swilling with a new, strong batch, and a shower was all she could think about. Catherine was at the play base, and she just had time for a quick wash before collecting her.

She simply had not noticed him. Her mind was busy as she hurried down the shadowed corridor and if she had been aware of the Japanese officer subconsciously, her thoughts were focused elsewhere. Raised voices drifted towards her from the dormitory down the passageway, and she wondered what the excitement was about. He too must have been listening. Her hand was on the door handle when the sharp bark halted her momentum and she spun towards the man.

The sting of the slap across her face exploded in her brain.

Her heart pounded. She gasped at the assault, and her cheek screamed as the nerves in her face protested. Tears sprung to her eyes and she stared at the little man with thick glasses. She saw the hand raised again and lurched forwards instinctively into the low bow that was expected of her. It was the lack of this bow that had offended the officer. Her nose ran and dripped unchecked to the floor as she retained the stance in self-defence. She heard the grunt of dismissal and still waited until his footsteps receded.

As she fell into the room, she saw Anna sitting on her mattress with Susie kneeling above her, trimming her hair. They had halted their excited chatter at the commotion outside the door and their eyes widened at the scarlet-cheeked Ronny.

Ronny growled, "Don't ask," and indeed it was self-explanatory. It had happened to both women on occasions and was a sharp reminder of who was in charge.

Irritated by the world in general, Ronny hissed, "He was listening to you. What were you squealing about? I could hear you from down the corridor."

Susie put her scissors away, and Anna hastened to make room for her. Susie, whose husband was in the military, considered herself the dormitory beautician, and had an extraordinary supply of potions and shampoos. Susie herself was wearing her hair wrapped in a turban, as the impossibility of getting her hair colorant was something she could not face. Turbans had become fashionable in camp. Susie wrinkled her nose at Ronny's proximity.

Anna explained, "Kodaki has told the committee overseeing this that they're going to allow limited repatriation."

"Repatriation! For whom? When?" asked Ronny.

"Apparently, Kodaki is considering it for when the exchange ship arrives."

"But that's far too vague." Ronny's cheek was still smarting. "I'd no idea that the Japs were considering an exchange. Will it be for you lot or us British?"

"Jap prisoners of war are being held by both countries."

Susie added, "Everyone will want to go. How will they work it out?"

Anna's voice was low. "I guess that's the committee's job. I hope the sick and the old get priority."

"Some hope! It'll be for those of standing with the committee. Repatriation for the important boys." There would be no getting it right with Ronny that day.

Susie snapped, "Oh, Ronny, shut up. What is that smell?" She brushed the hair clippings off Anna's neck and avoided Ronny's eyes.

Ronny slumped and moved away. "It won't matter who the committee recommends as the Japs will control the selection."

"I imagine it could be the transients. The ones who were en route for somewhere else and got caught here," continued Susie.

"You mean like the missionaries who were kicked out of China? How many are they talking about?"

"The number I heard is 350."

"And when's the boat due in?"

"The *Teia Maru* is expected later in September."

Ronny scoffed, "September? Why are we getting excited? That's almost six weeks away! There's plenty of time for the Nips to change their minds."

Anna put in, "It'll take that time for me to decide who to write to!"

"You've lost me," said Ronny.

"They're going to give out forms so that every person can write one letter home to be taken on the ship."

Ronny was silenced. Anna explained that they would be allowed to buy a sheet of paper and an envelope addressed to the Prisoner-of-War Service. One letter only would be allowed. Ronny knew that sending a letter back to London was something she needed to share with Pat.

She bounded to her feet. "Catherine! I almost forgot her!" The shower was forgotten as she headed out of the door.

—✦—✦—

The conversation was resumed in the slow shuffle of the chow line later that afternoon. Sometimes it took nearly an hour to reach the head of the queue. Anna had joined Ronny and Pat, and Daisy was keeping an eye on Catherine.

In the line, repatriation was the only topic of conversation.

Pat started. "Kodaki's ordered a survey on the question of repatriation. The men on my work shift are buzzing with it."

"Why a survey? Are there questions to be asked? It's obvious we all want to be freed." Ronny watched despondently as one couple queue-jumped blatantly, aided by friends ahead in the line.

"It's not so simple, Ronny. There's bound to be political aspects that we can't ignore."

"What are you talking about? Repatriation must be about prioritising and making sure that the evacuation is done on humanitarian grounds. Urgent medical cases and those whose lives are at risk should go first," declared Ronny.

Anna had concerns. "Have you thought about the families of those priority cases? What happens to them? Will they be allowed to accompany them?"

"I hadn't thought about that. I can see there would be a difficulty there," Pat stated.

"I imagine most people would only want to be repatriated if their families went with them, unless they were beyond making that decision. I know I wouldn't be prepared to go without

Marvin and Daisy, no matter how ill I was." Anna was missing Marvin, but presented a brave face.

Pat stuck to his original tack. "I'm talking about a different issue. Have you thought about what the Filipinos will feel if we are to be repatriated? What message will that give them?"

Ronny was startled. "Oh. You think this would play into the Jap's hands? You think they'd use it to convince the islands that the Yanks are deserting them?"

"Don't you see?" queried Pat. "The Nips couldn't lose! There'd be fewer mouths to feed and strong evidence to the locals that the Americans are leaving the islands for good."

Anna groaned, "Why does everything have to be so complicated!"

"On the surface it looks good, but I suspect there'll be strong divisions in camp about this." Pat had the last word as they approached the serving hatch.

—⊱—⊰—

As August wore on, Ronny was aware that inflation in the Philippines was rocketing. The prices in the little shanty stores were making even the wealthiest of internees think again. She heard that food scarcity was becoming so bad that the farmers were flocking into the city in the belief that the situation was better there. The importation of rice and rations had been severely curtailed. The cold stores had all closed down. Meat rationing was rigid, with carabao, pork and beef in short supply and only sold in public markets. The camp's internees appeared better fed than those outside, which reinforced the pressure on the Japanese to allow the families of interned men to join them.

Increasingly, there was no meat available, and the chow-line blackboard announced 'chilli sin carne', 'scrambled duck egg' and other meatless creations. Vegetables were becoming scarce, and the standby of vegetable hash no longer contained onions or cabbage. Garlic was the fallback flavour to such an extent that Ronny and Pat joked that only newcomers to camp reeled from this assault on the nose.

—⊁— ⊁—

Ronny was one of the crowd who jostled around the neat piles of luggage in the quadrangle by the main building, to see exactly who had been selected for repatriation on the *Teia Maru*. It was the morning of the luggage departure, three days in advance of the exodus of the chosen ones. They could tell who had been selected by the names on the labels on the trunks and suitcases. It had been a closely guarded and highly inflammatory secret for the last two months.

A woman in a green dress was frowning at a label. She turned to comment to Ronny. "I can see there are two doctors from the Rockefeller Foundation, but what about the people needing urgent medical treatment? I know of several who obviously haven't been chosen."

One of the nurses was at her side. "I know some who need surgery, but I haven't spotted their names yet."

Ronny had one piece of good news, "That fellow who lost one eye has managed to be included. His other eye is threatened if he doesn't get urgent treatment, so I'm glad for him. He learned about his transfer two days ago."

"I can see only five or six medical cases made it, which is pretty poor out of 127 leaving."

Ronny was shocked. "Only 127 people? What happened to the 350 Kodaki announced originally?"

The woman in green snorted. "You Limeys! When will you learn? You can't believe a word he says."

An elderly man with bushy eyebrows commented, "They kept changing the names right up to the last minute. Apparently, the Nips made twenty-seven substitutions."

"It's madness to guess at the criteria they used," concluded Ronny.

Quite a crowd was gathering and everyone had their opinions. "Why would they choose businessmen from Shanghai and Hong Kong, and their families?" asked one woman.

"Because they were transients. It seems fair as they were caught here just on the way to somewhere else," replied the elderly man.

A remarkably sallow man snarled, "Why fair? No one's here out of choice!"

The lady in green ignored him. "A couple of missionary doctors are amongst them, who were travelling back from China."

The sallow man was gathering steam. "It's not right. The sick should go. It's a death sentence to keep them here."

A new voice burst in. "I recognise the names of three newspaper men amongst this lot. Their organisations must have paid to get them out!"

Another chipped in, anger mounting. "And the vice chairman of the Executive Committee and his wife! Let me guess how they were selected!"

The crowd of unhappy label-readers broke up as Imperial Army officers descended on the quadrangle for some sort of inspection. At least twenty Japanese civilians, whom Ronny had never seen before, did the physical work of unpacking each suitcase and bundle with deliberation. Ronny drew back and joined the silent circle to watch what turned out to be the thorough destruction of the carefully prepared luggage.

Closely supervised by the officers, every gift or personal possession was unwrapped. Every hem and lining was systematically searched, and sealed jars were opened. Like locusts, they passed through the cases and trunks, discarding and scattering personal possessions then moving on in concentrated unison. They set aside every book that had been packed and every piece of paper that had been used as wrapping. Not one particle of written evidence was to be allowed to escape the camp. Photographs were removed from frames and examined carefully for hidden messages and those featuring people were confiscated. Ronny saw the photograph of a child joining the pile of material forbidden to leave. Chequebooks and bonds were taken, and the only currency to be allowed out would be Japanese. One businessman's stamp collection was summarily removed.

Ronny and the crowd watched in silence as clean clothes and underwear were flung on the dirty paving. The only sounds were the occasional guttural command or confirmation of intent by the military, and the distinctive clink of a breakage when fragile glass or china was dropped on stone. Anger gave way to genuine sympathy as they watched the brutal robbing and humiliation of the chosen.

It was only when the Japanese had left, carrying their plunder, that the buzz of voices arose again, this time in sympathy. The quadrangle was littered with debris, and Ronny joined the many willing hands ready to help with the repacking. She thought it was ironic that, because the Japanese were not monitoring them, any amount of written messages could be included in the packing. Tears were shed over breakages, but even more over precious photographs that could never be replaced.

—⊢—⊬—

Two days later, Pat announced "Guess what? Twenty-four members of the American consular staff joined the expatriation group! How's that for looking after the neediest?"

Ronny could only shake her head in disbelief.

Nineteen

————✠———✠————

6th August 1943
583 days in captivity

It was an airless afternoon in August, and heat bounced off every surface in the shanty. Ronny loved reading to her daughter, both curled up on Pat's mattress, but Catherine was fretful and fussing with her mouth that day. As Ronny inserted her finger to explore the problem, she was shocked to find that one of Catherine's tiny baby teeth was so loose in her gums that it fell out at her touch. The tiny tooth lay in the palm of her hand, its roots discoloured, weak and stunted. Horrified, she probed again and found other teeth were loose. It was only after she had rocked Catherine to sleep that she gave way to the despair she felt. Ronny had struggled to supply Catherine with sufficient calcium for her growth, and this was telltale evidence that she had failed. Breastfeeding had not been enough.

Swept with feelings of self-pity and frustration, Ronny vowed she would redouble her efforts to succour Catherine. The wealthy internees had food, and she resolved to approach the camp's elite and offer a specialised sewing service. One woman she knew made a living making sandals for the richer women in camp. Her English accent charmed the Americans and the offer of personalised tailoring could prove profitable. She was determined that Catherine would have eggs to feed her bones. By the time Pat returned, there was no evidence of Ronny's tears. She preferred to keep her failures to herself.

––×––×––

The little shanty felt crowded with Reg, Anna and Daisy as their guests, and Ronny wished for the hundredth time that they had an overhead fan to create a draught. Reg chose to sit on the floor, and Ronny studied him. In this world of make-do and mend, he always managed to look neat and attractive. How did he do that? It annoyed her slightly. He caught her looking and smiled briefly. He fascinated her and she wanted to draw him out, but he remained a closed book.

She blustered, "No cake today, I'm sorry to say! There's no more sugar to be had." Ronny was fooling no one.

Anna smiled and, like a conjuror, whisked a paper bag from behind her back. It contained two buns carefully cut into six portions, to include Catherine and Daisy in the treat.

Pat laughed. "Thank you, Anna. Aren't we the lucky ones? Shortages are getting worse everywhere in the islands."

"I don't understand how in such a fertile tropical place, we can be short of food. Who'd have thought it?" asked Ronny.

"Well, the Japanese should have seen it coming! The Philippines has always needed to import rice and other essentials." Reg had a deep, melodious voice, which was somehow at odds with his thin physique. "My greatest concern is that this threat of starvation is going to lead to an uprising. There's real unrest out there. The city's crammed with people from the countryside who thought there'd be food and work in the city, but now find it's not the case. There must be thousands of unemployed starving on the streets of Manila."

The whistle of the kettle on the charcoal stove brought Ronny to her feet, and she filled bowls with a weak pretence of jasmine tea, minus milk and sugar.

Anna focused clearly on Reg. "But if the farmers have left the land, where will the next crops come from? I guess if I were a poor farmer and saw my kids starving, I could be persuaded to think the city folk would have the answer."

Ronny mused, "Thousands of Filipinos probably believe the Imperial Army is going to look after them, especially now they're being offered independence."

Reg answered her. "*How wrong can they be?* Even with rationing, basics like vegetable lard, sugar, soap and matches can't be bought any more! There's so little available in the public markets that people are walking miles from one market to another, in the hope of buying anything on offer. It's a disaster."

"I agree the country folk are naïve. They'll learn that the Nips couldn't care less about them," said Anna.

"It's not a matter of caring. The Japs can't feed their own!" Pat declared.

Ronny put in, "Or us!"

"Did you know the Jap military-admin people are now charging rent to the families of internees living outside in their own houses? They've already evicted families who've failed to pay. I heard it from the Family-Aid Committee," confirmed Reg.

Anna wailed, "That's so wrong! Our guys are worried enough that their families can't feed themselves out there."

"They're desperate for their Filipino families to be allowed to join us. They've been trying for months now," confirmed Pat.

"There are 158 wives and 341 children on the list this week, who are trying to get interned." Reg always had precise figures to hand.

Ronny hid a smile; Anna looked impressed.

Pat's voice was quiet with intensity. "Surely all this is fuel for an uprising? I really fear for the people. If the Filipinos riot, there's no question that the Japs will react ruthlessly."

"They already show brutality towards the locals," Anna added. "I've seen beatings at the camp gate during package-line hours."

Reg looked grave. "I talked to a man this week who'd been out on a pass to a family funeral. He said that twenty-eight men had been executed in the cemetery last week. He was driven through the streets to the funeral, and saw Filipinos tied to trees or trussed up on the ground. There were groups of Japanese patrols going from house to house."

Ronny was alarmed. "That's terrible! I'm surprised there aren't already retaliation killings."

"But there are!" Reg's blue eyes were serious. "There are Japanese being killed in Manila on a weekly basis now. Some are stealth knifings at night, but some are executions in broad daylight. The whole thing is escalating around us." Reg stopped as if he had said more than he intended.

Ronny wondered where he got this information.

Pat broke the pause. "Do you think the big boom we heard this morning was connected to all this?"

Ronny, too, had been surprised by the sound, but had forgotten about it.

Reg answered, "It was a bomb attack on the east wing of the Manila Hotel. A Filipino protest, I imagine. An uprising wouldn't surprise me. Fort Santiago's full of prisoners again, including thirty leading Chinese civilians. The city's a dangerous place to be. We're safer in here."

The tea party had descended into gloom and soon broke up. Daisy led the way back to the dormitory, wending down little paths in the deep-pink sunset. It was a breathless, beautiful end to the day, heavy with perfume, and Ronny hated the confines of the dormitory. She carried Catherine, who felt a heavy a burden to her this evening.

Her thoughts were interrupted by Anna asking questions about Reg. Ronny's antennae switched in. Had she imagined an interest between these two this afternoon? *Surely not?* Anna was devoted to her husband, and Ronny was upset at the idea that Reg might have an interest in Anna, her only female friend. Besides, Reg was *her* friend, not Anna's! The women retraced their steps in silence, each deep in their own thoughts.

When Ronny had been contacted by one of the wealthiest women of Garden Court, she had been delighted. Her dressmaking service was getting off the ground, and she had come to the elegant shanty with a spring in her step. The reed-roofed house proved to be extensive, certainly the biggest that she had seen, and it was partitioned into sections. The owner, Lily, had created an interior that was totally incongruous with the world that surrounded her. Ronny was ushered in to wait for the hostess, and noticed a comfortable sofa and a cocktail cabinet in one corner. However, the most dominant feature, from the point of view of someone who had not seen one for nearly two years, was the full-length, freestanding gilt mirror.

Ronny stared at her reflection. Immediately, she saw that her clothes had become too big for her. She had not realised it was so obvious. With barely a hesitation she opened up her wrap around dress and gazed at what it revealed. Her breasts – free of the brassiere that had not survived months of washing, and gently swollen with milk – looked good. She frowned at her nipples. They had been abused by the little mouth once too often, and she was considering that, soon, enough would be enough. She noted that her stomach was satisfyingly flat. Ronny gazed at the woman she was by then. Her reflection showed that she had lost the softness of her youth. She had always been proud of her figure and legs, but whereas she had been gently slender once, she realised that she had become simply thin. The daily ritual at the communal washroom mirror had accustomed her to the gradual hollowing of her cheeks and the deepening frown mark between her brows. She had become used to seeing her face reflected, but seeing her figure as a stranger might was unsettling. She consoled herself that perhaps she was more striking at that point. Her hair was still her crowning glory, but her eyes looked deeper set and her gaze was no longer an open one.

Ronny wondered what Pat thought about her as a woman. She had been at Santo Tomas for six months, during which time Pat had not once approached her in a sexual way. They had sidestepped the issue carefully, and neither had spoken of it. They shared lots of hugs, and, for her part, she was satisfied with that alone, as Pat had always been the more enthusiastic about the intimate side of marriage. Just then, studying herself in the mirror, she wondered if she was still physically attractive to her husband or indeed to anyone. She found it mattered to her. Ronny thought about her conversations with Anna about the loss of libido in camp. Was Anna really interested in Reg? Was he attracted to her? She hoped not! Apparently, for some couples in camp intimacy had continued as she'd heard of one or two pregnancies in recent months, which had come to be viewed with greater tolerance by the Japanese. Ronny had not had her monthly bleed since becoming pregnant with Catherine and was happy to miss the premenstrual pain that had dogged her from adolescence. This was her body's response to the trauma and food deprivation of camp life, so she imagined she would not conceive even if she wanted to. Catherine was totally sufficient for her maternal desires, and she had no intention of bringing another child into her uncertain world.

Ronny had warning enough to cover herself quickly before Lily bustled in. Her client was a heavily made-up, plump woman for whom internee life was more an inconvenience than a struggle to survive.

Lily, with great condescension, showed her the work she required, which was a new dress for the Philippines Independence Day celebrations coming up on 14th October. Ronny found this extraordinary and wondered what world the woman lived in! She knew there was mounting anticipation in Manila, with reports that brightly coloured bunting had been erected on the main thoroughfares and a huge parade was planned. The excitement was due to culminate in a fancy ceremony for the inauguration of the president of the new republic. Ronny and Pat thought the event was a cynical distraction from the famine and unrest in the islands. The moment Lily dismissed her, Ronny left, carrying the material to be worked on.

The auspicious day of the celebrations finally arrived, and the blare from the tannoy was never-ending. Ronny was alone in the shanty. Pat had removed himself and Catherine to a quieter corner in which to amuse themselves, but Ronny had a work deadline to meet and tried to stick it out. Equipped with cotton earplugs, she bent over the table, intent on stitching the white linen, but still the scream of music and speeches encroached. Humidity hung in the air, and she could feel the sweat running down between her thighs. She persevered, stabbing the crisp linen with her needle, but, finally, when a salty drop of perspiration fell onto her work Ronny could bear it no longer. The noise and heat made concentration impossible.

She packed it in and decided she deserved to treat herself to a coconut juice in one of the little bars that straggled near the main drive. Still hot and suffering from the threat of a full-blown headache, she settled into the corner of the makeshift hut.

"Coffee for the pretty lady? What are you doing here?" The voice was immediately recognisable, and she looked up into the face of Reginald Winter Verney.

"Escaping from the loudspeaker they've positioned in the street! The shanty's too close to the wall, and I can't hear myself think!" explained Ronny.

"Yes, the parades'll be going that way up to the legislative building for the inauguration. It's going to be chaos and very noisy!"

Ronny sighed. "I, for one, will be relieved when it's over."

"You mean you aren't enjoying this celebratory holiday?"

Ronny gave Reg an old fashioned look. He did not expect a response.

However, she gave one. "Anna thinks this means the Philippines won't declare war on the US, and we'll be liberated or perhaps even transferred to Formosa."

"Bless Anna. She always has stars in her eyes," Reg replied dismissively, which Ronny noted. "There's absolutely no basis whatsoever for those ideas. Nominally, this event gives the Filipinos independence, but, actually, this is a dictatorship. There'll be no independence. Jose Laurel will be just a puppet of the Japs. Nothing will change!"

"If nothing will change, why have the Japanese been so paranoid about security recently? What with all the passes being cut, all communication with the outside forbidden and now this crazy seven o'clock curfew!"

Reg frowned. "They just don't want anything to disrupt the party! I noticed a new team of military police have come in to search the parcels at the package line."

"How did you know they were military police? I saw them, and they looked like civilians to me."

"No. Civilians wouldn't be acting with such precision."

"Tell me, if nothing is to change, why would the Nips go through with this charade?"

"It's just propaganda. Prime Minister Hideki Tojo is promoting his Pan-Asianism. Asia for the Asians, et cetera."

The hut was cool and intimate, and the world seemed a long way away. The aroma of coffee mixed with the smell of the earthen floor. Ronny relaxed. "Who is this Laurel? What do you know about our new president?"

"Jose Laurel's a fascinating character. A real survivor."

Ronny mused, "He must be in a very difficult position."

"Oh, he knows exactly what he's doing. He's been pro-Japanese since way back. He made sure he was their choice for president of the republic."

"Did President Quezon appoint Laurel to be the acting president when he fled to the US?"

"No, not Laurel! Manuel Roxas was Quezon's choice. When Quezon and the vice president escaped via Bataan, they intended establishing a government in exile in the US, and I imagine that's what they've done. But Manuel Roxas was in sympathy with the guerrillas and was soon rounded up by the Japanese."

"How come Laurel got past everyone?"

Reg laughed dryly. "Laurel's always been smart. When he was a law student, he was indicted for attempted murder when he almost killed a rival suitor to his girlfriend. He knifed him! He was a young man, still studying, but he argued his case himself and somehow managed to wangle an acquittal!"

"He sounds persuasive!"

"He gained his Master of Laws degree right here in Santo Tomas University. He then finished it off at Yale!"

"So, he's pro-American?" Ronny sipped her coffee slowly. Why was she drinking it? She knew that the camp's version of coffee disagreed with her, but somehow she had not wanted to say no to this enigmatic man.

"Not so! He was pretty clued up, as he was in cahoots with Japanese officials before the war. He received an honorary doctorate from Tokyo University and later sent one of his sons to study at the Imperial Army Academy in Japan."

"It sounds as if he saw all this coming?"

"The Japanese shot the Filipino chief justice, so Laurel stepped into his place. He was happy to serve the Jap military administration. He's held high posts with them since the invasion."

"Surely he can't be popular with the Filipinos? He must have made enemies!"

"Of course he has. Early this year, he was shot by guerrillas at the Wack Wack Golf and Country Club."

"Pull the other one! Wack Wack! Now I know you're joking. Wack Wack? For a golf club?"

"I kid you not; that's the name! Anyway, Laurel took four bullets, but survived it. The Japanese convicted and executed two guerrillas, and there was doubt about a third one. They arrested the man, a former boxer, but Laurel cleared him. The word is that this fellow pledged his life to him and has been his bodyguard ever since!"

"It sounds as if he may need him! What an interesting man we have at the helm." She could not help herself. "Reg? How come you know all this?"

There was a momentary blink in those blue eyes and he countered, "How come you don't? Come on, catch up, girl! I expect you to give me information next time." He smiled.

Suddenly, she saw that she had lost his attention and, at the same moment, she heard the noise. It was the roar of approaching aircraft, and her mind spun back to the balcony of the Baguio hotel on that fateful morning nearly two years ago. She knew that sound and her stomach lurched.

Reg was on his feet, heading for the door. "Come on!"

Ronny froze. All her instincts told her to scramble under the table as her mind raced for an explanation. The heavy drone was growing by the moment.

Reg spun midway to the entrance, took a step back and gripped her hand. "Come on Ronny!" The touch and grasp of the unfamiliar hand sent an unexpected tingle through her. It was foreign, in a world where no one shook hands any more, and her daughter's hand was the only one she held habitually. She felt the intimacy of it in a blinding flash and still held back. Her legs had no strength, but his hand was insistent. She allowed herself to be hauled out into the open air, her heart pounding as every instinct told her to remain under cover. Reg was then standing stock still looking at the sky, as were others gathered on the pathway. She followed their gaze.

From over the horizon, filling the sky with dark menace came a fleet of military aircraft. They were flying with great precision, very low, with their thunder preceding them as they advanced across the sky. As the vibration of noise intensified, she saw forty or fifty of them at a guess, flying in close formation. Were they Americans come to bomb Manila? Were they Japanese intent on finishing off the city? Her instinct was to fling herself on the grass, and she could feel the tingle of adrenalin coursing through her limbs. She wanted to run, but Reg still held her hand tightly. Reg squinted up into the sky with no apparent agitation; Ronny, wildly glancing around, found the crowd in the same stance; and they, too, appeared to be fearless.

The planes thundered over her head, and she saw the emblem of the Rising Sun. This had been a military flyover, just part of the Independence Day celebrations. She felt the eyes of her companion on her and knew she had betrayed her fear. This staged spectacle had triggered her panicked response, and she felt stupid and humiliated in the presence of Reg. How dare the Japanese interfere with her head? She had seen celebration fly-pasts before, but the weakness in her legs told her that something deep within her had irrevocably changed.

TWENTY

14th November 1943
684 days in captivity

Ronny stared at the flickering shadows cast by the animal-head shapes she made with her hands for Catherine's entertainment. The rain had not stopped since the morning, and the northwest wind was steadily increasing in strength. The window shutters were closed, and the guttering coconut-oil lamp was the only light to lift their spirits. Huddled together for warmth, listening to the roar of the storm outside, they were becoming anxious.

Pat's face was serious. "This shows no sign of letting up. If anything, it's getting worse."

A sudden squall set the windows banging, and its pressure forced rain through the cracks around the shutters. Ronny flinched at the cold spray and looked around for something to fill the gaps. Their home groaned and creaked and, for the first time there, Ronny felt vulnerable.

Pat made up his mind. "You must take Catherine back to the

dormitory. You'll be safer there. I don't know how watertight this house is."

"No! I can't leave you. You need my help to protect the house!" she cried.

"Ronny, I'm not arguing! I want my daughter in the dormitory. You should go right now. The storm's going to get worse and it'll only get harder for you to get back. There'll be branches coming down, and the stream will certainly rise with this rain. There's no time to waste!"

Ronny pleaded, "Can't you just pack up and come to the main building with us?"

"No, I'm staying here. There are things that I can do to protect the shanty."

Ronny recalled the phone calls she had made from Baguio begging Pat to join her and knew how immovable he could be. She was torn between her need to protect Catherine, and her concern for Pat and their home.

She tried another tack. "Pat, I'm not sure I'm up to carrying Catherine on my own. This wind's really strong. I'm scared it's going to blow me over and she'll get hurt."

Pat relented immediately, "Yes, of course. I'm sorry, I wasn't thinking. We'll go this minute."

They heaved on their waterproofs and slipped their feet into the *bakia* clogs by the door.

Pat reached for Catherine and – with a "Come on, Twopence" – picked her up, and she clung to him like a little koala, her legs wrapped firmly round his waist and cocooned inside his oversized coat.

The door threatened to tear away from their hands, but they managed to close it behind them and slithered down the ramp onto the sodden path. The sky was dark and unnatural for the afternoon, and the cold rain turned to icy daggers on their skin. They trudged to the little creek and blessed the foresight of the committee that recently had replaced the original bamboo pole with a thick, wooden plank for a bridge. Even so, the swiftly moving water had swollen until it licked the slippery surface threateningly, but they managed to get across. The journey back to the main building was fraught more with discomfort than actual danger.

Once they reached the main building, they could see that, in the security of the main hall, a crowd of men were encamped already having decided not to risk a night out in the storm.

Ronny turned to Pat. "Stay here. There's no point in going back. You're here now, so you may as well stay for the night or at least until the worst of the storm has blown over."

"No, poppet. I need to go back. I need to do anything I can to keep the shanty watertight," replied Pat.

"But it could be dangerous! Stay here! These men obviously think it's not worth risking their lives for some leaking roofs."

"I've got to go back, Ronny. You and Catherine will be safe, and I need to protect our things. The storm's getting worse and there may be flooding too."

"All the more reason to stay! It's crazy to go back again."

"*When are you going to listen?* I need to protect the shanty, and I can't do that from here. I've got to go now."

He would not budge. She extracted a promise that he would return to the hall if things became too tough. After a brief hug, she watched him disappear into the gloom of the growing storm.

—∗⸻∗—

Hours passed, and Ronny watched the worsening weather from the safety of the dormitory, dismayed by its gathering intensity. The storm was threatening to reach typhoon proportions. Rain was falling in sheets, pummelling the trees and gardens into submission. The howling of the wind chilled her to the bone. The evening meal in the dormitory was reduced to a banana each, handed out by the taciturn Beatrice. The electric light flickered in response to the gusts and somewhere a door was slamming without ceasing.

Ronny had descended to the hall a dozen times to see if Pat had returned. Each time, the hall was crowded with more disgruntled men, but Pat was not amongst them.

Catherine was asleep, somehow oblivious to the commotion, but Ronny could not settle. She paced back and forth.

"For heaven's sake, Ronny, stop it! You're driving us crazy," said one of the women.

Ronny was at breaking point. "It's all right for you! You're all snug in here away from the storm with nothing to do but bemoan the inconvenience! You don't give a cuss for anyone who's in danger as long as it doesn't disturb your beauty sleep!"

The answer was prompt. "Don't snap your cap at us! If you're such a saint, why don't you go and see whether your precious man's all right? At least we'd have some peace!"

There was no answer to this. She had seen a man bleeding heavily from a head wound on her last visit to the hall, and she could not bear the possibility that Pat himself was struggling or wounded. He was out there on his own and would surely need help. She turned to Anna and stated, "I'm not staying here. I've got to go. Would you please take care of Catherine?"

Anna paled. "Of course, but it's not a smart move! Quite apart from the storm, it's way past curfew and you don't want to be picked up by the patrols. You really should stay here."

"I can't see patrols being out on a night like this and I'm sure Pat needs help. I can't just stay here and do nothing."

Anna knew Ronny too well to argue further, and she produced a banana from under her bedding. "For Pat! Good luck!" was all she said.

Wrapping herself in many layers with her weatherproof coat on top, Ronny made a dash for the exit. She hardly registered the raised eyebrows in the hall and barely heard the shout of, "*Lady! You shouldn't be going out!*" as she battled to open the door; she slid out as it slammed shut again. She flattened herself against the building as she readjusted her eyes to the dark and summoned all her strength to set out on her rescue mission.

The wind was deafening and chilling. Ronny squinted through the rain, summoning her courage to leave the solidity of the main building. She did not wish to consider whether she was on a foolhardy enterprise or what her reception would be when she reached the shanty. She just knew she had to act. With a deep breath, she edged herself out of the lee of the wall. Immediately, the wind gripped her and bowled her along without mercy. She grabbed at tree branches to steady herself and tumbled her way up the centre drive, hugging tree after tree like she was performing some manic barn dance. Pausing for breath, she clasped one tree and looked back at the lighted main buildings; as she watched, the whole campus was plunged into darkness. The electricity had gone out, and her world became pitch black.

She did not know how long she hung on whilst her eyes adjusted to the inky dark. Then, following the edge of the driveway, she continued on her mad way. The wind picked her up when she released her grip and she was slammed forwards from tree to tree. She knew where to turn to enter the Garden Court area. Here, there were no longer any trees to give her respite, and she slipped and slid, trying to take refuge behind any halfway secure bush. Even though all the shanty shutters were shut tight, there was evidence that a few were still occupied, as chinks of light leaked through the cracks. The rain was stinging her legs. Her hands were freezing, but she continued along the water-logged paths. Fallen branches and twigs were a constant hazard, either whipping her legs or tripping her up. When she lost her balance and fell heavily on her side into a rose border, she cursed loudly at whoever had planted the thorny shrubs.

The path seemed endless. Ronny knew she was on the home straight when she heard the roar of the creek above the howling wind. Then, straining her eyes in the dark, she saw to her dismay that the plank bridge she had crossed only hours before, was no longer visible. The water, no longer contained by the banks, swirled dark and deadly. This was the hurdle that finally brought her to a halt, and she could have cried with frustration. What a fool she had been not to think of this likelihood! She had been too hasty. She should have used a different route.

She could not turn back, so she had no option but to focus her exhausted brain into forming some sort of plan. Ronny concentrated hard and, wiping the rain from her eyes, studied the swirling water where the bridge should have been. Judging from the lift of the oily, black torrent, the plank was still in place, but submerged. If she were to try to climb across using the bridge, she would have to hold on tight. She shuddered at the thought of submerging herself into the tumbling cascade. Weighed down as she was with clothes, she was frightened of being dragged under and swept away.

She looked around. The ground was littered with branches freshly sheared from trees, and she reasoned that if she could lodge the longer, firmer ones immediately upstream and side by side against the water-covered plank, she might get enough purchase to crawl across.

Ronny had no idea how long she laboured, dragging branches to the waters' edge, then throwing them in the hope that they would lodge next to the plank. She lost many downstream but in desperation kept at it. Finally, enough were jammed against the plank by the force of the water. She convinced herself that she would have guidance and something for her hands to grab whilst crossing. Her limbs were shaking violently with cold and fatigue.

Her hands were set like claws and her back was screaming for respite. By force of willpower alone, she waded to the edge and started to crawl gripping tightly to her makeshift handholds. The water was icy and its force terrifying. The submerged plank held firm as she scraped her knees along it, forcing herself forwards. She moved her body inch-by-inch, shaking uncontrollably and reaching from bough to bough through the fast-flowing water, until she reached the safety of the opposite bank.

Soaking wet, she staggered on down the path. The shanties here appeared in a worse condition and no glint of life escaped them. Finally, she saw the outline of her home. No light shone from it. With one last effort, she pulled herself up the ramp and pounded on the door. She no longer had the strength to pull it open against the force of the wind, and she prayed that Pat would hear her and come to help. She pounded again, and, finally, the door was wrenched open.

In the pitch black of the shanty, Ronny had a vague impression of Pat helping her remove her clothes and being rubbed dry, before she was helped into one of his shirts. She was desperately thankful to find him there. Speech was not possible over the howling outside and there was nothing to say. She was totally exhausted and collapsed on his mattress, whilst he lay down beside her. The heat of his body penetrated her back slowly and, with piles of clothes over the top of them, she succumbed to exhausted sleep.

She did not hear the ultimate violence of the storm when the shanty shook in winds of over sixty miles an hour. She did not hear the crash as 'their' banana tree gave up its fight and toppled over bringing down one end of the roof in its fall. The penetrating rain showered that end of their home immediately, but she remained unconscious in their burrow of clothes.

—*—*—

Ronny heard shouts from far away, and they would not go away. Slowly, she opened her eyes. It was day, the wind had dropped, and every part of her body ached. It all came back to her, and she saw the strange world she had woken up to. At the far end of the shanty, a large hole in the roof gaped open, and rain continued to soak all that lay beneath it. Pat, who still slept beside her, had put his evening to good use as their possessions were piled on the table, wrapped securely in a strange tarpaulin. She studied his sleeping face. She dreaded him opening his eyes and waited for the reprimand. The voices were outside by then, calling for answers, and her husband awoke. He opened his eyes, stared hard at her and shook his head as if in defeat, and they both remained quiet.

The American voices were insistent, and Pat struggled up and went to the door. There was a brief exchange before the leader of the shanty patrol pushed his way in. Ronny remained curled up, peeping out of the bedding.

The man with the grey crew-cut stopped short inside the door. His face was lined with fatigue and his eyes were pink-rimmed; his dripping, black waterproof coat shone like a seal. "Are you OK?" he asked. "You seem to have fared better than some of your neighbours! Five of the shanties have collapsed in this stretch alone!"

Pat answered, "Thanks, the roof needs fixing, but we're still standing."

The man spotted Ronny suddenly. "Lady, where did you spring from? You'd better keep quiet! I'm going to pretend I haven't seen you or I'd have to report you." He turned deliberately to Pat. "I guess you had a wild night. Most folks from this district were smart enough to come in!"

Pat responded, "Yes, it was tough! Thanks to your loan of the tarpaulin, I think our things will be fine."

The man persevered, "You told me last night that you were coming in, so why didn't you?"

"I left it too late, and then the trip seemed too risky. But we'll be fine now. Once we've fixed the roof, we'll be snug again."

"Not so fast! There's no way you can stay here! The water's rising fast and it'll be over your floor by lunch time. You've been lucky, my man, but it's time for you to evacuate."

"But—"

"No buts. Don't make my job even harder. I need you and your invisible dame out of here in the next hour." He dropped his voice, but Ronny still heard him. "We've killed a large snake that was clinging to the shanty next door, and there'll be more passengers as the water rises. Get the lady out of here!" The man walked away to leave, but then turned at the door. "Don't attempt to cut across the creek. Go the long way via the vegetable garden, and cut in near the carpenter's shop. That's your safest route."

And, with that, he was gone.

Ronny's body groaned from the severe beating she'd had from her journey in the storm, but she needed no further urging. They managed between them to lift the mattress up onto the table and piled their tarpaulin-wrapped possessions on top of it. Pat put a few necessities in the pocket of his waterproof, and Ronny housed more in hers. Getting into the wet coat again was grim, and, on thrusting her hand into a pocket, she found – to her disgust – one totally mashed banana. There was no funny side to it.

Leaving the shanty, they trudged, sometimes thigh deep, through the ever-rising water and were horrified to see devastated shanties, which had been uprooted and collapsed. The paths were only defined by the water pipes that stuck up at intervals. Wading with the necessary *bakias* protecting their feet made the going even harder, and Ronny struggled as she pushed through the water. She had no wish to know what other living things were in the water with them. She leaned heavily on Pat. They passed desultory men attempting to save their ruined houses, but no one exchanged greetings, and still the rain came down.

—⊁--⊁—

Once safely back in the main building, they parted. Ronny and Pat barely had exchanged words, but she knew that, inevitably, he would want to talk about her stupid risk-taking. Her crusade to rescue Pat had been irresponsible, and it was she who had ended up the liability. Pat went to seek accommodation in the education building, and she climbed to the dormitory.

Ronny was chastened when Catherine burst into tears at the sight of her mother. By the appalled stares, she knew her face was not a pretty sight, and Anna helped her to the washroom. A shower confirmed a multitude of cuts, grazes and bruises on her body, and she had gained a spectacular black eye. The previous night was just a jumble of images, and, bone-weary, she rejected Anna's suggestion of a check-up, and fell onto her mattress and slept.

Pat called round briefly in the evening, and his parting comment was, "Ronny, when will you learn that you're not invincible? You got away lightly last night, and it's time you grew up. You owe it to Catherine." It was his unemotional quiet tone that penetrated and shamed her.

—⊁--⊁—

The following day the rainfall stopped, having reached twenty-seven inches.

—⊁--⊁—

Ronny gazed out of the window at a flattened grey world. It was the third day of their existence surrounded by a sea of muddy water. Pathways and gardens had disappeared, and they were told that the worst flooded areas of the campus were as deep as six feet. A mantle of calm enveloped the scene, as if all the energy of nature was spent. Still without electricity, the internees were told the filtering plant of the Metropolitan Water District had collapsed, and tap water was no longer drinkable.

Ronny was pestered by the women for an account of her adventure, but she would not talk about it. Her spectacularly varicoloured bruised eye invited enquiries, which she deflected, reinforcing her image as a standoffish Brit.

Anna tried to encourage Ronny to make peace with the dormitory, so – as they wolfed down their cracked corn and coffee – Ronny sought to redeem herself.

"I'm impressed with how the Finance and Supplies Committee is managing to provide all this," she stated.

Anna supported the conversation. "Yes, all thanks to the volunteers. After the gas was cut off, we knew the kitchens were in trouble."

Susie joined in. "The men are heroes. They worked all night to build stone fireplaces in the corner of the dining shed. Ten, wasn't it? They're using charcoal to give us something hot to eat! They're great guys."

"Pat spoke to someone who said the stench in the kitchens was horrific. Sacks of rice have fermented, and the food from the refrigerators is all wasted. What's even worse is they've lost the vaccines and serums stored in them. Those are irreplaceable," explained Ronny.

Beatrice butted in. "I don't know what we're smelling now, but I suspect it's the men in the hall!"

"I think we all smell pretty rank," declared Anna.

Susie whined, "Three days without electricity! The smoke these burners give off makes my eyes water. I hate not being able to see enough to read by, and we can't go to bed any earlier!"

Ronny offered, "I think we're lucky. I gather it's really tough in the education building. It's so overcrowded that the men don't have enough space to lie down!"

Susie wailed. "No water to drink or wash in! How long can this go on?"

"I hadn't realised how many people lived in shanties now. There isn't a square inch in the hall between the men camping there," said Ronny.

Beatrice added, "It's not just the shanty people. The gymnasium has had to be evacuated too. The ground floor of the hospital is flooded, and the children's hospital is closed."

Anna murmured to Ronny, "I wish I knew how things are at Los Banos. I wish there was some way to know that Marvin is OK."

Having done her bit, Ronny was happy to exclude the others from the rest of the conversation. "It's really tough for you, Anna, but – selfishly – I'm so glad you're here. I don't know how I'd have managed without you and Daisy."

"Don't be silly! That's what friends are for!" Anna paused uncertainly before she made up her mind. "But I do have to tell you something Ronny. I'm requesting a transfer to join Marvin in Los Banos. I've put Daisy and my name on the list."

Ronny looked at her, devastated, then remembered her manners. "Of course I understand that you need to be with Marvin. I'm sure Daisy wants to join her father too." Ronny fought to sound generous. How could she survive in this dormitory without her only friend? "I'll certainly miss you, and Catherine will be lost without Daisy."

"I think that it's right to go and join him. Things have improved there. I'd like to think we can share a shanty at Los Banos."

Ronny gave Anna a sympathetic hug and wondered, for the hundredth time in the last three days, whether she and Pat still had their shanty to enjoy.

Twenty-One

$\longmapsto \!\!\!-\!\!\!\rightarrow$

29th November 1943

699 days in captivity

Ronny brought her fist down viciously on the tiny red ant that had bitten her. She had experienced enough of them! An onslaught of centipedes and ants, looking for new homes, had arrived after the water receded, but it was not going to be hers! She had worked hard at rescuing the shanty from the sorry state the floods had left it in. Luckily, water and electricity had been restored to camp finally, but fifty shanties were totally demolished and a further 300 needed urgent repairs.

Ronny repaired the hole in the roof, as the handymen in camp were fully employed, and Pat was the least 'handy' man she had ever known! His forte was finding the tools and handing them up as she sat astride the roof, monarch of all she surveyed. Ronny spent hours weaving the matting into place and securing it with nails. The unpleasant smell of mud still permeated the whole camp. The sun shone, but the landscape was uniformly dull: a sea of grey between the shanties, punctuated with broken trees. Not a flower was to be seen.

Ronny sluiced and scrubbed the shanty floors, banishing the mud slick that covered it. The tarpaulin-wrapped treasures had all survived intact; however, the mattress needed drying out, and the furniture needed repainting. Her garden was gone, and she would have to start again.

———✠———✠———

Ronny was repainting the legs of the table meticulously and decided to include images from Catherine's favourite book, *The Story of the Little Black Sambo*. Catherine loved to chime in when Ronny got to "I'm going to eat you up" and "Now I'm the grandest tiger in the jungle", with growls and little hooked finger talons! Carefully, Ronny painted little tigers peeping out from the vegetation that adorned the table legs. She sat back, satisfied that they looked enough like tigers for her daughter's delight.

"You are so talented, Ronny. I wish I could do that." Reg had an uncanny ability to materialise out of nowhere.

She smiled. "It's not great, but I think she'll love it."

If Reg noticed the remains of her black eye, he was too polite to comment. He settled himself on the floor beside her. "Did you know American Red Cross packages arrived here earlier this month?"

"No! What Red Cross packages?"

"That's the point! We know they arrived three weeks ago, and we still haven't seen them! Some of the internees helped to store them in the warehouse at the docks so we know roughly what came in."

"Oh, come on then. Tell me what we haven't got!"

He responded enthusiastically, "There are 4,511 food cartons, 110 boxes of medical supplies, 1,100 boxes of men's shoes and 165 cases of women's toiletries! Do you want me to go on?"

Ronny laughed. "I know you could! Enough! Enough!"

"Quite apart from the delay in us getting the relief, there're rumours that the military have been helping themselves to it, both from the pier and the warehouse. Kato's not happy about it, and there's a widening division between our commandant and the military."

"The military are a law unto themselves."

"Yes. We don't know how lucky we are that they aren't in charge. Things would be very different. What do you think of our new commandant?" The role had been held previously by the dual command of Kodaki and Kuroda.

"I actually like what I've seen of Kato. He looks refined and kind of classical, with that long face. We see far more of him than his predecessors."

"He was interned in Kensington House in London, which is why he speaks good English. He was part of the consular staff and was one of the first to be exchanged. He certainly knows our home country, but, from what I've seen, he doesn't seem concerned with our welfare."

"No real change then!" She changed the subject. "Reg, I never congratulated you on your appointment to the committee! That's a meteoric rise to power! You really are amazing!"

"Don't exaggerate! I'm only the property man who's 'in charge of camp tools and other property'! I've hardly joined the elite!"

"Well, I'm impressed, and you've obviously impressed others! What is it with you?" It came out all wrong! She had meant it to be just a throwaway remark, but something had crept into her voice.

He looked at her with that direct gaze, and she found herself blushing under his concentrated attention.

It was at this awkward moment that Pat and Catherine arrived, en route to the chow line for dinner. Ronny and Pat had been careful around each other ever since the night of the typhoon and had both avoided talking about it. She resented the barrier it had created, but was not going to be the one to bring it up.

Catherine was entranced by the little painted tigers.

They all left the shanty and headed for the chow line, where they waited in line to the sound of a trumpet playing 'When the Saints Come Marching In'. It was always a good day when Bumblebee Thompson, a handsome African American, serenaded the chow line with his horn. Catherine jigged to the rhythm. She adored him, and he always had a huge smile for the children in camp. His real name was Pendleton David Thompson, and he was assigned chef to the commandant, but – whenever he had the opportunity – he would share his extensive musical repertoire with his fellow internees. He was loved by all.

Watching the patiently waiting figures ahead of her, Ronny was stopped in her tracks as she recognised a figure coming back down the line. Her mouth went dry and she felt pure joy at the sight of the woman who had been so important to her. There was Dr Beulah Allen, with one child on her hip and another helping her carry the food containers.

"Beulah! Dr Allen!" Ronny called out.

The distinctive head turned in her direction. It was only after a moment's hesitation that the woman came over and enveloped Ronny in a warm hug. Ronny looked into the eyes of the woman who had delivered Catherine on that never-to-be-forgotten night in the kitchen.

"Ronny. I'm so happy to see you. And, wow, look at you, Catherine!" Beulah exclaimed.

"Hi Lee! Hi Hendy! Haven't you grown? How lovely to see you all. What're you doing here?" enquired Ronny.

"I've been here a couple of weeks. I came down with Dr Haughwart. It seems that Santo Tomas lost too many doctors to Los Banos, so the Nips ordered us here. You remember Dr Haughwart?"

"How could I forget our dysentery specialist!"

"We've worked flat-out since we arrived."

"It's lovely to see you. The little ones look well."

"Yes, they're great kids. Sam will be proud when he sees them again. Listen, Ronny, I'm supposed to be at the hospital. We're organising cholera shots for everyone. Tell me where I can find you, and we can catch up."

Ronny was more than happy to do so. The women exchanged hugs and parted. Ronny was delighted at this connection to her past. That day, camp life looked brighter, and she looked forward to their next meeting.

Reg was deep in conversation with Pat when she rejoined them. "I've been telling Pat how impressed I am with the job you did on the shanty. You'd never know the water was over the floor, except you seem to have gained four tigers!" He gave no indication that he had heard anything about her adventure, and Ronny was sure that Pat had been discreet.

"I'm relieved it's now clean enough to resume my sewing jobs. I was getting behind with my orders," Ronny stated.

"You're a lucky man to have a gem like Ronny," Reg told Pat.

"Oh, she's special all right!" declared Pat.

Ronny was alert to any hidden implication, but Pat continued, "Have you never been tempted by marriage, Reg?"

"I've never found the right woman!" said Reg. "I envy you, but, at this moment, it's a responsibility I would rather not have. I feel sorry for the men with families in the city, as many fared worse than we did in the typhoon. The appropriate committee is trying to get them into the camp, but Kato is immovable. They've asked permission for some of the Red Cross packets to be sent out to them, but Kato said that none of the American supplies were to be released. No American food, no American clothing and no American shoes!"

They shuffled slowly forwards in line.

Ronny was sceptical. "Well, we haven't even seen those packages yet! But why is he so adamant?"

"My guess is that he thinks the appearance of supplies from the US would reflect badly on the Japanese. He even refused to allow our powdered milk to be sent out for the children. The Finance and Supplies Committee suggested that the milk should qualify as medicine for the infants, but he wasn't buying it. He's trying to close down all outside communication. You mark my words! He'll get rid of the Filipino vegetable market and the little internee businesses. The package line will be the next to go!"

—⊩⋅⋅⊩—

It was barely a week later when Ronny sat in the dormitory watching in desperation as Anna packed. They had been notified that transportation for the move to Los Banos was ready, and her friend was going to desert her. Ronny felt miserable. She had always been the one to 'move on' and leave others behind, so this was a new experience. She could no longer deny Anna's departure, as she helped her sort her possessions to be packed. The limit was two small pieces of hand luggage per person. That evening was spent helping her friend make agonising choices.

"I wish I could have persuaded you all to volunteer to come too," said Anna.

"You might have persuaded me, but Pat won't budge. He's strictly in the 'better the devil you know' camp. Oh Anna! I can't tell you how much I'm going to miss you. It's going to be grim without you." Ronny held up a threadbare garment with a querying look, only to drop it on the discard pile at the shake of her friend's head.

"I'll miss you too, Ronny."

"I was naïve to think that we dormitory women were going to gel the way we did in Baguio."

"You had an exclusive group in the baby house. Also, you didn't have the numbers we have. It's the rat syndrome!"

"Rat syndrome?" Ronny raised her eyebrows.

"Yes. When you put too many rats in a confined space, they attack each other. It's nothing to do with not enough food; it's to do with space. Space becomes the most valued thing."

"Yes! I think that's the worst aspect of camp life. People! As long as you and Daisy were here, I didn't make any effort to connect with the others in the dormitory."

"You have Pat and the shanty. It's understandable. Privacy is what we all want. If you have the space of a shanty, why would you want to include others?"

Ronny bristled. "We've had you and Reg around a lot."

"It's not a criticism, Ronny! Your shanty's been a lovely escape for me too! It's certainly going to be more primitive in Los Banos."

Ronny was looking close to tears.

"Come on kid! Just concentrate on the positives. Don't forget, I'll be missing the movies and talks and all that good stuff!" Anna declared.

Ronny was not to be placated. "There's certainly lots of organised activities here, but everything's imposed on us: the endless gramophone records on the loudspeakers, the endless queues and the endless noise." She slumped, her packing forgotten. "I'm sorry, I'm just miserable about you going." She tried to change gear. "I really do hope that Los Banos will be better for you."

"Marvin says so! I hope it's true, though his two notes could have been sweet talk to lure me there. He says there are two barracks that have been specially divided into cubicles for married couples. We'll have one. I'm excited about the idea of being able to have my own room with Marvin. It'll be great to be a family again."

Anna's bedding had gone on to Los Banos earlier that day, so their last night together was spent sharing Ronny's mattress. It was a crush, with the two children taking pride of place, and there was little sleep for the two friends.

The sound of reveille blared out over the loudspeaker at three o'clock the following morning. It was December 10th, and the 177 women and thirty men were to leave before dawn. Half the camp showed up to send them off in the dark. Supported by Pat and Reg, Ronny kept a brave face in front of Anna. When the final goodbyes were said, they were so hasty that the full impact of her loss did not hit her until she was back on her mattress again in the grey of the early morning.

— ✂ ✂ —

The days progressed towards the third Christmas Ronny had spent under Japanese duress. Internees thoughts were dominated by food. There was no lard, sugar, meat or soap to be had. Vegetable stews predominated the chow-line menu, with the occasional night when meat gravy was served on the ever-decreasing serving of rice. Peanut loaf was a favourite, which was baked rice covered with a thin layer of boiled peanuts. Internees were starting to starve, and skeletal shapes were emerging, especially in the men.

The Red Cross kits had been transferred from the warehouses to the camp library, awaiting the Japanese pleasure. It was an incendiary provocation Kato finally had to address.

One morning, word spread like wildfire that the military had come into camp to inspect the kits. Internees were ordered to carry outside the hundreds of large, cardboard cartons – each weighing over forty-five pounds – to line them up in front of the main building. Ronny joined the crowd that gathered quickly in the sunshine to see the reality of the fabled 'comfort kits'. Each carton contained four food parcels, and uniformed guards stood around smoking until the full complement of boxes was arrayed before them. There were literally hundreds of containers, and the excitement in the crowd mounted.

Ronny watched as the Japanese soldiers armed with chisels and knives tore open the packaging, upturning the kits onto the ground. To her horror, they then turned to the kits themselves and attacked them with the same vicious determination. Chisels penetrated cans of meat, fish and milk powder, at the sight of which the murmur from the crowds grew to a growl of anger. Bodies pressed forwards against the rope cordons, and the air became charged with aggression as they watched the violation of the American aid helplessly. Jeers and shouts were directed at the men in khaki. The hungry crowd strained ever closer to them, and, sensing their danger, the soldiers hesitated and stopped their attack.

Upon a command, the Japanese turned their attention to the tins and packets, ripping off the labels, which they then inspected carefully.

A voice near her growled, "Why are they doing that?"

"They're looking for writing on the backs of them!" someone else explained.

A woman whined, "But it's the Red Cross! It's crazy to think that they'd try to get messages in. Anyway, these men can't read English!"

"Why are they chucking out all the packets of cigarettes?" another man queried.

An aged man with a young voice answered, "I heard that they discovered 'propaganda' at Bilibid prison printed onto the labels of the Old Gold packets. It was some publicity thing about freedom and our heritage, nothing specific, but enough to get the entire shipment confiscated."

"It's so petty. They should be ashamed!" the whining woman added.

Ronny had been scanning the military presence. She shouted over the crowd's noise, "*I notice Kato isn't here!*"

"Nor is his second in command! They're conveniently away for the afternoon!" declared the aged man.

Ronny knew she was experiencing something monumental. She was part of the anger of this impotent mass and was swept up in the fervour of it. The thin line of fear was the only thing that stopped the crowd, and it could have flowed over so easily into outright violence. Her heart was racing, and her legs were shaking.

As the shouts and calls tailed off, a deafening silence descended on the crowd, which held its own menace. For the watchers, time stood still, and the soldiers lingered over their task. The sun beat down, but not one of the crowd moved away from the scene.

Finally, a group of internees were assigned to reassemble the opened parcels once the cigarettes and labels had been removed. They did the best they could with the damaged cardboard. Ronny noticed that, as well as damaged tins, food such as sugar, dried fruit and prunes that were contained in paper had their packaging torn, and ants were making their way into the open kits. She stood, thirsty and weak, her eyes glued to the scattered debris of good food that was out of her reach.

Only when the soldiers had departed did the Finance and Supplies Committee members take over and dispersed the crowd. Apparently, there were more cartons still in storage to be opened on the following days.

—⊬—⊬—

Later that afternoon, everyone in the annex was presented with four of the kits.

Ronny, Pat and Catherine sat on the floor and took it in turns to draw out goodies slowly, like children on Christmas morning. The Americans had done them proud.

"Corned beef, Spam, ham, salmon!" announced Ronny.

Many with their labels removed had to be guessed at.

"Twelve tins of butter and four cheeses!" speculated Pat.

"Powdered milk, jam and prunes!" Ronny suggested.

"Packets of chocolate and tins of coffee!"

"Sugar cubes, bouillon powder and soap!"

Ronny was laughing and crying. "Vitamin pills! And there's more to come when you get yours, Pat!"

The sight was overwhelming. A cornucopia the like of which they had not seen for two years. Catherine was confused by her parents being hysterical over the packages, and Ronny recognised that she was fascinated by the packaging, but the contents meant nothing to her. The tins and packets were small, but more precious to them than jewels. They cried out to be eaten, immediately!

"We've got to be clever about this, Ronny. Of course, we're going to give ourselves a treat, but we need to make it last," said Pat.

"Let's just have something to reward ourselves with. Please! I can't think straight until I have something in my stomach. Then we can be sensible," Ronny responded.

After much deliberation, they chose a tin of Spam, which they followed up with one cube each of the condensed chocolate. Catherine relished her small portion of the meat with much smacking of lips, but her first taste of chocolate was a shock, and she spat it out, much to the amazement of her parents. Afterwards, they settled down to a mug of real coffee. The smell alone was heavenly.

Pat broke the companionable pause. "I've been put on guard duty for three hours tonight."

Ronny gaped. "Guard duty?"

"Well, patrol duty really. The Department of Patrols is giving all shanty dwellers three-hour shifts throughout the night from now on. It's because of the escalation of Filipinos breaking in to the camp to steal things."

"I heard about that. Men have been coming in over the wall during the night?"

"Yes, there was a young chap caught a couple of nights ago, and they tried to frighten him a bit before putting him back over the wall. He was lucky it was us who found him rather than the Nips. The Department of Patrols is having to tighten up security."

"How sad that it's come to this. They must be desperate to break in to camp to steal. We've so little. What do you think it says about the conditions outside?"

Ronny watched Catherine in her new game, rolling tins up and down the floor. She was struck by the irony that, whereas she and Pat knew these containers were potential life savers, for the child they were gleaming, new toys.

"Since Kato's forbidden the Red Cross food to be shared with families outside camp, men will be selling their kits to give money to their wives in town," Pat divulged.

"There'll always be rich internees who'll buy it. It's so unfair," stated Ronny.

Pat's forehead was furrowed. "Poppet, we're going to have to hide this food. We can allow ourselves one or two things a day to make it last as long as we can. The perishable stuff will have to be eaten first, before the ants find it."

Ronny looked around. "Can we bury it under the shanty?"

"It's a bit obvious, but I don't think we have any choice. At least it wouldn't be easy pickings by night raiders."

"I don't like the idea of you patrolling! Your night vision isn't great, and it means that the shanty will be left unprotected. How I wish I were allowed to sleep here."

"I've been approached several times to let another man share the shanty."

Her response was immediate and from the gut. "No! It's ours! We're not sharing!"

"Ronny, we may not have a choice! They're expecting nearly 300 folk in from Davao, any day now. The Housing Committee is tearing its hair out to accommodate everyone."

"I know that! Anna and Daisy were hardly out before someone had their space!"

"How would you feel if I asked Reg to move in with us?"

"Reg? What are you talking about? I don't want to share our home. We're cramped enough as it is, what with my sewing and Catherine's things."

"Reg could be the solution. He's our friend, and we know how busy he keeps himself, so he wouldn't be here much! He'd probably just sleep here, and then we could take it in turns to protect our shanty."

Ronny struggled to sort out her thoughts. Reg was certainly an answer, but there was something in her relationship with him that she found difficult to manage. Ronny was never totally at ease with him. She found herself trying too hard in his company, and then would feel exposed and silly. Ronny also hated the thought that Reg would sleep here when she could not. She remained mute.

"What do you think, Ronny? Inevitably, someone will be placed with me, and I'd prefer it to be Reg. We'd be doing him a favour. Shall I ask him?"

Pat would not let her sidestep the issue, and she knew it made sense. Seated on the floor with an array of packets and tins surrounding her, she knew she had much to be thankful for. They had a supply of food for as many days as they could make it last, and the promise of more clothes, shoes and medical supplies still to be distributed. Finally, she gave her consent.

TWENTY-TWO

30th December 1943

730 days in captivity

Christmas arrived, accompanied by a succession of carol services and concerts. Santa Claus made an appearance, and everyone was cheerful, especially following the delivery of the Red Cross packages. Ronny, Pat, Reg and Catherine exchanged little gifts. Ronny created a shirt for Pat and a dress for her daughter, and hand-painted a little wooden box for Reg. The package line brought in a large amount of parcels for the fortunate, although no visitors were allowed.

Ronny mused, "Considering how tough it is for the Filipinos, I'm stunned at their generosity."

Pat responded, "I'd feel ashamed to accept gifts from them."

"They're all Roman Catholics. I don't mean their religion's behind it; I think it's their nature to be generous."

Reg seemed much in demand over the period, but Ronny and Pat chose a quieter time. They took Catherine to the double film show of a Donald Duck film and *Dumbo*, and, although the little girl nodded off, her parents thoroughly enjoyed it.

Sharing the shanty with Reg was not as difficult as Ronny had imagined. The only evidence of his presence was the knotted mosquito net hanging from the ceiling over his rolled bed mat and a small pile of possessions. He took himself off during the day, and she was happier knowing Pat had company at night. She enjoyed their conversations in passing and found she was disappointed when he wasn't around. There were material advantages too. Reg produced an endless supply of whatever tools they needed and brought with him a locking metal box, which they used to store their Red Cross allocation securely. They had almost reached the end of their Red Cross supplies by then, but congratulated themselves that they had been self-disciplined. Many had glutted themselves initially, and suffered stomach ache and no lasting satisfaction.

─────

One morning, Ronny was surprised to find both men still in the shanty when she arrived, and realised quickly that something had happened.

Reg, clearly agitated, only acknowledged her with a nod, before stating, "I heard it directly from a committee member. It's really bad news. The camp's been placed under the military department of the Imperial Army. We will no longer be governed by civilians."

Pat was lingering, halfway out of the door, when he asked, "What does that mean?"

"The military will supervise all prison camps and civilian internee camps directly. Although the guards have been drawn from the military, their actions have, up till now, been restricted by civilian leadership. General Morimoto will be in direct charge," explained Reg.

The two men looked tense.

Ronny strove to understand. "Yes, but how will this affect us?"

"I've absolutely no doubt that things will toughen up considerably. For a start, all activities will be restricted and permits certainly will be cancelled. Any civilian leniency will be stamped out once our status is changed," posited Reg.

Pat was late for his refuse shift, but was reluctant to go. "I was told the guards at the gates were doubled yesterday."

Reg continued, "They've already announced a change in the distribution system. Instead of the per capita allowance, the army will furnish us with supplies directly, no longer giving the Finance and Supplies Committee cash to buy our own."

"Could that be in our favour with this inflation?" queried Pat.

"No, Pat, the opposite! A committee man told me what's been proposed, and I jotted it down." Reg reached for his note pad and read. "For adults per day there'll be 100 grams of fish; 400 grams of some form of cereal, made up from corn, rice, beans or *camote*; 200 grams of vegetables; 20 grams of sugar; 20 grams of cooking oil; and 1 gram of tea. Luxuries of meat, eggs, milk, coffee, and vegetables such as tomatoes or onions won't be provided. Children under ten will only get half the adult allowance. There'll be no special allowance for the old or sick."

Pat grimaced. "That sounds serious! I'm late, old man, but we'll talk again after work." With a perfunctory peck on Ronny's cheek, he left leaving her to study Reg closely. Their friend was noticeably pale and distracted.

She queried, "Talking in grams is difficult for me to follow. Once the kitchens have prepared the food, will it be so different from what we have now?"

"Ronny, don't act dumb! It's not just the food! You've no idea what it's going to be like under the military. You've no idea what we have to fear!" There was a sharpness in his voice unlike anything she had heard before. The Reg she knew was always in control. She and Pat sometimes smiled behind his back at his love for exact statistics, but they relied on him never to get ruffled.

"What are you suggesting? We're still civilians and not military."

He started to pace the room seeking an outlet for suppressed energy, then spun and hissed impatiently, "Open your eyes! Being a civilian makes not one iota of difference to the military. You've no idea how they can behave."

Ronny was stung. "I do have an idea. I've seen the beatings."

"Beatings? This is a holiday camp compared to what our military are surviving."

"Do we actually know what's going on? All we have is rumours."

Reg glared at her. "How can you be so naïve?"

Ronny reacted to his tone of voice and responded instinctively. "So, you're the authority suddenly? What do you know?"

Reg shouted. "I've been there! I've been their prisoner! Believe me, I do know what it's like and I would rather take my own life than go through that again."

She was shaken to the core. "Reg, I had no idea! You never said a word. I'm so sorry."

The words then came tumbling out of his mouth as if a dam had been breached. "Don't ever underestimate what they can do. They are brutal."

Shame flooded her. How could she have been so unaware that he was hiding a great hurt? She had never seen this side of Reg before.

She could not bear it, so she stepped forwards and put her arms round him. After the briefest hesitation, he returned the hug. He was only a little taller than her, and they stood entwined in an embrace. He made no sound, but she could feel the deep suppressed trembling that shook his body. When she looked in his face, his eyes were haunted, and there were tears on his cheeks. They stood like this until his breathing slowed.

"Do you want to tell me what happened? Can you talk about it?" she questioned.

He stepped back and chose his words. He paced again, but this time slowly and his voice came from far away. "Panay wasn't taken until April 1942. We were too remote an island to bother them much. The Japanese military took us to a municipal building in Jaro, along with some Filipinos. There were no mattresses or mosquito nets, and no food except rice and a few bananas. There weren't many of us. A month later, we were transferred to the provincial jail in Iloilo. Other prisoners joined us until we were about fifty in total." He stopped.

Ronny felt compelled to prompt him. "What was the jail like?"

"It was revolting. The cells were dirty and far too cramped for all of us. The toilets were unspeakable. Water was unreliable. The jail was infested with vermin. When you can't get clean you become the host of vermin and become vermin yourself." His voice shook in disgust. "We were hungry all the time, and survived on a little rice and beans. The Filipinos were singled out by the Japanese for especially cruel treatment."

There was a flatness in Reg's tone, a disengagement. He continued, "We sorted out a routine amongst us to keep sane: cell cleaning, and meal and water distribution; anything to create a routine. There were seven Spanish priests amongst us, and they were impressive. And then, after a month, they left!"

"The priests left?"

"No, everyone! All the internees were transferred, except five of us. It was after the two British guys were shot!" Reg's voice broke up.

"They shot two Brits? Civilians? I don't understand!"

"Yes, civilians. They were friends of mine." Reg struggled for words and Ronny waited transfixed. Finally, he could speak again. "They left us. We were five men: three Brits, one Swiss and one Scottish/American. We were left in the jail under the military."

She waited, then asked, "How long did they hold you?"

"Seven months and twenty-eight days exactly."

"Why? Why you?"

Reg started to shake again, and Ronny urged him gently to drop to the floor where they sat leaning against the wall. She kissed him on the cheek and cradled him in her arms.

She heard his muffled voice saying, "The military don't need reasons. We were beaten with clubs. We were interrogated. Daily. We were tortured. We were starved. We were humiliated. We became nothing. I just wanted to die!"

"Oh Reg. Dear Reg. I'm so desperately sorry. I don't know what to say," murmured Ronny.

His voice was stifled and disjointed. "They wanted answers from us. Who knows why us? The Kempeitai thought we had information. Walter Saul, Jimmy Redfern, Gilbert Cullen, Max Iller and me."

"These men are in camp here?"

"Gilbert's a retired doctor; he's seventy-five years old. What happened to Japanese respect for elders? He's been in hospital ever since we arrived, and I doubt he'll ever come out." There was a long pause again. "The others are here. Max is Swiss and only twenty-five, so he probably survived the best of us. We never talk about it, even amongst ourselves."

What could Ronny possibly say? She continued to hold him. This morning, Reg had opened a door he preferred to keep closed and was, without doubt, already regretting the weakness. She had 1,000 questions she wanted to ask, or did not want to ask.

She tried asking something safe. "They finally let you rejoin your original group?"

"Yes. Last January, we were released suddenly. There was no explanation. We joined the group at the Central School in Iloilo under Commandant Yano. We were like scarecrows and desperately ill, but we had survived!" He drew away from her and gave a cracked, false laugh. "The internees thought that Yano was a cruel tyrant, playing vicious tricks on them, but he seemed lightweight to me. He was a civilian. We were transferred here in June. Everything that's happened since has felt insignificant in comparison!"

"Reg, does Pat know about this?"

"Pat may know something, but he's a wise man and doesn't ask questions. There is no gain in revisiting the past. I don't ever want to be singled out again." He moved away from her and crossed the room, regaining his own space.

She felt a tug of loss and wished he would rejoin her.

Reg continued, "I can be useful and busy here, and this gives me a chance to heal."

She could not help herself, but blurted out as she moved towards him, "You're an extraordinary human being. I can't bear to think they tried to break you."

He stared at her, with that disconcerting look that stripped her bare. "Ronny, if you want to help me, leave this conversation between ourselves. Talking about it isn't helpful."

"I'm so sorry. I wouldn't hurt you for the world." What could she say to someone who had experienced something so far outside her own small experience? She stepped forwards and hugged him again.

He mumbled, his mouth in her hair, "It's not your fault. I was upset and just needed to talk to you. Just promise me you'll keep your head down, Ronny. Pat knows how to do that, but you seem to have a problem. For my sake, please keep your head down!"

Something had passed between them that morning: an acknowledgement that they had some sort of special relationship. It was not till later, when the shock of Reg's disclosure had abated, that she wondered why the Japanese chose him to be investigated. Since the first time Ronny saw Reginald Winter Verney, she felt that he stood out amongst the herd. He was a natural leader who kept his own counsel. His obsession with statistics could be put down to his accountancy training, but she always felt that, even though he was happy to share his knowledge, there was much stored behind those intelligent eyes that he did not disclose. *Could he be in the intelligence services?* Ronny wondered. Surely, the very mannerisms that made him stand out meant he could not be an agent. Agents were chosen for their ability to blend in. Could the Japanese have got it right? One thing she was sure of was that Reg would never tell her.

When she saw him again that afternoon, she looked for some sign of their new relationship, but the waters had flattened out, and the self-contained man was back in place.

—⊱⊰—

It was the first day of February, and Ronny turned over to shut out the morning before the fog of sleep cleared. Then she distinctly heard the tune of 'Here Comes the Bride' blaring out over the camp speakers and remembered that her long-standing wish had come true. Finally, the Japanese had bowed to the inevitable, and women were to be allowed to sleep in shanties from that day forward.

She could not wait to leave the inhospitable dormitory and rose with a smile on her face. She had known about the commandant's decision for a week, so had already transferred most of her and Catherine's possessions. At first, Reg expressed concern about encroaching on their private space, but both Ronny and Pat begged him to stay. There would be little change in their arrangements in the shanty. The fact that they would all be sleeping under one roof was no problem, as camp life had killed any expectations of sexual intimacy or privacy. Catherine was excited to be joining her daddy and Uncle Reg, and moving-in day was a welcome transfer.

That afternoon, deep in thought, Ronny crossed the grass after her work shift only to be halted as a Japanese patrol crossed her path. The soldiers were grim and focused, and her eyes went to the fixed bayonets that were then attached permanently to their rifles. This was visible evidence of the change that had come over the camp in the last two weeks, and the men appeared unusually tense that day. It was only later that the significance of the soldiers emerged when an agitated Pat burst into the shanty.

"I saw it all. I thought there was going to be a riot," he declared.

"Calm down, Pat. Saw what?" queried Ronny.

"The package line! We knew there were going to be problems when they announced they were going to close it, but their timing was unbelievable! On Sunday afternoon! Everyone was trying to get their orders brought in."

"Slow down."

He took a breath. "The final deliveries had been ordered for this weekend, so the streets were jammed with crowds planning to deliver packages and goods. There was a huge crowd outside and in. I was just passing the entrance, and, at that moment, the Japs decided to close the line!"

"That was a real power statement! What happened?"

"The Finance and Supplies Committee tried pleading with the commandant, but to no avail. The Filipinos outside just kind of settled down and waited. They just went silent and tense before they hunkered down. No one was moving."

"Were there internee families out there?"

Pat was genuinely upset. "Of course! I caught a glimpse when the doors were opened. They were just sitting in the road, rows and rows of them, just inches from the armed sentries. I was scared that the Nips would start shooting. All the crowd were."

"I can imagine! What happened?"

"The standoff must have gone on for well over an hour, as nothing had changed when I returned the same way later. The committee members were getting nowhere and the people outside seemed to have no intention of going home. The mood was getting really ugly."

"Whose mood? The Nips?"

"No ours! There was a real swell of anger in the crowd waiting inside. You could feel it in your bones, as if something was going to burst."

"I know what you're talking about! I felt it when the Japanese were messing with our food packages, and we could do nothing but watch. It felt like we were in a pressure cooker!"

"Yes, the same feeling exactly! I really thought there was going to be a massacre, Ronny." He gestured impotently. "The Nips must have felt it too, as, suddenly, the sergeant in charge waved his arms and said, 'I will let them come in. My gift to the camp!' The guards stood down, and the Filipinos poured in to deliver the goods. The tension changed to a real carnival atmosphere. Many internees even managed to talk to their families through holes cut in the *sawali* matting."

"And the guards didn't stop them?"

"No, they did nothing! It was an extraordinary sight. I couldn't stop watching."

"It sounds as if the Filipinos won this round!"

"Oh, the Japs will close the line tomorrow without a doubt. The crowds outside were so strong and quiet, and loyal to us. I don't know what the Yanks have done to deserve such loyalty!"

"Yes, we're better off than they are, and yet they're still putting themselves in danger trying to help. Would we do the same? I'm ashamed to say, I think not!"

They fell silent. They had not benefitted personally from the package line, but the closing of it meant that all internees would be relying on the chow line for food, which would mean less for all. More importantly, the feeling of isolation was the biggest blow to their spirits. Ronny thought about Reg's warning about the military takeover, and this deliberate action felt as ominous as he had predicted.

—⊦— ⊦⊦—

The two men had decided that moving-in day warranted a special celebration and somehow had conjured up a tiny cake to share after the evening meal. An excited Catherine had been tucked into 'her' corner to sleep, and they settled down for a relaxed evening. Ronny was content, seated between the two men, knowing that no curfew was going to drag her away.

They were talking about the shift in the internees from able-bodied to infirm and the increase in the number of the seriously ill. Filipino doctors and nurses were no longer permitted to enter the camp. Total isolation was the obvious goal.

Pat giggled unexpectedly. "Ah, but we've got our secret weapon!"

"What secret weapon? What are you talking about?" asked Ronny.

"Not what, but whom!" Pat put his finger to the side of his nose. "We have our Haughwout!"

Ronny looked at Pat more closely. There was no mistaking it, Pat was tipsy! She had been unaware that there had been secret drinking going on.

"Our saviour Haughwout is a parasitologist, *par excellence!*" exclaimed Pat.

Reg joined in. "Haughwout is a protozoologist, beyond measure!"

"Here's to Haughwout!" Pat declared.

And the two men raised their glasses in a salute.

Ronny's response was complicated. It was lovely to see Pat relaxed and happy, but alarm bells were ringing that could not be ignored! The Pat of old, without a doubt, liked his liquor, and there had been times when he had accused her of being a wet blanket for restricting his intake. Ronny also enjoyed a cocktail or two, but it was historically evident that she had the stronger head. She never lost it as swiftly and completely as he did, and he never knew when to stop.

Quick as lightning, Ronny seized Pat's glass. "I'll drink to him!" she stated, and, before her husband could stop her, she downed the glass of water. The explosion in her head rocked her. This was firewater indeed.

She spluttered, "What in heaven's name is this? Great Scott, it's strong!" She laughed at the two shocked faces. "How long did you think you could keep that a secret?"

Reg responded first. "It's not how it looks. This isn't a regular thing! I'm the guilty party, as I've been saving it for a special event, and this is it!"

"How lovely! But you didn't think to include me?" she enquired.

"Pat said you didn't drink!" Reg offered.

"Not to excess, for sure, and this stuff's formidable! Or perhaps it's just been too long and I can't remember! What is it?" Ronny asked.

"Another one?" was Reg's response.

"I think I'll pass, thanks!" She eyed Pat as she saw him reach for his glass again and down another one. She was about to remonstrate, but this was a special night and she knew that Pat rapidly would succumb to bleary quiet. Reg was another matter;

he appeared totally unaffected by the drink. Reg obviously thought that Pat had drunk enough, and corked the bottle and put it away.

"It's a clear native rum. I was given it for a favour a few weeks ago," Reg explained.

"You sound as if there's a lot of it around!"

"Oh, it's common enough amongst the shanty aristocracy! The Nips will never be able to stop it coming in. Until he was caught, the commandant's Filipino chauffeur was bringing in four or five bottles a day! There's no chance of that now the package line's closing!"

Pat was in a world of his own and sang softly in a high falsetto voice, "They can't close the package line!"

Reg's glance dismissed Pat and concentrated on Ronny. "It's just another step to isolate us. I warned you that life would change drastically once the military took over."

"Yes, you warned me!" agreed Ronny. "I heard that they're threatening to abolish the Executive Committee, so we won't have any representation. How are the Japs going to make it work?"

"With fear, that's how! There won't be even pretence that we have any control. Food will be cut back again."

"But we've already only half the calories per day that we need. They can't expect us to do physical work on that."

"They do and they will, even if we're starving! I heard today that they're ordering us to build a barracks for them at the front gate."

"Come on, old man, where've you put that bottle?" broke in Pat.

Ronny started at the sound of his voice. She had almost forgotten him. This was an old pattern from a distant past, and she was sad that her first evening was to be ruined because of alcohol. With a sigh, she turned to remonstrate with him.

TWENTY-THREE

———✁——✁———

2nd March 1944
793 days in captivity

Ronny lay flat on the floor and watched the heavy wooden-paddled fan rotating slowly, gathering its strength till it became a hazy whir above her.

"What's wrong? Are you all right? I didn't know anyone was waiting," said a voice, unexpectedly.

Ronny sat up smartly, embarrassed. Dr Beulah Allen stood above her.

"I'm sorry. I'm fine. I shouldn't have let myself in, but I couldn't resist five minutes under a fan! Watching it has made me quite dizzy!" Ronny explained before she scrambled to her feet and smiled guiltily. Her friend did not respond.

"How can I help?" Beulah said wearily. She looked distracted and drawn.

"It's Catherine's birthday soon, and I wanted to invite you and the boys to a little party for her. I'm hoping the Stewart family can come."

Ronny studied her old friend, who was grim-faced and tense. It had been harder to keep in touch with Beulah than she had imagined, as the doctor's workload had tripled since the days in Baguio, when she had found time to lead the ill-destined suffragette movement. Letting herself into her friend's inner sanctum had not been a smart idea after all.

"I'm sorry, Ronny. It's not good timing," stated Beulah.

"No, I'm sorry. It was presumptuous. I'll catch you another time!" Ronny declared, but the slump of the other woman's shoulders brought her to a halt. "What's the matter, Beulah?" she asked softly.

Beulah's resistance melted in the face of her friend. "I've just been talking to the two army doctors whom they brought in from Bilibid prison. They're nice fellows: Captain Bloom and Captain Noell. I was trying to get news of Sam. It's been nearly two years since the fall of Bataan. I've been so worried, and it's been my first chance to get news of him, but now I wish I hadn't asked."

"Did they have news of him?"

"They couldn't tell me anything about Sam specifically, but they knew what happened to his division. They were reluctant to tell me, but I guess they knew I'd learn about it at some stage. Oh Ronny! I can't bear it. What went on since the surrender is awful, and Sam's division couldn't have escaped it. I remember, way back, Sam got a message to me that our troops were poorly equipped, and physically and morally exhausted. These doctors told me the Japanese have captured over 70,000 American and Filipino soldiers!"

Beulah paused to pick her words. "They were forced to march for five days, about sixty miles, north from Bataan to San Fernando. Those devils made them march in the heat of the day. They took away their canteens, and forced them to drink water from irrigation ditches or buffalo wallows. They were only fed thin rice gruel twice a day and, of course, dysentery was rife. It was cruelty in the extreme. Thousands of people died. Are you sure you want to hear this, Ronny?"

"We all need to know. For their sakes, we need to know."

"They told me that our guys arrived every night at campsites where they found hundreds of dead or dying men who had been left behind from the previous day. They were forced to move or bury them to make room before they could lie down for the night. The places were filthy, and, every morning, the men incapable of moving were left behind. If they tried to help a mate on the march, they were beaten, bayoneted and even beheaded. Dear God. They told me about a brutal massacre en route at Pantingan. Five days, the march went on for, and thousands died."

Ronny thought her friend had finished, but Beulah continued, "Even when they got to San Fernando, the horror didn't stop. They were forced into corrugated iron boxes for transportation to Camp O'Donnell; 125 men sandwiched in a box. They told me that hundreds more died at the camp of dysentery and exhaustion." Her voice broke. "Sam must have ended up there. He's got to be there!" She dissolved into tears, a broken woman. "It happened two years ago, and I've only just heard the details! I've no idea if my husband is alive or dead."

Ronny hugged her. "Your Sam's a survivor. You've always said so. He's got you and two beautiful sons to live for. He'll come back, Beulah. You'll find him." Her words sounded hollow, but Ronny's determination was clear. She had to believe that there would be an end to this nightmare, or what was the point in going on? Beulah had to believe that her husband would survive and the stories of atrocities were exaggerations.

The silence that bound the two women was encroached upon by internees gathering outside the clinic, and Beulah needed to compose herself for her job. They had one last hug and the promise to make more time for each other, before Ronny slipped out into the blast of heat and humidity.

———— ⸻ ————

It was St Patrick's Day, Catherine's second birthday, and Ronny wanted to put a smile on her daughter's face. There was so little that made her smile. With her grey eyes, curly lashes and wispy, blonde hair, she could have been a pretty child, but for the obvious signs of malnutrition. Her little tummy protruded; she was growing up bandy-legged, which was evidence of rickets; and her teeth were a mess. Ronny had learned to accept all this, but the look of suspicion in her daughter's eyes broke her heart.

Ronny had a plan. One of the wealthier shanty owners had a cat that had produced kittens, and Ronny bartered a sewing job for the prettiest tom. She was excited by her idea, but knew Pat would not be happy. He would consider it madness to take responsibility for a pet in their situation. She knew it was madness too, but persuaded herself that the cat would only need a little milk and a bed, and would fend for itself once it was old enough. Pat could deny Catherine nothing, so Ronny decided that she would live with his displeasure, after the event!

She squared her shoulders, concentrated on her daughter and handed her the cardboard box. Pat raised his eyebrows in enquiry.

"Happy birthday, sweetheart. This is from Daddy and Mummy, and all yours to keep," Ronny announced.

The box shook and a little mew gave the game away. Catherine's eyes widened, she looked uncertain, and Ronny prayed under her breath. Solemnly, the little girl investigated and then let out a squeak of delight, as two little black ears and two bright eyes emerged from the box.

Catherine looked straight to her father. "Mine?"

Ronny watched as Pat's mouth fell open, but, to his credit, he gave no inkling to his daughter that this addition to the family was unwelcome.

"All yours, Twopence. What will you call him?" asked Pat.

Ronny's relief was short-lived as his glance at her was cold.

"Tom," was the little girl's immediate response. She hugged the kitten tight and gave her parents her long-awaited, gap-toothed smile. The deed was done and no matter what the fallout, Tom's place in the family was established.

—⁂—

As the months passed, Ronny suffered from increasing bouts of illness and fatigue, and this intensified her fear of her oppressors. The increased military presence cast a dark shadow over the camp, and the restrictions of the Japanese military became more and more onerous. By then, there were roll calls twice a day, and they were much more formal than previously. The loudspeakers barked out orders from the commandant for increased productivity on a daily basis. Even those moments when she could lose herself at a concert or film showing were curtailed abruptly by announcements of more demands from the Japanese. The camp was to be further isolated from the outside world, as more bamboo matting was erected within the original walls to cut off sightlines into the street. Supplies of gas and electricity became more sporadic, and hunger was a constant stalking companion. The camp was sealed with yet more barbed wire; the screw was tightening and spirits were lowered accordingly.

—⁂—

One evening, when Catherine was asleep, Reg was entertaining Ronny. She needed her spirits lifting and she thought he was pulling her leg. She laughed, but his face remained straight. This was the funniest thing that she had heard for a long time. Pat's name had been put forward to join the team of cooks!

"This is ridiculous! Pat can't boil an egg! If there's one person less competent than me in the kitchen, it's got to be him!"

Reg explained, "It's not his culinary skills they want, but his honesty! The cooks are in trouble with the Finance and Supplies Committee. The first cook's team walked out and the second's given a week's notice! The committee's got to recruit, and fast!"

"Everyone knows the cooks get privileges, and it's a closed-shop set-up. What's made them strike? It must be something serious."

"As you say, the kitchen workers have been untouchable, but they went too far this time. They helped themselves to some of the ham sent by the International YMCA to celebrate the emperor's birthday. The committee found out and sent two guards into the kitchen to monitor them."

"Well, good for the committee!" Ronny was still visualising Pat being approached to be part of the elite group. It really was too funny.

Reg ignored her sniggers. "The cooks believe that their job's a tough one. They do a disagreeable job in unbearable temperatures for long hours, so they consider that they deserve their perks. Most are ex-marine catering staff and putting two internee guards in their kitchen was considered the ultimate insult, so they staged the walk out."

"A bluff?"

"Well, one they've lost! The committee is adamant!"

"So, Pat's name has been put forward? This is good news for us, Reg." She smiled thinking it would be bad news for the camp, unless Pat was closely supervised!

"It's no picnic, Ronny! Because, with the lack of gas, they're relying on the wood and charcoal stoves they built during the typhoon. Pat is going to have his work cut out."

"I think it's to our advantage! He'll get to stop his refuse shift, and he'll have access to extra food to bring home."

"His honesty is why Pat's been chosen! I don't have to tell you that he's not going to bring food home!"

We'll see about that, Ronny thought grimly.

At that moment, the subject of the conversation appeared, looking grim and breathless from his night-patrol shift.

Pat blurted, "I've just heard they're going to pull down all the shanties that are too close to the wall! That may mean us!"

Ronny could not believe her ears. "What! They can't do that!"

Reg looked shocked, "Are you sure? What's the thinking behind that?"

"All shanties within ten feet of the wall are going to be pulled down in the next month! Two hundred shanties, apparently. They say that it's to stop messages going out over the wall, but also to stop Filipinos from climbing in to steal. It will make patrolling easier."

Ronny was instantly close to tears. "They can't take our home!"

She looked around at their beloved space, which was so essential for their emotional wellbeing. *It's not going to happen,* she told herself fiercely. She let out an unconscious groan; sunk, in misery, with her back against the wall, hugging her legs to her chest; and heard the voices of the two men as if from a distance.

"It seems the building of the barracks at the front gate is to go ahead, and they're talking of digging some sort of moat within the camp. It doesn't make sense. There's more barbed wire going up too. The commandant's ordering the internees to do the work!" Pat clarified.

Reg's deep voice answered, "The commandant will find problems there. How can we be expected to work when we're so malnourished? The Work Committee knows there are very few men left who are up to doing physical work."

"The Japanese keep contradicting themselves and seem to be panicking now. Everything points to a rescue by the Americans. I'm surprised that they're still allowing *The Manila Tribune* in."

Reg scoffed, "That four-page rag! The Nips think it's safe because they edit it! They've never cottoned on that we learn more from the paper's refutations of 'false' Allied reports than any other source. I imagine even that rag will go soon."

"I think the military are beginning to feel really threatened, Reg. Why else would they be making such efforts to increase camp security?"

"All we have to work on is rumours, but I'm sure the tide is turning, and the Yanks will be coming soon. Even the Japanese are reinforcing that with all the security measures they're instigating!"

Pat's lighter voice continued, "I think the military are creating a stronghold for themselves here. The more secure they make this place, the better off they would be if they had to retreat inside it. I saw the copy of Roosevelt's speech that's been going the rounds, and he says the war will be over by next Christmas! Without a doubt, the Nips are feeling the pressure!"

"Are you suggesting that they'll use us as human shields? Or that they'll simply get rid of us and keep this place for themselves?"

The men dropped their voices instinctively, but Ronny was listening intently.

"They won't have to do much to eliminate us; we're starving to death as it is," said Pat.

The reflective silence was broken by Reg. "The commandant's expecting the internees to sign an oath of loyalty."

"Anything we sign isn't worth the paper it's written on, as it's done under duress. I'll sign anything."

Ronny shut off the conversation. She loved her precious home, and the threat to pull it down overwhelmed all the other difficulties the men were talking about. She looked around at her domain. The coconut-shell lights threw out a soft light, and the men's shadows danced gently on the walls. Catherine, in her corner, was curled up on the little patchwork-cotton mat, her figure appearing diffused by the mosquito net that hung from the hook above her. She clutched her battered bear and, with her thumb in her mouth, slept on. Tom kitten was sleeping in his box. The silky knots of the mosquito nets were hanging above their mattresses, with Reg's over in the furthest corner. She looked at the bookcase full of treasured, old friends, and the chess-set figures placed incongruously on the highly painted, little table. The indispensable folding chairs were stacked against the redundant charcoal-fired cooker. Filipino baskets held their few clothes and possessions, and, in the dimmed light, blended into the matting on the floor. This quiet haven housed four lives and was, in reality, her little family's first and only home.

She let out a sob of despair. "I can put up with anything, but they can't take our home!"

It was Reg who squatted down and put his arm round Ronny's shoulders. He said, "The commandant changes his mind every few days. Do you remember the debacle when the Japanese wanted to use the swimming pool to breed fish, rather than for water storage? That idea lasted only a couple of days. This will be another one of those, you'll see! Don't despair, Ronny. We'll get through this."

She smiled, grateful for his protective words, but no one could assuage the fear that gripped her heart.

—✳ ✳—

Ronny massaged her legs as she sat on the floor with Catherine in Beulah's waiting room. She was worried. The loss of sensation in her feet was barely detectable at first. By then, she had stubbed toes that were once sure-footed and no longer relied on their messages to get off burning stone paths. When she first noticed the creeping lack of sensation, she was not concerned, only a little surprised. The soles of her feet felt as if they were protected by a layer of cotton wool beneath the skin, accompanied by a not-unpleasant tingling. She only became worried when fluid started to accumulate in her legs and ankles, and, dictated by this tightening band of fluid, her movements became limited. At first, all righted itself after a night's sleep, but the day came when a night's sleep made no difference, and she started to worry in earnest.

When her turn came, Beulah Allen smiled at her. "What's bothering you, Ronny?"

"I feel as if my body's turning against me. I was getting used to my legs and ankles being swollen, but now I'm getting concerned about my hands too. I'm scared that it will get worse."

The doctor examined her carefully. "Of course malnutrition's at the core of this. You'll not be surprised to hear its beri-beri, due to lack of thiamine."

No, Ronny was not surprised, only terrified!

Beulah continued, "It's unpleasant, but it's not life-threatening. Your discomfort's aggravated by the humidity. I could tell you to put your feet up, but I know it's impossible. In a different world, we could put you right pretty quickly with a good diet of vegetables, eggs and meat."

"Is Catherine at risk of catching it?" Ronny queried.

"It's not something you can catch. It's your body's response to the deficiency. I wish I could do something for you, but I can't! You aren't alone; about a third of the camp is down with it."

Ronny came clean. "Beulah, I'm frightened. I've seen people in a really scary state. They look totally bloated with fluid, as if they're about to burst. Is that where I'm heading?"

"No Ronny. There're two types of beri-beri. The people you've noticed have the wet sort. They, poor dears, are really suffering. They can put on sixty pounds of fluid in the course of a day. It's all water. They have to have the fluid drawn off them by puncturing them, and it's not always successful. You're lucky. Your beri-beri is the dry kind, which will only affect your extremities and possibly your face."

"My face?"

"I won't lie to you. It's possible. Your face could become puffy. But I can only reiterate that, when you get the vitamins you need, you'll make a full recovery."

Ronny said bitterly, "There's not much chance of that then, is there?"

Beulah looked hard at her and then turned her attention to the little girl. "How is Catherine doing?"

Ronny knew she had gained nothing except for a medical name to put to her plight. With a sigh, she started to talk about her daughter. "She's as well as can be expected. We never got that milk and eggs in May that the commandant promised for the children. To be honest, I worry most about what's going on in her mind. How does she make sense of all this? How will it affect her long term?" She looked at the doctor over Catherine's head.

"Children bounce, Ronny. They adapt. Just give her as much stability as you and Pat can manage, and try to always be there for her. You two are her core strength, and, emotionally, she'll take her lead from you. That's all you can do. As for your beri-beri, we'll keep an eye on it."

Ronny looked at her feet dubiously and wriggled her toes. The only sensation she could feel was the tingly obstruction as her then pudgy toes responded sluggishly. She rotated her feet in the limited circle she could manage by then. She just had to pray that her face would not be affected. *Please,* she prayed to her gods. *Please spare my face.*

TWENTY-FOUR

———⊦—⊦———

25th May 1944

877 days in captivity

The white sampaguita flowers released their distinctive scent into the warm air, and Ronny inhaled the mixture of dust and light perfume. She and Catherine were on an expedition to inspect the gash of reclaimed land that ran along the north boundary wall of the campus. The vacant space replaced the 144 homes that had been dismantled and moved, and the only indication of the previous community was then scattered in the baked mud. Clearing it had been a mammoth task, as the shanties were forced to either huddle closer to their neighbours or totally relocate. Ronny had kept her head low and stayed at home, listening to the sounds of others' lives being torn apart. Despite reassurances that her shanty was safe, she believed doggedly that she needed to remain present to stop the destructive swathe from encompassing her home. Within two months, the ordered clearing of the ten-foot passage had been accomplished and she knew the shanty was safe.

Catherine picked her way carefully along the uneven track, lingering whenever a flower or beetle deserved closer inspection. Gardens had been trampled underfoot, and the little girl squatted down and lifted tenderly the broken heads of red and yellow canna lilies. She brought the broken heads to Ronny, who gathered them gently to display for one extra day of life. She hoped that the land would be used productively for growing more food, which was a project that she would endorse!

Mother and daughter meandered slowly down the cleared strip, with flowers in their hands. Amazingly, there was no other person in sight. In the heat of the day, for these few minutes, she could hear no sounds of the burgeoning population of the camp. It was bliss. Catherine was quietly content in her world of exploration, and Ronny, watching, envied her innocence. She thought about the differences from what she experienced in Camp Holmes and how she missed the laughter she had shared with the women in the baby house. Humour had helped in every situation, and she knew she had changed. Social interaction was a thing of the past, and she made no attempt to mix with people by then, even for the occasional game of bridge. Catherine, Pat and the rarely seen Beulah were the only people she was comfortable with. And Reg, of course!

As Catherine was absorbed in watching a trail of busy ants, Ronny rested her back against a sturdy banana tree that was putting out its first blossoms in defiance at its close shave. Ronny thought of Reg. She thought about the way his eyes seemed to strip her soul bare, about the little mannerism of sleeking his hair back from his face when he was disconcerted. She thought about his clever, tapering fingers; his extraordinary ability to retain facts; and his secretiveness. It was, by then, Reg she turned to for advice, entertainment and comfort. She wondered if she was as important to him as he was to her. Ronny frowned. This was dangerous territory, and she briskly called Catherine and continued on her walk.

Her mood changed as she switched to thoughts of Pat. Things were not good between them, and she thought about the row they'd had the previous night. It had started after the evening meal, with a surprise statement from Pat.

"It's not good enough, Ronny. We can't go on like this," he declared.

"What do you mean?" questioned Ronny.

"Your habit of excluding me, as if I have no say in matters that should involve both of us."

"You're paranoid! I haven't the faintest idea what you're talking about!"

"You no longer consult me about anything. I'm just the mug who does what he's told! We don't talk any more."

He stared at her, and she glowered back, not knowing which way this was going to go and feeling guilty.

He continued, "You just think that we'll all fit in with your whims. We're supposed to be in this together, but it feels like a one-way street to me! The cat is a prime example."

Pat was a slow burner, but this was ridiculous!

Ronny countered, "I wondered how long it would be before you brought that up! It's been over two months. Yes, the kitten was my idea, and it was a good one."

"But it wasn't your sole decision to make! If you don't consider my opinion counts, what about Reg's? Did you think of consulting him? He lives in our home too, you know? Did you ask him what he thought?"

There was a silence.

"I thought not!" Pat stated.

"But look at how much Catherine loves Tom! She'll never forget this gift!" She added an afterthought, "Reg had no objection anyway."

"Of course Catherine would love Tom! But we have to make sure the cat is fed, the cat stays healthy and the cat doesn't run away."

Ronny's anger mounted. This was unfair. "I've taken responsibility for all that! I've never asked you to do anything for Tom! I make sure it's my food he eats, and I clear up any mess whilst he's learning. Look at how happy he makes her!"

"And what happens to Catherine if something happens to him? There's no guarantee that he'll survive! There're lots of predators around and some are two-legged. And if he does survive, what happens to the cat when we're liberated and go back home? You never think ahead, Ronny!"

What was Pat really upset about? Surely not the cat? Why did she feel guilty?

Furious, she went on the attack. "Of course I make my own decisions. You're never here! You're gone most of the day, working in the kitchen. You may have dropped the refuse job, but you're still on the emergency delivery team! You're doing your night patrols. You're dead tired most of the time, and your daughter rarely sees you now!"

"I thought you were pleased when they asked me to work as a cook!"

"Yes, and you know why! I thought, in my stupidity, that you were going to bring some food home to your family, like everyone else on your team."

"You know that's not true. You know that's why they changed the cooks! They wanted honest men in there."

Her constant hunger fuelled her fury. "You can't eat honesty! You've got a family that needs food, Pat! Haven't you heard charity begins at home?" Her stomach churned and she felt sick.

"I can't talk to you when you're like this. I have a responsibility to the whole community. I'm doing everything to see that we all survive this hellhole. If you don't see much of me for the time being, then that's the price we have to pay. Don't you think I miss spending time with you both?"

"You have options, Pat! You can give up some of your duties! I know it's great that everyone thinks you're wonderful and noble, but all we have is the downside. We never share a meal together. You're never here to read to Catherine at bedtime. She misses you! I miss you! You're too tired to come to a cinema showing, and I have to talk Reg into coming with me. You're never around now! And what do we get for it? What compensation? Do you have money to spend on us? No! Do you have extra food to give us? No! What does your family get for you being the camp's most hard-working and honest man? You tell me!"

She was still trembling when Pat headed for the door. Ronny wanted a fight, a real fight to clear the air, but Pat, as always, headed for the door. And it had not ended there. Hours passed, and she had started to worry, especially after curfew. She put Catherine to bed in a distracted way, and paced the floor until Reg returned from his patrol. Embarrassed she explained Pat's absence, and Reg went back out into the dark immediately to find him. Another hour passed.

The husband Reg brought back finally was quiet and thoughtful. In the past, he might have been the worse for wear, but not here with alcohol being so difficult to obtain. Fundamentally, Pat was a thoroughly good man, if sometimes misguided in her opinion, and she knew he would make an apology later in the day and expect her to laugh the matter off. Nothing would change. He would always put his community first before himself and his family. She scuffed the dust in irritation before she took her daughter's hand and headed back home.

—✂——✂—

Ronny had been surprised to find she had green fingers and derived great pleasure from growing plants in her fertile patch. She experimented with any seed she could lay her hands on, and was not past pinching cuttings from other people's lots. The ground had benefitted from the flood, and the dappled shade from the trees surrounding the shanty gave protection from the relentless sun, enabling her garden to flourish. She found that squatting down, coolie fashion, helped her back and she spent happy hours, in thought, working with her hands in the cool soil.

The military commandants came and went with alarming regularity, so Ronny no longer bothered to learn their names. The Japanese demands continued to increase, and she ran over the last month's restrictions in her mind. Internees had to hand in any building materials and any privately owned electrical and gas appliances. All open meetings had to receive the commandant's seal of approval and be closely monitored. The military authorities ordered the sealing of many of the camp's helpful businesses, such as the electrical repair shop and the soap-making plant. All sports activities in the camp were discontinued, and so the list went on. Daily, new restrictions reflected the military's jittery response to rumours that the American forces were getting closer. Three sentry boxes were erected at the main gate by internee labour, and the gymnasium was vacated for Japanese use. Soldiers took over the accommodations on the ground floor of the education building. Blackout and searchlight practices became a common event.

Ronny interrupted her weeding efforts to stroke the little black cat as he rubbed himself against her thigh. Stroking Tom was a sensuous experience in a world where nothing was soft and seductive. She loved his soft, black fur, and would lift the cat and bury her face in its warmth at the slightest excuse.

Next to the tactile pleasure of stroking Tom, food was the closest to a sensory delight she could think of. Thoughts of food were always with her and were the constant topic of camp conversation. Since the military had become the sole source of supplies, food had become even scarcer, and starvation was visible in the crowd around her. Ronny thought the men were the sorriest sight, with their muscle wastage making their weight loss screamingly obvious, and she was grateful that the wearing of G-strings had never been permitted in this camp. The morning meal was cracked corn with a small spoon of sugar every other day. A banana was served morning and evening. Small fish were served three times a week, but it was merely a gesture. Meat, even in soup form, had long vanished. Coconut milk was unavailable. The evening meal was red rice with either boiled whole corn or radish. Ronny's intestines found both the corn and radish hard to digest, and she was often in pain. She sighed unconsciously.

The little cat whisked its tail and moved to its favourite spot in the deep, cool shade below the shanty. Ronny stood and stretched. She felt a sudden gripe in her belly and hoped that it was just indigestion. They had taken it in turns to nurse each other through dysentery over the months, and Ronny hoped that she was not in for another bout. There was no question that the death toll in camp was rising, and Reg told her that the Japanese had directed the doctors not to list malnutrition as a cause of death.

— ⊁— ⊁—

It was a wet August night, and Ronny was glumly turning the collar of one of Reg's threadbare shirts to extend its life. She had made the rounds of her wealthy clients to solicit work, but cutbacks finally had reached even the richest of internees, and they made it clear that their only outlay from then on would be for food. Skill, ability and persistence were no longer enough to earn her the pittance she had been relying on.

She stretched her back as the coconut-oil lamp coughed, spluttered and mercifully settled again. The steady drumming of rain on the roof was comforting, Catherine was sleeping, and

Reg was reading his collection of handwritten recipes, with the little black cat curled up on his lap. Reg had joined the craze of exchanging recipes, the more exotic the better, either verbally or written on scraps of paper. He read and reread them avidly. The passion for exchanging recipes was rampant in camp, even for those who did not cook. Tom obviously thought that it was time for attention and patted the little pack of paper scrawls until the man was forced to turn his attention to him. Reg would never admit it, but he loved that cat.

Pat was out on night patrol. Theft was a constant occurrence by then, from Filipinos coming in over the wall and internees themselves stealing from each other. She had not protested when, with the worsening atmosphere, Pat and Reg decided that one or other would always be in the shanty at night.

For some, starvation meant that any code of ethics was long forgotten. Only this morning Ronny had overheard a conversation when she had taken Catherine to see the experimental, little farmyard set up within the campus by the Japanese. They had been looking at the litter of piglets when she was startled by a rough voice at her elbow.

"All the eggplants from the camp gardens has gone to those little blighters. They're better fed than we are!" said a yellow-faced man, who leaned over the stockade fence, too close to Ronny for comfort.

As he turned his eyes in her direction, her heart had missed a beat. The whites of his eyes were yellow, a stronger hue than his comparatively pale irises, and she shuddered at the reptilian quality it gave him. Advanced liver disease was the obvious cause, and she knew she should feel sorry for him, but those snake-like eyes made her recoil.

He was joined by an unpleasant-smelling friend, who commented, "I heard that they get sweet-potato peelings too! They'd better be worth it!"

"We might not be around by the time they're big enough for slaughter. And who's to say we'll benefit anyway? I'd be surprised if the Nips don't take the lot!" Ronny heard the reptile man's confidential mutter. "That one there's never going to grow. The runt of the litter, it is! How about we take it right now? Why should we wait for the official kill?"

The morning's interlude ended abruptly as she distracted Catherine's attention decisively.

Ronny looked up as Reg broke the companionable silence when he saw her concentration was flagging. "The commandant's told the Work Committee that the war in the South China Sea has intensified," he offered.

"Of course it has. We don't need blackout practices to indicate that," Ronny responded.

"He's asked the Work Committee to oversee the construction of air-raid shelters. He actually said that American bombing of Manila was inevitable. They want a shelter near the commandant's office for him and his staff, and other shelters for the hospital. He's asking internees to volunteer to act as firefighters and first-aid teams."

"I hope any bombing will be confined to the harbour area and the airfields. They wouldn't bomb the camp, would they?"

"My dear, there are no guarantees in war. Obviously, the Japs are alarmed. The commandant's talking about storing emergency water. We must anticipate increasing shortages of the goods being delivered to camp as he spoke of the need to cultivate every inch of spare ground for food production. In order to do that, he's stepping up the compulsory labour hours for us all."

"But that's not possible! We're exhausted as it is! What is he expecting, Reg?"

"Women, children and old men have to do three hours a day. Children from fifteen to seventeen and men in their fifties are to do four hours, and all the other men must do five hours a day. We're talking about hard physical work: construction or gardening. All our regular work is to be done on top of that!"

She was tired just listening to him and said bitterly, "The Nips seem intent on wiping us out. Will we still be here by the time the Americans arrive?"

"We've survived this long. Of course we'll be around to greet them. We're survivors, Ronny. The war is on the turn. The Jap behaviour itself is telling us that. It can't be much longer now."

"I'm sorry." Ronny sunk her head down onto her arms. "I hear the stories that if the Americans come, they won't find us alive and all evidence of us will have been covered up. They're intent on making this a fortress for themselves. I'm not blind. I saw the convoys of Japs bringing army boxes into camp to be stored in the gymnasium. I saw the red cross being painted on top of the hospital roof. They're just securing a good base for themselves, and we're expendable." She sighed deeply. "I'm so tired of it, Reg. I'm tired of feeling hungry and unwell. I'm tired of worrying about Catherine's future and our future. I can't help thinking that we don't have a future."

"I don't ever want to hear you talking that way, Ronny. You have to keep strong. We do have a future, and we'll come out of this fighting. You have to keep believing that there will be a life after Santo Tomas."

"What sort of future will that be, Reg?" She looked across at him sitting there, quietly domestic. "I can't imagine a future without you living with us! What would it be like not to be together? I can no longer imagine it!"

There was a silence. The distance between them seemed infinite. Reg jettisoned Tom from his lap swiftly, moved to her side and enveloped her in his arms. He murmured into her hair, "Promise me you'll live, my dear Ronny. With or without me. Promise me!"

She felt the strength of his arms, and breathed in the intimate smell that was unique only to him. Her world halted, and she stayed perfectly still, relishing the moment. Seconds later, Reg stepped back and into his role once again. He stooped to pick up the indignant, little black cat and – breaking the tension – joked, "We're going to have to save you too!" And the tension retreated.

Later that night, she hugged herself beside Pat's sleeping body. She went over the conversation moment by moment. What madness was this that she was getting into? There, not four feet away and shrouded in the silk of the mosquito net, lay the man that she wanted to be held by. The tender man of secrets who fascinated and delighted her. She could no longer deny that she sought out Reg's company whenever she could. She cherished their moments alone and sulked when she had to share him. She could no longer ignore her desire to intensify this intimacy. This was madness indeed, and someone was going to get hurt. She shifted on the mattress to try to find a cool spot to soothe her fever.

TWENTY-FIVE

———✂———✂———

2nd September 1944
998 days in captivity

Ronny wiped the sweat out of her eyes, and called Tom's name over and over again until her throat was parched. Neither she nor Reg heard any responding mew. They had been searching since early morning, and by then the midday sun beat down and all sensible internees were sheltering in the shade. They had noticed his absence after morning roll call, and paired up in their normal pattern, Pat with Catherine and Ronny with Reg, to scour the camp for the runaway cat. They looked under shanties and peered into trees. Ronny's cheek was scratched and they were exhausted. Slowly, over the hours, concern had turned to despair and, finally, they had to admit that Tom was nowhere to be found. Tom would not be coming back.

Ronny and Pat slumped exhausted on the shanty steps, with Catherine between them. They all loved Tom, and the thought of never seeing him again was unbearable.

Pat broke the news. "It's no good, Twopence. Tom's gone. But I think I know what's happened to him."

"Where's he gone, Daddy? I want him to come back." declared Catherine.

"I think he's gone to a very happy place. I think he's found his way to a place that is wonderful for cats. A special place where he has lots of friends and lots of good things to eat. He can play all day."

Catherine wasn't buying it. "But I want him here. I want him back, Daddy."

"Twopence, he's on a big adventure and he's with his friends. He may come back to see us one day when he's bigger."

Ronny butted in, "But, right now, he's having fun, in a new place, with new friends."

Catherine let out a wail, and Ronny backed off and left it to Pat to pacify her. He had always managed to give her the reassurance that Ronny had never managed to provide.

Later, Pat joined her as she squatted in her garden, her hands deep in earth, seeking the balm she could rely on.

He stood over her. "I don't want to say I told you so, but I told you so! It was inevitable, Ronny! He was a meal once he'd grown large enough."

She looked up at his frown. "You think a Filipino got him, from over the wall?"

"Possibly! More likely it was someone right next door! There must have been hungry eyes on him for a couple of months now. Curried cat was never out of the question."

She prodded the earth distractedly. "We should have been more careful. I just couldn't believe anyone would hurt him." She felt the constriction of her throat. "Tom was so friendly and gentle."

"Too friendly for his own good. Catherine's really upset. She's cried herself to sleep. There'll be no more pets, Ronny. It's just not fair to her."

Ronny had no answer. He was right and always had been. A POW camp was no place for a pet, and she had been crazy to have thought otherwise. She just hoped Catherine would get over it quickly.

Over the next few days, Ronny watched Catherine carefully and with concern. The little girl never mentioned Tom again. It was as if he had never existed. Ronny removed his box and scrap of blanket, and all traces of the pet. Occasionally, when one of the adults mentioned the little cat, Catherine appeared totally disinterested and, apparently, unhearing. Although it made it easier for Ronny, she was disturbed by her daughter's attitude and her apparent ability to block out something that was too hurtful to acknowledge. Catherine was only two and a half. Was that normal?

— ⊬ — ⊬ —

For her part, Ronny went about her daily communal chores, but she found it hard to concentrate. It wasn't Tom she was thinking about. All her thoughts revolved around Reg. She was gripped by something that she could not resist and could no longer deny. She sought Reg's company continually and planned her days around times when she thought they might meet even if only fleetingly. Only last week, in the midst of a group discussion, Reg had taken her hand in jest. The electrical charge that she had experienced was so strong that she was surprised that no one else noticed it. She let her hand lie in his as long as she dared and then, to her shame, she waited for the next opportunity to touch him. Was it like this for him? Could he be feeling one fraction of the magnetism that she was experiencing? It was total madness, but Ronny felt helpless to do anything about it.

— ⊬ — ⊬ —

There had been no explanation, but, suddenly, Reg wasn't there any more!

He was always busy with the committee he was on or some other duty, and she missed him. His keen, blue eyes never seemed to look directly at her any more, and he became evasive and distracted. It was not just she who noticed the change; Pat had too. Reg appeared to be so much in demand away from the shanty by then that Pat started to jest about it. A secret lover was created in Pat's imagination, and he took great relish in teasing Reg about her existence. Ronny could only watch this pantomime with a rigid countenance, which her husband put down to a lack of humour. The more Reg withdrew, the more Ronny sought his presence. She was confused and hurt, and cast about her for a likely explanation. Had she been wrong about their special relationship? Had she deluded herself that he had sought out her company above all others? Finally, after two weeks of confusion, she could bear it no longer and feeling foolish and desperate, she resolved to confront him.

The opportunity came one day when Ronny had brought a sullen Catherine up to the camp's little farmyard. She watched her daughter with a pain in her heart. Catherine's little legs were bowed, her chest was slightly concave and her stomach protruded. These signs of malnutrition could be rectified if they were rescued, but the emotional impact of Catherine's early experience of life worried her more.

She studied the fair head of her daughter as Catherine lent her forehead against the wooden railings and stared at the animals. The litter of pink piglets squealed and thrust their snouts at the patient sow, and Catherine smiled. Just a little. Although the frantic scrambles in the pigpen were easy to enjoy, Ronny could not forget that these bundles of fun would be destined for the pot soon enough. It was a joy to watch Catherine unfurl slowly in response to them. If only all life were that uncomplicated. In the next compound were two sway-backed, cream-and-coffee-coloured bovines, their ribs clearly visible, but tranquillity in their eyes. Doubtless they were destined for the pot too.

A vivid splash of red caught her eye. A tall woman and her little boy, sporting a close crew-cut, who were instantly identifiable as American, wandered up.

The mother called across, "Hi there. Isn't that Catherine? I recognise her from Chester's group."

Ronny glanced down at Catherine.

The woman went on, "Is it OK with you if they play together?"

She really did not want to make the effort to be civil, no matter how friendly this woman in red was, but Catherine clearly liked the boy. They were already laughing at the scruffy cockerels, who strutted about freely, scratching the dust and picking at the lobster-pot-like wicker baskets in which they were usually contained. Ronny didn't want to make conversation as her thoughts dwelled on Reg and his hurtful absence.

Then she saw the opportunity that had presented itself. She introduced herself and said, "It's a bit of a cheek, but if the children are happy together, would you mind Catherine for a little while? I really need to see someone urgently."

"But of course. Don't be a stranger! I'm happy you asked," the woman replied.

Ronny beamed. "May I see you here in an hour?"

"Take your time, and if we aren't here, we'll be back at the play base."

Before her idea was fully formed, Ronny was walking swiftly towards the education block, and Reg's work shed. There, she believed she would find him. She didn't allow herself to formulate a plan; she just needed to confront him and understand this apparent change in their relationship.

As she neared the building, luck was on her side, as she spotted his familiar figure leaving the granite building, and – at her call – he turned and stood with concern on his face.

"Ronny. What is it? Are you all right?" he enquired.

"No, not really." She then wondered how to continue. This was crazy. She was mortified that she had exposed herself like this, but it was too late to retreat. "I need to talk to you alone."

"Of course. Let's go to my office."

She wanted to tell him that she loved him and that she couldn't bear to be estranged from him. She mumbled, "Any chance of that?"

He shuffled her back into his small office and bolted the door. They stood and stared at each other. It was a cramped, musty-smelling room, with a dirt floor and a desk full of paperwork. It was really for tool storage, but – at this moment – it offered privacy, and that was what she wanted. She looked at him. What could she say? Her heart was pounding so loudly she thought he was bound to hear it.

"I miss you." It came out as a croak, and she thought he hadn't heard her. "I miss you. Where have you been?"

He was standing like stone, his face pale and his eyes huge.

His voice was muffled and she strove to hear him. "Dearest Ronny, I didn't mean this to happen. I have to tell you that I've fallen in love with you," he declared.

She let out her breath slowly, shocked and exhilarated by his words. All she could say was, "I know."

"It's crazy. I just can't think of anything else."

"Yes, my dear. I feel the same way."

They moved towards each other, and she was swept up with the dizzying sensation of Reg's lips on hers as she melted. His arms were strong, his mouth was hard and the demand of his body was undeniable. This was everything she wanted, and she wanted it right then. She felt triumphant and urgent and weak all at once.

They stepped back and gazed at each other. They were both breathing heavily.

She said, "I can't do this!" Where did that come from? Of course she could. Somehow they would be together. But she heard herself saying again, "We can't do this."

"I know, my dear. God knows I've fought it all along," he confirmed.

"You've fought it?"

"I knew you could cause me heartache from the first time I met you. Do you remember? I called in to play chess, and you were there. I knew then that you could be my undoing."

Eagerly, she wanted to hear more, every detail. She wanted him to confess all. She wanted to hear that she was as essential to him as he was to her. "You knew then?" she encouraged him.

"Dearest, you looked so pretty. You were wearing your polka-dot dress and you seemed so sure of yourself, so collected."

"I saw you before that. I saw you the very day you arrived in Santo Tomas. Isn't it odd that even then I was drawn to you? I didn't know what to make of you, but I knew you were special. I never meant it to go this far, Reg."

"Neither of us set out to make this happen. We are not to blame. It's just sad that we can't take this any further."

"It was cruel of you to remove yourself so completely from me. Why did you do that?"

"I'm so sorry, my dear. I wouldn't hurt you for the world. I just knew that, for all our sakes, I had to step back."

"But without any explanation? Did you really expect me to just accept it?"

"No, not you! I just couldn't think straight. I can't be sorry that I'm in love with you, but I am sorry for the pain."

She studied his face. She saw the crease marks rising from the corner of his eyes, his slender nose with its slightly flared nostrils, but, most of all, his wonderful, direct, blue eyes that just then appeared warm, vulnerable and, for once, readable. He wanted her. She knew that with total certainty.

"Kiss me," she demanded.

He did, with mounting passion, but it was Reg who broke away first.

He explained, "As you say, it's not possible. I love you with all my heart, but we are not going to take this any further. God knows I want to, but we mustn't, for the sake of us all."

Despair filled Ronny. All she wanted was to be in Reg's arms and blot out this ugly world that surrounded her. She did not want to think about Pat or Catherine. She wanted to follow her heart and part of her screamed in anger at the injustice of denial. She deserved some happiness after all she had gone through! How dare Reg be noble? She wanted him to be selfish and base and self-seeking with her, to hell with the consequences. But she knew it was not right for either of them.

"Oh Reg, I need you to know that I love you so much. I always will. I can't think straight at the moment. Please hold me again before I have to face rights and wrongs."

He did, swiftly and gladly and they sat on the floor, listening to the gradual diminishing of the beat of their hearts. In this sordid hole, sitting on the dirt floor curled up next to this dear, dear man, she could think of nowhere that she would rather be.

"Ronny my dearest do you want me to move out of the shanty? I'll do whatever you say to make it easier for you," Reg offered.

She stared at him in horror. "No, I couldn't bear it. You are part of my life." She clung to him again. "I won't even consider it."

"No, I can't consider it either, unless you insist. We have to learn to live together without ever referring to this again. Pat must never know."

She did not want to talk about Pat. Not at this moment. In time, master her behaviour she must, but not just then. Ronny had no idea how she was going to face the coming days and live in the same room as the man she felt so passionately about. She had no right to make Pat or Catherine suffer for the way she was feeling, but she could not deny the overwhelming joy and pain of this long-desired embrace.

They kissed again, slowly and passionately.

When Ronny and Reg finally parted, it felt as if a part of her had been torn away. The assurance that he was experiencing the same grief was no help, and she almost turned back. But she did not. She rushed back for the belated rendezvous with Catherine, almost blind with tears. She missed the curious looks her flight generated. They had made the commitment that Pat would never know. They would stop this right there, before anyone else got hurt.

Ronny was battling with their charcoal-and-wood stove. Matches were so precious, and she had already wasted two without getting a flame going. She wondered why she bothered. If she did manage to get it to work, it would only billow out smoke, and no culinary offering would be worth the streaming eyes and the lingering smell.

The days that followed her and Reg's tryst had passed in a blur of misery. She dragged herself from one chore to another, and her deep pain was unrelieved. She wondered whether her anguish was worse when she was with Reg or when he was absent. She hated the stove and hated her squalid existence, and she could not think of one pleasant thing that could take her mind off her loss. Life felt unbearable. Anna was gone. Her little comforter, Tom, was gone. She knew she was guilty of having withdrawn from her friends. Reg was as good as gone, and she missed the pleasure of talking to him. She tried desperately to put on a good front for her daughter and her husband, but she was tired of trying.

She was tired of everything, and turned her back on the stove and any idea of cooking the banana skins into a semblance of potato crisps.

Pat had been watching her surreptitiously and broke into her thoughts. "I don't know what's got into you, my girl. You've got the face of a sour lemon. Lighten up, will you?"

"I'm sorry, Pat. Personally, I don't think there's much to smile about right now. I hate that stove. I wanted to make us something different. I'm fed up with mush! Mush for breakfast, mush cakes pretending to be bread and mush for dinner with gravy. Endless mush," she griped.

He tried levity. "How about Luago? The stuff of all life in camp!"

"That runny, white blancmange? I don't care if you guys manage to make flour out of it or a version of American popcorn! I hate it! And before you open your mouth, I hate *camote* too! It turns out far too watery. That's not what I would call food!"

He gave her a wise look. "Is your stomach playing up again?"

Water-lily leaves were often served by then, and sword beans, which Ronny hated with a vengeance for the damage they did to her intestines. They all veered between struggling with diarrhoea or suffering from constipation, as the amount of food available was totally inadequate to keep their bowels working normally. The doctors did not offer laxatives, as they were too weakening.

"Ronny? What's really the matter? Is there something you're not telling me? You've been so terribly unhappy recently. What can I do?" asked Pat.

At his kind words, Ronny burst into tears. "How can you pretend that life's even remotely bearable?"

At his quizzical look, she cast about for an acceptable explanation and did not have to look far. "Can't you see what's going on, Pat? The Japanese are turning the campus into a fortified camp right around us. Our role is to be human shields. Look at all the air-raid practices, the blackouts and the watch towers internees have been forced to build. We're going to be sitting targets when the Americans arrive."

"My dear, we'll get out of here and we'll do it in one piece. I'm sure of it," Pat confirmed.

She allowed herself to be gathered up into his bear-like hug. It wasn't Reg's chest, but it was solid, kindly meant, familiar and comforting.

—*—*—

The dull plopping of tropical rain that afternoon released a distinctive cloying perfume from the dust. Ronny sat sheltering on the shanty steps, brushing Catherine's hair. The trees above her head rustled and swayed, and there was the promise of coolness that was tantalising after the recent humidity. That day might be their lucky day in that the rain might last long enough to disburse the sticky heaviness that was so oppressive.

She leaned forwards and stretched out her arms so delicious drops of water bounced off her parched skin, like little missiles of nourishment. Catherine watched her guardedly for a minute then copied her. Ronny edged down a couple of steps until she was totally exposed to the downpour. She offered up her face, her mouth open to receive this bounty straight from the gods. She was pleased when her daughter joined in this celebration of life.

Ronny stood up, walked into the unprotected glade and twirled slowly in the rain, her head back and arms akimbo. She could feel the fever-quenching liquid running in rivulets down her back, and she laughed. It did not matter that she was unable to feel her feet, that the pain in her back rarely seemed to go away any more or that her heart had been broken. She spun and laughed.

Catherine followed her mother's lead, and the serious child giggled and squealed. Obviously, her mother had gone mad! Ronny bent down and hugged her. Without hesitation, she stripped the dress and panties off her little daughter gently, urging her to dance in the rain, naked. How she wished she could do the same. She wanted her to experience the joy of dancing naked in a rain forest, without censure and restrictions. She saw her daughter turn and turn, her little exposed body running with water and her delighted laughter bubbling up from deep within her. Ronny wanted Catherine to live fully, exposed to everything good that life and nature had to offer. She wanted a life for her beloved daughter.

Her laughter took on an edge of madness, then failed. It was too late for her. She had made her adult choices, and she was surrounded by adult parameters and constraints. The tears on her face were washed away by the rain as Ronny started dancing more savagely. She did not feel the squalid mud beneath her feet, but she saw the trees spinning above her head. She wanted to dance into oblivion. She wanted this world to vanish and take with it the pain in her heart. She spun and spun more savagely. Water stung her eyes and streamed down her face, her throat constricted, and, forgetting her company, she let out a primeval howl of anguish. In the savagery of her dance, she failed to see her little girl stop and watch, her face creased up with uncertainty at the strange behaviour of her mother.

Twenty-Six

— ⊁— ⊁—

21st September 1944
1,017 days in captivity

Frowning over the family washing in the communal laundry trough, Ronny thought the growing roar was the start of another Japanese air exercise. These days, she had become used to mock dogfights and planes drawing sleeve targets behind them for anti-aircraft practice. She had come to recognise the timbres of the different planes, and they had become just another intrusion into the silence she craved. She reached for another shirt, then hesitated. That day's sound could not be dismissed. She halted and listened more carefully to the intensifying growl.

Something was different on this late September morning!

She felt the resonance of the approach of heavy planes in her chest moments before it assailed her ears. She recognised the tightening in her gut, and she froze. Squinting up into the light, she saw the sky had been darkened by the approach of a heavy formation of planes coming out of the cloud bank. She barely registered the air-raid siren. They came from the north-east, and were large bombers with little planes darting here and there around the formation. The bottommost bank of planes loomed low, their roar preceding them, and she saw other formations towering above them, intent and menacing. She stared in disbelief at over sixty planes! They were set on a course, and she knew instinctively that the camp was not the target.

Ronny let out a whoop. "*They're here!*" she shouted to the world in general. "*They're here!*"

The group of women surrounding her were shouting too and embracing each other with tears streaming. This was the moment they had been waiting for all these years.

"*Our boys are here!*" was the unanimous shout from all quarters.

Cheers left 1,000 throats as all eyes turned to the skies. Another plane formation came into view from the north-west and then turned on their bombing run, and the Japanese anti-aircraft fire sprang belatedly into life, but the American fleet seemed impervious to it and flew on. Japanese aircraft were scrambled, and Ronny saw the glint and shine of small planes as they swooped and crossed in a dogfight above her head. Time stood still. One little plane burst into flames. She cheered loudly, not knowing whether it was friend or foe. Release was coming, and she could see the evidence with her own eyes.

"I saw it from the start." A woman ran up to greet her friends. "I saw the little plane in front of them. The white star on blue. It flew low over us and rolled over from side to side even though the guards were shooting at it!"

"A victory roll!" Ronny gasped. "I wish I'd seen it. How wonderful!"

The planes banked and separated into smaller groups heading for targets outside their vision, and the heavy anti-aircraft fire did nothing to halt them as they proceeded on their run, strafing as they went. Ronny watched transfixed, oblivious to the danger she might be in.

"It's the port they're after!" somebody shouted.

"And the airfields!" added someone else.

This was confirmed by the columns of smoke that billowed up into the air from the north and the south of the city. They could hear the heavy thudding of the bombs landing on Manila targets above the shriek of the air-raid sirens. The air was dense with noise. Ronny could pick out the puffing of the pom-pom guns, the rattle of the machine guns and the thin whine of shells from the anti-aircraft cannons. This surely must be the start of their liberation, and it could only be a matter of days by then. She caught the markings of a few Japanese planes amidst the solid mass of the American Air Force. It was little David against Goliath, and this time she was rooting for the massive Goliath.

Someone tugged her arm, and she resisted, not wanting to miss a moment of the spectacle, but the pull on her arms was too strong and, stumbling, she allowed herself to be swept into the shelter of the annex. The throng of excited men and women jammed the areas nearest the windows, and she had to settle for shouted commentaries. Ronny, restricted in the crowded building, was desperate to share this moment with her family in the shanty. Another wave of bombers followed the first an hour later.

It was not until the end of the morning that the loudspeakers proclaimed the all-clear. Her washing forgotten, she ducked through the door and stumbled as fast as she could towards home. With a stitch in her side, and breathless with exhilaration and exertion, Ronny was disappointed to find their home empty. Where were Pat and Catherine? Where was Reg? She called out, and Pat's answering call came from beneath her feet, as he and Catherine wriggled out of the shelter in the shadows beneath the shanty. When Pat and Reg dug out the bomb shelter, Ronny had paid it little attention, as she was convinced that their earthen dug-out offered little protection from direct bombing. Pat had pointed out that shrapnel was the main concern and had then taken full advantage of the security that it gave them. Pat had foreseen the danger, whilst she had been standing exposed, her mouth open, drinking in the battle above her head. Guilt hit her. What sort of mother was she to have lost herself in the spectacle without thinking about the danger to herself or her child? The air-raid warning had been just that, an instruction to take cover, which she had blithely ignored.

A semblance of lunch was served in the annex, a little fish gravy and a piece of toasted rice bread, and the atmosphere was electric, as everyone felt the end was in sight. By the time the air-raid siren started again, heralding the next wave of American bombers, Ronny and Pat had decided to stick with the crowd in the main building. The afternoon was easier for them, as Catherine was distracted by other children, and they took it in turns to recount what could be seen from the overcrowded windows. The menacing planes appeared from the same direction, but at a greater height than the previous ones, and Ronny prayed that their targeting would be as accurate as in the morning. Heavy firing could be heard, and, at one stage, everyone in the room was silenced by a huge explosion from the bay area.

Voices opined and argued:

"That's got to be a boat. A munitions barge perhaps?"

"It must be one of the Japs."

"Not necessarily. We could already be in the bay as a prelude to landing."

"Surely Luzon would be the obvious place for the Yanks to land?"

"Where do you think these planes are coming from? There's bound to be aircraft carriers and battleships out there. It can't only be the Nips in the bay."

"We're hardly going to bomb the bay if we're already there!"

The speculation was interminable, but the mood was animated and excited.

—+— —+—

Ronny spent the next few days in a fever of anticipation, as the bombing raids continued daily. They heard mighty explosions and witnessed more dogfights. Her spirits sank when the first identifiable American plane was shot down and then a second one, only to be elevated again when she saw a troop of 1,000 Japanese soldiers marching past the campus walls, heading east out of the city. The emotional rollercoaster was exhausting.

Then, suddenly, as swiftly as it had arrived, all went quiet.

Week followed week with no sightings of American planes, and even Pat, the most optimistic in the group, had to admit that liberation was not to be immediate. Ronny could find nothing to lift her spirits, and the drudgery of internee life once more resumed its death slide to starvation.

———※—※———

Pat was looking pleased with himself. He hummed a little tune, and Ronny could feel his eyes resting on her. She bent closer to her feet and tried experimentally to press a twig into the numbed flesh of her soles, but her calloused feet were as unaware of sensation as a pair of leather shoes. She wondered if her emotional responses were then as deadened as her feet appeared to be.

Pat said, "Do you know what day it is?"

"It's 16th October or thereabouts, give or take a couple of days," answered Ronny.

"It's 14th October to be precise."

She responded impatiently. "And?" She tried to splay her toes, but they no longer responded.

"The 14th October," Pat repeated.

Ronny looked at his expectant face and wracked her brain. Was she supposed to be doing something? She waited and, suddenly, the significance of the date came to her. "It's our wedding anniversary! But I have nothing to give you to celebrate."

"Well I have! Tonight, my dear, you are going to feast like a queen! It's all arranged. We've dinner for two in our shanty paradise, after Catherine is asleep. All you have to do is make yourself pretty, and I'll do the rest."

She laughed awkwardly. Pat looked so pleased with himself that she had not the heart to spoil his pleasure. "That sounds lovely but surely you mean dinner for three?" she queried.

"Reg is going to be away this evening. He said he has something special going on."

"You mean you told him it was our wedding anniversary, and he has tactfully withdrawn?" Ronny would have been irritated with both men if this had been the case.

"No, my dear! I might well have said something, but he beat me to it. He was on some secret mission that he wouldn't talk about, but I have my suspicions!"

"Suspicions?"

"I'm sure he's found a woman!" Pat tapped the side of his nose irritatingly, oblivious to Ronny's glare. She found it hard to supply the expected smile. She had made her decision with regard to Reg, but the thought of him being consoled by someone else was not to be contemplated. She turned her attention fully on Pat.

He was triumphant. "Whatever his reasons, he told me he would be sleeping over at the education building tonight, so we can have an anniversary meal in our own home together. I have it all organised, and I don't think you'll be disappointed."

She straightened her shoulders and turned the full beam of her smile on him. "Oh Pat! I'm agog to see what you've managed to rustle up."

—⊁—⊁—

Catherine was sleeping soundly when Ronny and Pat settled down for their meal. The little table had been cleared of its chess game, and Ronny had contributed a bunch of flowers. Having committed herself to making an occasion of this evening, she had washed and towel-dried her hair. Normally, it was secured up for coolness, but this evening, as a special gesture, she allowed it to hang loose.

The shutters were down, and there were three coconut candles to light the shanty. They settled down to celebrate the fourth anniversary of their married life, and Ronny was determined to make it up to Pat for her recent straying emotions. She had never set out to hurt him and felt confident that he had no inkling about the turmoil she had endured. This was a good time to start repaying him for his constancy, and she focused entirely on her husband on their anniversary evening.

It was blessedly cool, and Ronny had tied a shawl around her shoulders. The patter of rain on the vegetation outside added to the intimacy of the occasion, as did the intermittent roaring of the wind. It reminded her of the night of the typhoon the previous year, although this storm held none of the ferocity of that unforgettable event. That night, she could stay cosy and safe with her husband.

And Pat surpassed himself. He had managed to conceal their share of a recent Red Cross allocation of one twelve-ounce tin of corned beef for every four adults, to which he had added a few spoons of beans and the watery rice from the chow line. It was a feast indeed. To top it off, there was a tiny bottle of native alcohol that Pat had purchased at some cost from the camp's black market. Mercifully, the alcohol was not of the savage variety, and Ronny was determined to enjoy every last drop of it. They sat at the little table, with their heads close together in order to be heard against the storm outside.

Ronny became sentimental. "I can't imagine there are many couples who have photographs of themselves together when they were children!"

"It's amazing that I survived your family! You were always leading me into trouble," chided Pat.

"We just had normal adventures!"

Pat laughed. "Normal? I can cite a dozen times when you got me into difficulties! You were a tearaway, my girl, and nothing much has changed!"

"Do you remember when Moppity had her puppies under your bed, and Mother insisted that you shouldn't move them?" She smiled, remembering Moppity, their grey Irish Wolf Hound and childhood companion.

"I had to sleep with them there, and Moppity was so large that she pushed against the mattress whenever she moved. Why didn't your mother move me or them? I think all your family are a little mad!"

"Possibly!" She laughed. "Why are they always my family when it's negative and our family when it's positive? The home helps were distinctly odd, do you remember?"

"I remember Lavender, the gardener. Do you really think that was his name? I remember Elsie the maid, and how she used to catch wasps in her fingers and crush them to death against the window panes! She never got stung."

"Do you remember the time when you and I were in one of the lanes near Painswick and we came across the horse and cart that had overturned?"

Pat nodded. "It was the coal cart, and the horse was lying with one of the shafts underneath it? It was in a terrible state."

"Yes, the man asked for our help."

"It's curious that I don't remember any blood! The coal was all over the lane and one of the wheels was broken, but I don't remember being aware that the horse was hurt. Only, that it couldn't get up, and kept neighing wildly and rolling its eyes, struggling."

Ronny continued with the familiar story. "The man wanted one of us to sit on the horse's head whilst he went for help. He asked you first, but you wouldn't do it!"

Pat countered swiftly, "Only because I knew you were dying to. You were always up for new experiences!"

"Come on, Pat, admit it! You were far too chicken to sit on its head!"

"Far too sensible! I think I had my good clothes on, and your mother would have been annoyed if they were covered in coal dust! Anyway, you didn't take much persuading to sit on the horse, covering its eyes under your frilly skirt."

"I've often wondered about that. Do you remember how quiet the horse was once I was sitting on its face? It was as good as gold, as if it knew there was help on the way."

Pat toasted her. "I will now admit that you were pretty brave. I do confess I wasn't keen on the idea."

"Its head was warm and I tried not to wriggle. We were there for an awfully long time. It was getting dark, and we were going to be late for tea. You stayed with me and sang songs!"

"Did I? They must have been ones I learned at school. Anyway, I always stood by you, didn't I?"

"I wonder what happened to that horse, Pat? We were shooed away pretty smartly once the fellow and his chums returned. We never found out!"

He grimaced. "I suspect that a bullet dispatched it once we were out of hearing. I don't know what else they could have done."

"You never told me that! I'm sure that the grown-ups said that all was well." She smiled to herself at her use of the word 'grown-ups'. How idyllic their childhood had been in the Cotswolds valley.

"Of course they did! What else would they say?" Pat had something else on his mind. "Now we've eaten, I have a present for you, poppet. I want you to know just how much you mean to me, my dear."

Ronny wanted to stay in their shared childhood past. "Hush Pat, you don't have to say anything." She did not want any speeches. She did not feel she deserved them.

"But I want you to hear me out." He took her hand in his familiar clasp. "I know I wasn't your first choice of husband. You wanted someone far more adventurous and exciting."

"I chose you, Pat. Please don't say any more."

"I'll look after you, my dear. I'll make this up to you."

"This isn't your fault. It's just our bad luck. Wrong place, wrong time."

"I know you don't love me as much as I love you, but, for my part, I'll be eternally grateful that you're in my life. You and Catherine. I'll always do everything I can to make you happy."

"I know that. Please hush." With every word he spoke, she felt worse about her recent duplicity. She did not deserve his unquestioning love.

"I have a gift for you, Ronny. You deserve more, but it comes with my undying love."

He let go of her hand, reached under the table and presented the gift he'd wrapped in banana leaves. She stared in anticipation at the little, vibrant, green package and, although she was pleased to be receiving a gift, she steeled herself for disappointment. She had no expectations, and she arranged her face so as not to hurt this dear man. In accepting this gift, Ronny felt she was again accepting a wedding ring and all the implications of fidelity that she had promised then. Fleetingly, she thought of Reg. Her path had come to a fork, and she had chosen this husband of hers. With all his foibles and irritations, he could still surprise and please her, and he was the one she had chosen to remain with.

Ronny opened the leafy wrapping and exposed the bamboo bracelet that nestled at its centre. She let out a gasp. She was genuinely thrilled with what lay in her hands. The circular band was intricately carved on its exterior side and secured invisibly in a perfect round, and she held it close to examine it in the flickering light. It was a work of love and care, a work of precision and infinite patience. Tiny leaves and flowers had been carved into the bamboo in different depths, giving it the look of a sculptured scene. Enchanted, Ronny slipped it over her wrist. It was light, fragile and whimsical, but deceptively strong.

"Thank you, Pat. It's lovely. Where did it come from?" she asked.

"I saw a chap in the carpentry shed making it. I knew it would be perfect for you! It took some tough haggling and a few chess lessons to get him to part with it!" admitted Pat.

"Thank you. I will always treasure it."

With shining eyes, she moved into his arms and snuggled against his familiar chest. She was content to stay this way, listening to the storm outside as it drummed its way through the tropical foliage. Neither of them spoke. She reached her arm out and twisted her wrist this way and that, and the dancing light gave the impression that the tiny leaves were moving and alive. Dulled pleasantly by the alcohol, she thought she had never seen anything so enchanting.

"We'll have another life, my poppet. It's getting closer all the time. I know it's disappointing that the Yanks appear to have left us, but don't give up. We've now seen the strength of the American forces, and they know exactly where we are. Our future is just round the corner."

"What are they waiting for?" Childlike, she asked, "They're out there somewhere, aren't they, Pat?"

"Yes, my dear. They're out there and getting closer. They won't give up. It's only a matter of time now."

Pat stroked her hair absently, and they murmured together of a world after liberation.

They allowed the dream of a different life to take substance in their imagination. They dipped their toes into previously forbidden territory by talking of whom they would see first once they were liberated, where they would go, and how surprised and pleased family and friends would be to see Catherine.

The visualisation of a life worth living fed a dormant desire in Pat, and Ronny was surprised when his embrace became more insistent. She felt him kiss her damp neck and taste the scent that lingered beneath her fall of hair. She allowed herself to be swept along with the mood of the moment. She was here with her dear, familiar husband; her child was asleep; and the shutters were down against the falling rain and prying eyes. Pat led a slow exploration of her body, and she melted with his growing need. Time stood still as they both held their breath. Their physical response to each other was strong, after being shrouded by separation, starvation and deprivation. They found they fell naturally into the old, familiar patterns of their lovemaking from so long ago. For Ronny and Pat, the world outside faded away.

TWENTY-SEVEN

4th November 1944

1,061 days in captivity

Over the next couple of weeks, Ronny helped the two men extend the bomb shelter under the shanty. Pat and Reg, despite their fatigue, managed to dig, and Ronny overruled her unreliable legs and helped disburse the soil. Reg seemed confident that the Americans would avoid bombing the university campus, but mistakes could happen. The threat of stray shrapnel or explosives from the dogfights was always there. Anti-aircraft fire from the Japanese was sometimes successful and the descent of burning planes could certainly harm them. Guerrilla activities in Manila had endangered the internees on a few occasions, with stray mortar fire raining on the camp.

Reg had warned Ronny about possible damage to their eardrums from bombs, and had presented Catherine with a wooden peg to carry round her neck on a string. The idea was to get her to clench the peg between her teeth to lessen the pressure.

Catherine went through the motions, but Ronny was pretty sure that she would forget in an emergency.

The festering boil of Ronny's relationship with Reg had come to its natural head and been lanced, leaving only soreness after the initial pain. She derived some comfort knowing it was a shared experience and that no one else had been hurt. She loved both her men in different ways. Having turned her back on temptation, she concentrated deliberately on improving her relationship with Pat, and it was paying off. If her nightly dreams sometimes wandered down forbidden paths, her morning determination reinforced her original decision. Watching Reg over the weeks, she believed he was more relaxed too. They had enough difficulties in their lives, Ronny thought ruefully, without self-created ones. They managed to live harmoniously once again, and if she had lost the frisson of passionate intrigue, she had gained peace of mind.

The night of intimacy between Ronny and Pat on their anniversary had not been repeated. It remained a secret that had been as delightful as it had been unexpected.

—⊩—⊮—

Ronny's lack of stamina forced her finally to give up her cleaning rota, and she got demoted to a daily three-hour duty in the lavatory block. She hated the job, but at least she could sit down whilst she handed out the statutory two pieces of toilet paper to all comers. It was in the middle of one of her latrine shifts that Pat came storming to find her.

He exploded, "They used her! They used Catherine for begging! I'm mortified. A Finance and Supplies Committee man said that it had to stop."

Ronny was embarrassed. "Calm down. What are you talking about?" She glanced around, as they had become the object of curiosity.

"A committee man's been to see me. Apparently, that little posse of so called friends who've been borrowing Catherine have been begging from the commandant's kitchen! For sugar and sweets!"

"Not Judy and Jimmy, surely?"

"No, not them. The little American tykes used Catherine as a front, because she's pretty and quiet, and then they shared the proceeds! Apparently, there's been a Jap complaint, as they had become a nuisance."

Ronny had been aware that the neighbouring older girls had adopted Catherine and was happy for them to take her out on little excursions. Inevitably, the girls were American, and Ronny no longer bothered to correct Catherine when her vocabulary became colloquial. Cars became automobiles, sweets became candy and rubbish became trash, but Ronny relaxed, secure in the knowledge that Catherine was happily occupied.

She looked up at Pat, as she continued methodically to hand out sheets to the by then amused queue. "And Catherine hasn't said a word?"

"Of course not! Why would she? They probably bribed her to secrecy! I had no idea they were going right across to the commandant's quarters," he blustered.

Only then did Pat become aware that he had become a spectacle. He muttered, as he took himself off, "I should have kept a closer eye on her."

Guilt dogged Ronny. Was she, too, supposed to be indignant? She simply did not have the energy. She confessed to a sneaking admiration for these streetwise girls, although she was not happy they had used her daughter. Unbeknownst to Pat, she had made her own stealthy visits to the refuse bins outside the commandant's kitchen annex. She would wait until the coast was clear, then take anything worth salvaging for her family. Ronny would get food any way she could and considered her captors fair game, although she drew the line at stealing from other internees. This was sadly rife. One of their neighbours was serving time in the camp jail for stealing two aubergines from the kitchen.

———⊁———⊁———

From her mattress, Ronny watched the dismantling of their little table with horror. Reg had taken an axe to it, and the fragile legs broke easily. Why had he bothered to use an axe when anyone could see that it was easy to break up without such violence? She saw the scuffed little tigers she had painted on the legs so long ago, and felt unsummoned tears blurring her eyes. Her paintings were a personal gift to her daughter from a story where a little boy's guile defeats the terrors of fear and savagery. The chess set always graced the table as a symbol of civilisation, both ancient and modern, with the rules never changing. And then, by order of the Finance and Supplies Committee, furniture was being commandeered to keep the kitchen fires burning.

Ronny knew she was deteriorating and watched the process dully. The beri-beri, although not particularly painful, left her lethargic. To her dismay, her teeth were starting to lie down in her gums and could no longer be relied upon to chew. She could have coped with that, but the nausea that was laying her flat every day was debilitating. It robbed her of what little energy she had left, and she spent many hours on the mattress in deepening depression.

Her senses were fuddled after a broken night, disturbed by an escalation of explosions and the howl of the air-raid warnings. Her throat was parched, and her eyes felt as if they had grit in them. Long gone was the time when the bombing raids were exciting, and the last two months had felt like one long rollercoaster. The exhilaration of actually seeing the American air power in September contrasted with months of depression when there was no action in the skies.

The previous night, the bombers were back, but, despite this, Ronny found it impossible to hope. She was convinced that death by starvation would be the outcome for them all, and there was plenty of evidence surrounding her to reinforce her impression.

—⊬—⊬—

On Christmas morning, Ronny stayed in the shanty whilst Pat collected the breakfast. Reg had been called away on a matter of urgency, and Catherine was curled up next to her, anticipating a special day ahead. She sang remembered old Christmas carols softly to her daughter. 'In the Bleak Midwinter' and 'Good King Wenceslas' painted a picture of conditions that could have been from another planet! Ronny was determined to make it a pleasant third Christmas for Catherine.

A children's party in the play base had been planned for in the morning, and all the participants were to receive two pieces of coconut and muscovado sugar, which the Finance and Supplies Committee had managed to buy through the Japanese. Ronny had made Catherine a tiny, fabric mouse out of her worn out polka-dot dress, and was pleased at the little girl's delight in it.

Pat had taken an inordinately long time in bringing back the slightly sweetened mush, the coconut milk and the coffee that they had been promised on that special day, and when he arrived carrying their cans, he was grinning from ear to ear. "Look, Ronny! Look! This is our Christmas present!"

He waved a scrap of paper under her nose, then, seeing her hesitation, pushed his glasses up onto his forehead and read it to her. "The Commander-in-Chief, the officers, and the men of the American Forces of Liberation in the Pacific wish their gallant allies, the People of the Philippines, all the blessings of Christmas, and the realization of their fervent hopes for the New Year. Christmas, 1944."

Smiling, he waited for her response. "There were handfuls of leaflets dropped from a plane in the night."

Ronny stared at the pencilled copy in his hand. "I can't believe it! Oh Pat! Happy Christmas!"

"They were found this morning. I imagine they're all over Manila. The Yanks must be close now, Ronny. They've got to be close."

She looked up into Pat's face, which was wreathed in smiles, and she wondered if she could allow herself to believe what he was saying. Was freedom close? Was she going to survive this?

She tried to follow his mood. "So, what's on the Christmas Day menu?"

"We're serving lunch today! Only thick soya-bean soup, but at least it's an extra meal! This evening, we have a special treat for everyone! Dinner is going to be fried rice in oil and vegetables... drum roll... and tins of canned meat! A veritable feast for us, poppet."

There could be no containing his enthusiasm, and Ronny managed a laugh at the spectacle of Pat, chef by default, taking credit for a feast! Secretly, she thought even last year's Christmas was luxurious in comparison.

It was Reg, looking grey and serious, who punctured the balloon when he returned. "There's been a knifing this morning, near the gymnasium. It was a dispute between a fellow and his room monitor. It's serious."

As if to reinforce his words, they heard the soft rumble of distant bombings.

Reg said bitterly, "What a way to celebrate Christmas!"

"That's awful. Today of all days! Has anyone been killed?" asked Ronny.

"No one's died this time! But one chap's been hospitalised. Tensions run high this time of year. Everyone's upset because they were counting on the Red Cross kits being distributed today, but there's no sign of them."

"There'll be no visitors or gifts allowed this year. The men with families outside have always had Christmas Day visits, so they'll be disappointed."

"Emotions are bound to be stretched! But the knifing of one internee by another! That's really frightening."

The brightest moment came in the afternoon with the distribution of jam. Real jam! There may have been only two spoonfuls for each person, but it was utterly delicious. It was a YMCA donation. It came with half a disc of native chocolate, which Ronny intended to make last all week.

—⊬——⊬—

It was another airless afternoon. The sky was an electric blue, and the heat sucked all the energy out of the air, like a huge vacuum. The shanty benefitted from the dappled shade of the trees, but Ronny's only relief was the bamboo fly-swat that she waved feebly in front of her face. Several flies were buzzing in their death throes, the sound drilling into her head, but she did not have the energy to put them out of their misery. She lay listlessly, listening to the murmur of conversation between the two men, who were seated outside on the shanty steps.

"Pat, things are bad. The Finance and Supplies Committee has calculated that, on the present rations, the life span of internees is two or three weeks at a maximum. The situation's desperate. They think that unless the Americans arrive soon, we may not be here to greet them," explained Reg.

"That's no surprise. We all know the writing is on the wall. Was it two weeks ago that all the farmyard animals were slaughtered?" Pat enquired.

"It makes me so angry that the Japs took them all for their New Year celebration. It was criminal gluttony, and our kitchen didn't benefit from one animal!"

There was a silence, and then she heard Pat's voice again. "I miss salt most. I never realised how important it is. I always took it for granted."

"In this heat, we dehydrate so fast that it's vital. A lack of salt is what causes the muscle cramps!" declared Reg.

"I know! It was your turn to cry out last night!"

"Sorry, pal! It took me by surprise. Did I wake you?"

"We take it in turns. Why are the Japs withholding salt from us? It doesn't make sense."

Reg responded, "The commandant says the Philippines is now a battle ground, and the army needs to divert any they can get, for making munitions."

"I'm surprised at their honesty!"

"Well, how much can they hide now, with their troops living in the ground floor of the education building, and the piles of oil drums and munitions they're storing here. They can't pretend ignorance of the American advance."

Another silence.

"Reg? Is there anything we can we do about Ronny?" Pat enquired.

At her name, Ronny pricked up her ears.

He continued, "I'm really worried about her. She's always had a weaker constitution than us, but she's lower than I've ever seen her. She was vomiting again this morning, and she can't afford to become so dehydrated."

"What does Beulah Allen say?" replied Reg.

"I went to her clinic, but she isn't able to call round and has nothing to offer. She just said to give Ronny as much bed rest as possible."

"What's new? Bed rest's been recommended for us all as a way to preserve our energy."

"There's no hope of that with all the demands the Nips are putting on us! We're still turning out for endless roll calls, and the Work Committee is still under pressure to make us do more gardening."

"They're on a hiding to nothing. The chow line is the only excursion that most people can make."

Ronny heard the men moving away, and switched off. She was disgusted with herself at her inability to throw off this sickness. It was pathetic. The only real effort she made was in the presence of Catherine. Her daughter's pet wail of "I don't want to do anything!" had become a relief to her. Both Pat and Reg were kind and caring men, and she was lucky they were so supportive. She knew she was snappy with them both constantly and regretted it. Her last thought before drifting off was that she must try to be nicer to them.

Ronny's deep, exhausted sleep was cut short suddenly. She had not heard the background roar of the approaching planes, but she was jerked awake by the familiar scream of "DaddyMummyDaddy". Unquestionably, it was Catherine. Ronny hauled herself up off the mattress, slipping as her feet scrabbled for balance on the wooden floor, and made for the door. Weak as she was, she nearly fell down the ramp in her haste. She floundered instinctively towards the source of the screaming and was grimly aware of the huge, black, lumbering presence of bombers over her head. Fear gripped her. Where was her little girl? She stumbled, uselessly shouting Catherine's name, her voice obliterated by the deafening noise. The B-24s were back with a vengeance, like huge sharks in the sky, ignoring the endless ack-ack fire that streamed up to meet them.

Suddenly, there was Catherine, lying down flat on her tummy, exposed on the grass. The child looked up as Ronny grabbed her shoulder. Her mouth was stretched in a grimace, her teeth were clenched onto the wooden peg and, somehow, she was managing to scream at the same time. It broke Ronny's heart! In this moment of confusion, her little daughter had attempted to do a version of what she had been directed to do. Roughly, Ronny pulled her to her feet, and half-carried and half-dragged her, still screaming, in the direction of the trees.

It was then that Ronny heard, with a sickening certainty, the whistle of an incoming shell. She checked her stride and pushed Catherine down violently onto the grass. The cry of protest was checked as the wind was knocked out of the child, and Ronny scrabbled to cover her totally with her own body. If the shell hit them, they would certainly die or if it hit concrete, flying debris could be as lethal as the shrapnel itself. In that instant she prayed. Seconds felt like hours.

The sickening thud between Ronny and the trees released her. The soft ground had absorbed the impact, and the immediate danger had passed. Adrenaline ruled her limbs. Trembling violently, she got to her feet and, once again, sweeping up the then silent child, she stumbled on. A glance at the crater was all she allowed herself. The image of what could have been their fate was not to be dwelled upon. Later, she had no idea how she managed to reach the shanty and their earthen refuge. The boom of the bombs rolled in like a tsunami. They were too close to the camp. Too close.

As mother and daughter curled together in the cool damp of the air-raid shelter, Ronny was furious with herself. How could she have been asleep when her daughter needed her? Catherine was quiet and shaken, and Ronny knew she had been lucky, this time. The bombs had dropped just outside the camp, and the stray shell had taken its toll on her mind but not her body. She was totally spent. The energy she had consumed in her rescue mission had used her last reserves, and she lay in a heap, inhaling the warm musk of the earth that encased them. She vowed she would never again allow Catherine to stray far from their bunker beneath the shanty. They had to lay low and stay alive. As the bombers had returned, surely it could only be days before the Americans arrived? She had to make sure her daughter survived.

Over the next week, Ronny spent all her hours on the mattress or in the shelter. Her rescue mission had drained the last vestige of reserves from her body, and, despite her resolve to guard Catherine more carefully, she was unable to look after even herself.

Ronny looked uncomprehendingly into the face of the doctor. She could not believe her ears at the diagnosis; she was aghast. "But I can't be!"

Beulah raised her eyebrows. "An immaculate conception, Ronny? I'm not sure I can wear that one!"

"But it was only the once, on our wedding anniversary! Just once! I never dreamed that I might conceive. I haven't had a period for nearly three years! There's got to be some other reason."

"Ronny. I know my stuff, and you're pregnant, my dear. There's no doubt about it. I'd say congratulations are in order!"

Ronny's face was ashen. Congratulations were definitely not in order! She could not imagine less welcome news. "I can't have a baby, Beulah! I can barely look after myself. I can't have a baby."

"My dear, it seems you have no choice. You're going to have to come to terms with it. That kind husband of yours will be delighted, and I'll do all in my power to keep you as well as I can."

"No! No! I can't think of worse news. I'm not going to survive this, Beulah. This is going to kill me. I know it is."

"What rubbish, Ronny! Where's your fighting spirit? You may not have conceived at an ideal time, but you have your husband at your side and liberation is closer than it's ever been."

Ronny turned away from her friend and threw her arm across her face. Inside, she was screaming, *Please, please get rid of this baby that should never have happened.* She knew Beulah would not consider a termination even if she was able to perform one. Beulah had two children to care for without her husband at her side. Ronny's plea to release her from this pregnancy must stay in her heart and not be voiced.

Ronny needed time to assimilate this terrible news. How could she have let this happen? She screamed internally at the injustice of the world. She was going to die because of one moment of warmth and tenderness amidst years of deprivation. Wildly, she grasped at straws. Surely no foetus could survive what her body was going through? She would not tell Pat and Reg. Not yet. Hopefully, not ever. She closed her eyes and wished the doctor away as she wished the news away. This baby was not going to make her cry. This baby was not going to thrive. This baby was not going to happen.

Twenty-Eight

15th January 1945

1,102 days in captivity

Ronny felt drained and sickened over the next days as she acknowledged her situation finally. Her only hope was for a miscarriage, as her body was suffering such hardship, but, as time passed, her conviction grew that the pregnancy had sealed her fate. She was going to die. She had not told the men, and the longer she left it, the more impossible it became. She dreaded the joy her news would give to Pat just as much as the shock she imagined she would inflict on Reg.

Ronny lay curled on the mattress. The night was dark, and the shutters were sealed close in accordance with the nightly blackout; the only light was a single coconut candle. There had been air-raid warnings all day intermittently. She thought about the ruin of her life. She could have survived if the Yanks had come sooner, but they were still a distance away and there was no guarantee that the camp would be liberated. She considered it likely that the Japanese would slaughter them before the Yanks arrived, and what did it matter? Ronny believed she was being attacked from within; the new baby was a parasite, stealing whatever nourishment was available. Her pregnancy was utterly unwelcome and deadly. She was totally alone and locked in her misery.

Pat and Reg were huddled on the floor, with the chessboard between them, but their thoughts were elsewhere.

Pat said, "I can't believe that David died just like that! I stood next to him in the chow line yesterday. He looked weak and pale, but not noticeably worse than we do."

"It was his heart. Starvation affects the heart muscles, and they just stop working," clarified Reg.

"I think it's in the mind. Some people just give up. Was it four who died yesterday? Why would people give up at this stage? We can see with our own eyes that help is not far away."

Ronny made a huge effort to contribute to the conversation when all she wanted was to close her eyes and sleep forever. "Beri-beri can make you want to give up."

There was a pointed silence.

Irritated, she met their eyes. "Why are you looking at me? It's the wet sort that distorts the thinking, not what I've got. Although, if I had to endure what they go through, I would have ducked out by now."

Reg rebuked her. "Let's have no talk of ducking out. We're a team, and we're all going to survive this. It's only a matter of time." He was interrupted by a dull explosion. The night sky was lit up with a flash of electric white before it settled down to the warm red of constant burning, which had become customary in the last two nights. "The demolition squads are at it again."

Ronny reflected quietly, "I don't understand the Japs' thinking? What's the point in demolishing Manila?"

"It's not indiscriminate, Ronny. The Japanese are taking out the railroad yards at Calcoocan, and the shipyards at both Malabon and Navotas. As for the port, I imagine that they are blowing up the harbour breakwater. They'll also be sinking ships strategically to block the fairway," confirmed Reg.

She persevered, "I haven't the energy to understand the logic of that. Wouldn't that be cutting off their own exits?"

Pat snorted. "When did you last expect logic from the Imperial Army? Aren't you forgetting 'death before dishonour'? The Imperial Army is never going to surrender."

"But we saw that mass exodus of Jap troops going north?" queried Ronny.

"Yes, to fight. Not to run away!" concluded Pat.

The next explosion sounded nearer. Pat went outside to see if anything could be seen in the night sky, and Ronny heaved herself slowly over to check Catherine. The child was sleeping soundly, and she stroked her soft cheek. She thought it was tragic that Catherine had grown so used to the nightly bombing, the air-raid sirens and the explosions that she simply slept through it all.

Ronny felt Reg's eyes on her and he moved in close, dropping his voice. "Ronny, my dear. When are you going to tell, Pat?"

"Tell him what?" She stared at Reg, her eyes wide.

"That you're pregnant, my dear. He needs to know."

She was shocked. "How did you find out? Did Beulah say something?"

"I watch over you, my dear. Of course I noticed. I didn't need to be told. But, for Pat's sake, you must tell him."

Tears sprung instantly and coursed down her cheeks. "I don't want it, Reg. It's going to kill me."

"Nonsense!"

But did she detect a shake in his voice?

"Where's your fighting spirit? This is a wonderful gift. This is the best reason to live," he chastised.

The dam had opened, and she sobbed irrepressibly. She couldn't find words to express her horror and her conviction that this foetus was sucking the life out of her.

Pat's alarmed voice broke in. "Poppet! What is it? What's the matter?"

Reg moved aside, and her husband's arms surrounded her. She was incapable of speaking.

Pat had turned to Reg. "What's going on?"

"I think Ronny has something to tell you, and it's important that it comes from her," Reg responded.

She turned her desperate eyes to her husband and saw concern written large. She was looking at the face of a man expecting a mortal blow.

"What is it, Ronny? You've got to tell me, dearest girl. Have you had bad news?" Pat asked.

She still remained mute and turned her eyes back to Reg. How could she speak to Pat with Reg listening?

Instinctively, he responded, "I'm just stepping outside. I'll be out there if you want me."

"Pat." She swallowed hard and wiped at the tears. "I haven't found the right time to tell you."

He was looking at her with his beautiful, grey eyes, wide and fearful. He waited unable to help her.

"You know I've been feeling really ill, and Beulah came to visit me. She examined me." She paused on the precipice. "Pat, she says I'm going to have a baby."

She watched the dawn break over his face. The relief was followed by incredulous joy. Then she watched his eyes cloud over with fear as he understood the full implication. She would not have to spell it out.

"My dearest one!" was all he said as he held her in his arms.

It felt like a long time later when he continued. "I know this is not what you wanted and that you're frightened, poppet. I can see that. But you have to believe that we will all survive this. I'm convinced the Yanks'll be here within days. This baby will be the start of our new life together. You'll be healthy again by the time it arrives. You'll have the baby in comfort, not like the last time. Our baby and Catherine are the most precious gifts to come out of this miserable experience."

She was exhausted and drained of tears. "Oh Pat. How can this have happened?"

"It's a miracle! Really! The little tyke in there certainly was determined to have a life!" He smiled at her. "It saw its only opportunity and was determined to survive, and the same will go for you. Help and food is on its way. And if you think I'm going to let you slip away at this stage, you'll have to think again. We'll be a two-child family." He stroked her shoulder. "Very soon, this life will just be a bad dream. I love you so much, and I'm going to make sure that nothing bad happens to you. We'll start by making a rule that you are not going to exert yourself in any way. I'm going to wait on you hand and foot, and I'm going to keep you safe."

For his sake, she smiled. She smiled to protect him from the truth, as if he were the child. She knew she was not going to survive.

When Reg burst back in with, "Well? May I be the godfather?" Ronny turned her back on the men without bothering to respond. She did not have the energy for their games any more.

—⊁—⊁—

Over the next week, Ronny sank into apathy. Pat veered between talking animatedly about the future baby and watching her, heavy with concern. She refused to get drawn into the former and she hated the latter, which invaded her privacy. Both behaviours were exhausting. Reg was no better. She was irritated by his enthusiasm and his request to be the godfather, and thankful that she had not succumbed to her passion, as it meant there was no question that Pat was the father. Not that it mattered just then, as she would soon be dead. The two men tried to look after her, and she knew she never showed appreciation. Listening to her ungrateful self, she was horrified to hear her own curt responses to their enquiries. Nothing they did could satisfy her. She hated men in general for putting her in this position, but she hated herself most of all.

Ronny refused to go into the shelter any more, much to Pat and Reg's concern. Whereas once she had found the shelter womb-like and comforting with its earthy smell, by then she could not bear it. The hole in the earth resembled the grave that she was convinced she was destined for before long. Dreams of this haunted her sleep, and she resolved that, as long as she was alive, she was never going to descend into that hole again. She would prefer to die in the shanty.

Ronny was too ill to leave the mattress. She felt guilty about Catherine, but the little girl clung more and more to her father, and Ronny convinced herself that the child was better off without her. She could feel herself growing weaker, and she just wanted it all to end.

She heard Pat's voice. "Ronny, you've got to keep going. You can't give up now. Ronny, listen to me. I've just been to the education building, and I saw six or seven American light planes flying low over camp. Really low, Ronny. They weren't being fired at, and one dropped something over the side onto the ground. Everyone was cheering. Do you know what it was, Ronny? It was a pair of aviation goggles with a message inside. 'Roll Out the Barrel', it said. My dear, you must hang on. They're on their way!"

She heard Pat all right. Everyone was talking to her as if she were the child, not carrying one. She wondered if that was what happened when you were dying. You were treated as if you were porcelain. She drifted in and out of consciousness.

——✂——✂——

Later in the evening, Ronny awoke to heavy machine-gun fire coming from the north. She lay there and listened to it dispassionately, as the gunfire appeared to multiply and spread to other parts of the city. She could not define from which direction it came. Was it from the front or the rear of the camp? Did it matter? The loudspeaker system conveying urgent Japanese instructions to the internees was suddenly cut off, mid-sentence, and silence descended.

"That's the electricity gone." Reg said.

Pat responded, "It's got to be the rioters. The Nips will be shooting looters."

"Why do you say that? Why can't it be the Yanks?"

"There've been truckloads of Japanese coming and going from the education building. They must be out in force to stop the rioting."

"There's too much gunfire just for looters."

"Can the Yanks have made it this quickly?"

"The Yanks can't come a moment too soon."

There was a pause and Ronny knew that both men were looking at her. What was it people said? The last thing to go was your hearing. She could still hear; it was having the energy to respond that failed her.

Reg's voice came again. "Well, it may be past bedtime, but I'm not taking my shoes off tonight in case we need to move quickly."

——✂——✂——

A prolonged low growl was coming from the north of the city. Ronny could not imagine what it could be and could not place the sound. It bothered her.

Pat's voice cut across her thoughts. "It's tanks! It's got to be!"

"It has to be the Yanks!" declared Reg.

"Come on, Reg. I've got to see this. I've got to see what's happening."

"I'm with you. Let's just have a quick look."

Pat leaned over her. "Ronny, we won't be long."

She heard them heading for the door. They were going to leave her! The strength of the voice that left her lips surprised even her as she said, "No!"

They halted mid-stride and turned uncertainly.

"No," she repeated.

"Ronny?" asked Pat.

"I want to see this!" she demanded. She could see the conflict in their faces. She croaked, "Please help me. I beg you to take me."

They hesitated still.

"Please!" she said.

True to form, they went to her aid. Despite her body's resistance, Ronny pulled herself up on her arms and, supported by the men, struggled to lift herself off the mattress. With shaking hands, she attempted to put on her shoes, but Reg stooped and did it for her. Pat lifted the sleepily protesting Catherine into his arms, and they all headed for the door.

Ronny's first sight of the world outside the shanty was unreal, tinged as it was through a mist of deep pink. It had the quality of a dream. The night sky was lit by fires in the city, giving it the appearance of a gentle, red glow, highlighted by the lack of competition from electric lighting. From the streets outside the compound, the heavy growl of machinery on concrete was loud and ever increasing, and they stumbled down the shanty ramp to join a throng of people all headed for the central plaza. Barely aware of Reg's considerable effort supporting her, Ronny forgot her body's limitations. She had to see what was going on.

Sporadic machine-gun fire cut through the babble of the excited crowd as they jostled towards the main building. Ronny, Reg and Pat, with the then wide-eyed Catherine in his arms, kept bunched together and saved their voices.

There was enough shouted clamour surrounding them as voices rang out triumphantly shouting, "*They're here! Our boys are here!*" only to be answered by other voices stating, "It's the Japs. They're coming back!"

Some people were laughing; others were crying. Everyone was jostling. Ronny hung onto Reg as they struggled through the bruising mass.

They rounded the corner of the education building, and she saw Japanese sentries standing guard nervously, with their bayonets drawn. The sound of a hand-grenade explosion came from the main gate, and there was no time to lose. Reg half-dragged her on towards the main plaza to get as good a view as possible. Pat kept close beside them, shielding Catherine from the elbows of the stampeding crowd.

Ronny heard the crack of rifle fire coming from ahead of them, and, as one, the sea of people came to a halt, staring through the glowing dark towards the action. She was shaking uncontrollably, bombarded by a mixture of exhilaration and uncertainty. Were the Yanks outside the gates or was it a platoon of retreating Japanese soldiers who would execute them all?

Her thoughts were voiced by a hysterical woman next to them. She was crying hard and tugging at her companion. "It's the Japs! We need to hide! They've come to finish us off!"

"Don't be stupid. The Japs wouldn't be sending in tanks! It's got to be our boys!" her companion responded.

"No, no! We need to run. It's the Japs!"

Ronny looked away and searched in the pink-tinged gloom, trying to see if any of their Japanese guards were part of this throng, but she saw none. Where had they gone? Was this a trap? The only Japanese she had seen were the sentries she had passed, and she assumed all the others had retreated inside the education building.

The noise of another hand-grenade explosion at the front gates grabbed her attention. Reg and Pat urged her on, and they wove a path through the onlookers to a place on the grass with an uninterrupted view of the far gate, from which sounds of gunfire were coming. With the loss of electricity, it was impossible to see what was happening, which made it even more frightening. Ronny wished she had never left her mattress in the shanty and hugged close to the men amidst the confusion

Suddenly, huge searchlights shone out from the direction of the advance, flashing right across the campus. They bounced off the solid buildings and the vulnerable watchers. Seconds later, rockets shot up, illuminating the whole camp and the tense and restless crowds. The entrance gate sprang into sharp relief, and Ronny saw, as if in a dream, the dense black of a tank breaking through the *sawali*-matting inner gate and pushing it aside as if it were made of gossamer. A collective gasp silenced the internees. The vast block of the tank came on, ominous and threatening against the scarlet, fire-illuminated background. Colours being bleached out by the flat, white lighting from the flares, which tailed away and died only to be replaced by others, added to the sense of unreality.

Ronny stared at the lumbering tank coming directly up the drive towards the plaza. Her legs gave way, and it was only the combination of Pat's and Reg's arms that stopped her sinking to the ground. As they supported her, one on either side, Catherine whimpered on Pat's other hip and covered her ears with her hands. Ronny could only smile at her briefly in reassurance. She could not stop looking at the gash that was once the solid and imprisoning gate.

Another tank turned in through the gaping opening and another and another. Her mind was stunned at the steady approach of these metal hulks, and she counted five tanks in all. Two figures were walking in front of the lead tank, but, in the intermittent and moving light, she could not decipher whether they were friend or foe. The crowd surrounding her surged forwards and backwards according to their hopes or fears, but, in a tight knot, the four of them remained still in the ebb and flow. The noise of the approaching monsters was deafening. It could only have been minutes, but, to Ronny, it felt like hours before the four tanks ground to a halt in front of the main building, whilst the fifth rumbled on, round towards the rear.

Distinctly, she saw the hatch lift on the lead tank and a head emerge. Did she really hear the "Hi folks!" the American soldier called out, or was it her imagination?

The waiting crowd responded with a deafening cheer. These were indeed their boys who had come to their rescue. This was the moment they had been waiting for all these years.

Ronny turned her face to Pat and Reg, and her tears of joy and relief were mirrored in the faces of her two dear men. They grinned at each other through unashamed tears. They had made it. They had survived all the starvation, humiliation and deprivation. They were going to be free. They were going to live.

People were cheering. People were weeping. People were dancing. The sea of humanity around her jostled and bobbed with sheer exhilaration and elation. The atmosphere was electric. Tall American soldiers seemed to be materialising and joining the crowded lawn from all directions. Ronny saw a group seize one or two of their liberators, and carry them, shoulder high, up the main stairway of the main building. Their purpose was clear, as – like trophies – the soldiers were displayed on the main balcony so that everyone could get a look at their saviours.

Ronny stared up at them. They were so tall! They were so young! They were so healthy! To Ronny, they were young gods indeed!

Pat shouted over the noise, "*We've made it Ronny. We've made it, dear girl. Here's our future. It's arrived at last.*" He broke away and danced a little ungainly jig.

Catherine bounced on his hip, and giggled at his antics and the world gone mad.

Ronny reached out and pulled both men's head's close to hers. There was something that she needed to say urgently, something that could not wait. "I'm so sorry, my dears. I'm so sorry I've been such a monster. Will you forgive me? I'll make it up to you, I promise."

Pat placed a large kiss on her cheek, and Reg did the same. Catherine followed the men's examples, and they stood entwined in a huddle, excluding the pandemonium surrounding them. They were united, and they had survived.

Reg said something to her, smiling broadly. She strained to hear him above the cheers, and he had to press his mouth close to her ear to repeat the question.

"Remember this date, Ronny: 3rd February 1945! The day we were rescued! Now will you let me be godfather to your baby?"

Ronny laughed and laughed. She had survived over three years and a month under the Japanese tyranny. Her apathy, her weakness and her surrender to death were a thing of the past. Here was the helping hand she had craved all these years. Here was a future worth fighting for. Another sort of life had become possible, as she carried another life within her. She, her husband, her dear friend, her child and her unborn baby were going to live their future after all.

Around Ronny, 1,000 voices began to sing 'God Bless America'. Once the voices were released there was no stopping them. The roar of 'The Star Spangled Banner' and 'America' followed and filled the night sky, throbbing through her body as strongly as any flyover. Her world had opened up. She was liberated. She had a life to live.

HISTORICAL FOOTNOTE

The tanks of the 1st Cavalry Division of the US Army entered Santo Tomas Internment Camp on the evening of 3rd February 1945. The Japanese guards, who had retreated into the education building, held over 200 internees as hostages and refused to surrender until 5th February. On 7th February, the Japanese shelled the camp, wounding ninety people and killing fifteen. Japanese snipers, shells and mortar fire continued to menace the camp as the Battle for Manila raged around it. The US Army was feeding and clothing the internees, but leaving camp was restricted as it was still unsafe. On 23rd February, the first wave of 360 internees left the camp to be repatriated; this was the same day as that on which the camp at Los Banos was liberated. Manila was declared free of Japanese in early March, leaving much of the city destroyed and over 100,000 Filipinos dead. The camp was closed officially on 14th July 1945.

Ronny, Pat and Catherine left the Santo Tomas camp on 10th April 1945 and headed, by truck, to the port area, to be carried by landing craft out to the *SS Cape Meares*. The freighter travelled first to Leyte, then south to New Guinea and, finally, arrived in San Francisco on 12th May 1945. The family stayed in a hotel in San Francisco for two weeks before crossing the US by train to New York. They returned by plane to England, only arriving a few weeks before the birth of the author, Merilyn Sheila. Within months, Pat was posted back out to the East to work for the Hong Kong Shanghai Bank in Shanghai, and he was followed quickly by Ronny and the two children, and the Stewart family, who remained good family friends.

Reginald Verney left the camp on 10th April 1945; travelled to San Pedro, California, on the *USS Admiral Eberle*; and then made his way to England. He became the author's godfather, never married and continued to support the family closely till the end of his life.

Joy, Mother, Felicity, Pat and Ronny 1917

Pat and Ronny Pre-war 1941

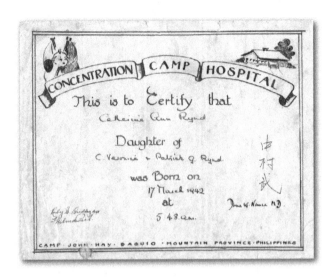

Birth certificate *created in Camp John Hay*

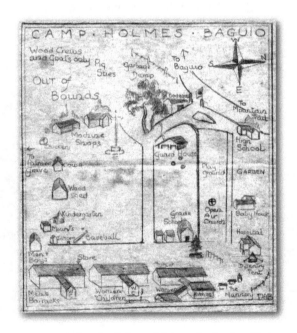

Original sketch of Camp Holmes *by Daphne Bird*

**Wendy, Jim, Judy, Catherine, Michael and Mary Frances
after liberation** *(courtesy of George Stewart)*

The Rynds' shanty after liberation *(courtesy of George Stewart)*

Catherine after liberation *(courtesy of George Stewart)*

Ronnie, Pat and Catherine after liberation *(courtesy of George Stewart)*

Aerial view of Santo Tomas 1945 *(courtesy of National Archive)*

BIBLIOGRAPHY

Stevens Frederic H. *Santo Tomas Internment Camp* Stratford House INC, USA 1946

Wilkinson Rupert *Surviving a Japanese Internment Camp* McFarland & Co, Jefferson, North Carolina, USA 2014

Hind R.Renton *Spirits Unbroken* Howell-North Press Berkeley, California USA 1946

Goldhagen Juergen R. editor *Manila Memories* Old Guard Press, Shearsman Books Ltd, Exeter, UK 2008

McCall James E. *Santo Tomas Internment Camp STIC in Verse and Reverse* The Woodruff Printing Company, Lincoln, Nebraska USA 1945

Hartendorp A. V. H. *The Santo Tomas Story* McGraw-Hill Book Company, New York USA 1964

Brown Grace *Amazing Grace* Argyll Trustees Ltd, Fortrose, Scotland 2015

Martin Therese *In the Presence of My Enemies* Therese Hackett Martin, Castle Rock, Colorado USA 2006

Griffiths Stephen *Guerrilla Priest* Dancing Moon Press, Newport USA 2016

Angeny Helen Frances Buehl *Behind Barbed Wire and High Fences* Sunbury Press, Pennsylvania USA 2012

Whitfield Evelyn *Three-Year Picnic* Premiere Editions International Inc, Corvallis USA 1999

Colquhoun Robert translated and edited *A Free Frenchman under the Japanese* Troubador Matador Publishing Ltd, Leicestershire UK 2015

Lucas Celia *Prisoner of Santo Tomas* David & Charles Publishers Newton Abbot, Devon UK 1988

Tong Curtis Whitfield *Child of War* University of Hawaii Press Honolulu USA 2011

Bailey Fay Cook *Only a Matter of Days* 3rd Edition Merriam Press, Vermont USA 2012

Miles Fern Harrington *Captive Community* Mossy Creek Press Jefferson City, Tennessee USA 1987

Crouter Natalie, edited by Bloom Lynn Z. *Forbidden Diary* Birt Franklin & Company New York 1980

Stephens Margaret *Woman & Marriage* Frederick A Stokes Company New York USA 1910

ACKNOWLEDGEMENTS

This account of my family's life in the Japanese prisoner of war camps in the Philippine Islands during World War II would not have been possible without the assistance and guidance of many patient individuals.

Thank you Maurice Francis, who allowed me to join his 'gang' and whose dogged and meticulous research into the histories of the Philippine internees allowed me access to numerous men and women who were surviving internees of the same camps.

I would like to name John Ream, Annarae Hunter, Carol Wion, Cliff Mills and his Philippine Internment site, Curtis Brooks, Derek and Jacine Bird, Evelyn Bolling, Iian Brown, Katie Krsobeck, Robert Colquhoun, Rod Hall, Sally Marshall, Terry Martin and last but not least Stella Boswell who have all generously given me their time, personal knowledge and support.

Thank you Jimmy Stewart and Judy Harding who remained lifelong family friends and who supplied internment photographs. The unique photographs taken in camp after liberation are their father, George Stewart's work.

Terry Coughlin, I thank you for all your professional expertise and support. Thanks to Troubador Matador for their excellent and patient services of copy editing and printing and advice launching The Bamboo Bracelet.

I have been fortunate to have intelligent and supportive friends who have assisted me in this, my first venture into writing. You know who you are. In particular I would like to thank Deborah Lee who gave me an infinite amount of her time and advice over the process. My son Luke and my daughter-in-law Robee are responsible for the cover design and the map, and so much more. Lastly, I thank my husband Owen for his patience over the years of writing this and my sons Ben, Adam and Luke who gave me the motivation to tell their grandmother's story.

Merilyn Brason was conceived in the prisoner of war camp, Santo Tomas, in the Philippines during World War II when her mother was imprisoned by the Japanese. She has lived in mainland China, Nigeria and Australia where she worked in radio journalism. She is now a retired psychotherapist with three adult sons, and lives with her husband in Gloucestershire, England. *The Bamboo Bracelet* is Merilyn's first book, triggered by her mother's unfulfilled urge to write the story of her extraordinary war.